# Praise for *Are We Done Fighting*

A fresh, studious and very readable book on how to live peace in today's chaotic world. Matthew Legge's helpful hints for individual or group action are in the best Quaker tradition.

—Hon. Douglas Roche, O.C., former Senator and former Canadian Ambassador for Disarmament

No, we are not done fighting, but we can fight in a better way. This book tells you how.

—Johan Galtung, founder of the academic discipline of Peace Studies, and founder, Transcend International

I recommend this extremely inspirational, accessible study book with its extensive practical exercises. I love the way it accepts that peace is possible, so in an interdependent world, it is everyone's responsibility to create positive change that fosters sustainable peace.

—Professor Elisabeth Porter, University of South Australia

This book is a joy. ...[it] offers new material (stories and science) to those who have been doing this work for years, and a great way into peace for those just getting started. I especially appreciate the group discussions and exercises. No one should do peacework alone!

—Stephanie Van Hook, Executive Director, Metta Center for Nonviolence

...an invaluable contribution to the ongoing quest to ensure peacemaking rather than violence is utilised to resolve conflicts, be they between individuals, groups or nations.

—Andrew Feinstein, author *The Shadow World: Inside the Global Arms Trade*

This transformative book presents a refreshing and innovative exploration of how to visualize and actualize peace in global society, in our families and relationships, and in our own minds.

—Douglas P. Fry, author, *Beyond War*, and co-author, *Nurturing Our Humanity*

... a much-needed antidote to the risk of depression and despair. In page after page, and with a multitude of sources to back up the arguments, Matthew Legge gives us plenty of hope stemming from experience.

—Paul Rogers, Emeritus Professor,<br>Peace Studies, Bradford University, UK

This is the book many peace, justice, and reconciliation advocates have waited for. Enabling, practical, and clear-minded, Matthew Legge offers readers—individuals or groups—a road map to transform our deepest conflicts.

—Paul R. Dekar, Emeritus Professor and co-founder,<br>Peace Studies program, McMaster University, Canada

... exceptionally valuable and timely ...Matthew Legge offers practical solutions that make a difference in our own lives and in the broader communities that surround us. ... Not only to be read, but put into action.

—Alex Neve, O.C., human rights lawyer and Secretary General,<br>Amnesty International Canada

For those who are working to decrease the madness of violence and increase the sanity of peace, lock arms today with Matthew Legge. Tomorrow is too late.

—Colman McCarthy, Director,<br>The Center for Teaching Peace, Washington D.C.

# *are we done* FIGHTING?

## Building Understanding in a World of Hate and Division

**Matthew Legge**

new society
PUBLISHERS

Cover design by Diane McIntosh.
Cover illustration: ©iStock: iStock-179520278

Printed in Canada. First printing April 2019.

Inquiries regarding requests to reprint all or part of *Are We Done Fighting?*
should be addressed to New Society Publishers at the address below.
To order directly from the publishers, please call toll-free (North America)
1-800-567-6772, or order online at www.newsociety.com

Any other inquiries can be directed by mail to

New Society Publishers
P.O. Box 189, Gabriola Island, BC V0R 1X0, Canada
(250) 247-9737

LIBRARY AND ARCHIVES CANADA CATALOGUING IN PUBLICATION

Title: Are we done fighting? : building understanding in a world of hate
and division / Matthew Legge.

Names: Legge, Matthew, 1983– author.

Description: Includes bibliographical references and index.

Identifiers: Canadiana (print) 20190080531 | Canadiana (ebook) 20190080558 |
ISBN 9780865719088 (softcover) | ISBN 9781550927016 (PDF) |
ISBN 9781771422970 (EPUB)

Subjects: LCSH: Conflict management. | LCSH: Peace. |
LCSH: Interpersonal relations. | LCSH: Reconciliation. | LCSH: Peace of mind.

Classification: LCC HM1126 .L44 2019 | DDC 303.6/9—dc23

New Society Publishers' mission is to publish books that contribute in fundamental
ways to building an ecologically sustainable and just society, and to do so with the
least possible impact on the environment, in a manner that models this vision.

# Contents

# Foreword

*by George Lakey*

Matthew Legge has given us a considerable gift: guidance for expanding our capacity as peace advocates. Whether this is our first peace-related book or our fiftieth, reflecting on the issues raised here can increase our knowledge, skill, and confidence, even in situations when conventional wisdom insists that violence is the only answer.

In our world, violence is still promoted as a solution on many levels, including individual self-defense, community protection, challenging injustice, and international conflict. That means we can explore peaceful alternatives wherever we're most challenged by violence in our own lives. As we become aware of where we're stuck for answers, and experiment with ways of getting unstuck, we grow our capacity and courage. Because this book operates on multiple levels, it supports us on our way.

While teaching at Swarthmore College I encountered students who were concerned about the threat of terrorism and at the same time wondered if "the war on terrorism" was in fact recruiting more terrorists. I therefore offered a course completely focused on nonviolent responses to terrorism. I was deluged with students, who went on to develop nonviolent defense strategies for a variety of countries currently threatened by terrorism.

Back in the 1960s, even though many people were singing "Give peace a chance," the institutional decision-makers remained sure that power = violence, just as the flat-earthers were sure centuries ago that safety depended on being able to sail near the coastlines.

Since then the old violence paradigm has become raggedy—
Matthew Legge tells us that wars have almost never been won since
the US invaded Grenada in 1983! But most decision-makers still
cling to the old belief.

This is a Good News book, one that encourages new thinking
and experimentation in more effective ways of relating to conflict.
It contains stories that may surprise even people who have already
sailed out of sight of the coastline to explore the possibilities of
peace. More than that, the author is a coach as concerned to empower us as he is to fire our imaginations. He shows us proven
means of communicating the Good News to people who are still
hugging that coast, so we can join them in mutual exploration.

The mutuality is encouraged by Matthew's presentation of peace
methodology not as dogma but as an unfolding set of practices. He
supports this approach with numerous studies from social psychology and political science. Once we've digested the finding that mass
movements seeking freedom from dictators have twice as good a
chance of winning if they choose nonviolent struggle rather than
violence, we're more open to tantalizing experiments from the field
of unarmed peacekeeping, which as yet haven't been fully studied.

I remember how important exploration was to me when I joined
the first team of Peace Brigades International's Sri Lankan project.
It was 1989; no one could be sure that human rights lawyers who
were being assassinated by hit squads could be kept safe by nonviolent accompaniment. Still, the experiment needed to be done,
and as it turned out, we kept everyone safe who we accompanied.
An important part of the effort were the peace workers back home,
who supported the experiment and backed us up by communicating with the governments involved. As experiments of this kind are
tried and found successful, we gain more confidence that we can go
beyond the old violent paradigm that is failing us.

The book invites all of us into a collaborative search for peaceful
alternatives, a search that is bold enough to make the discoveries
we need without pretending in advance we were certain of the outcomes. Then as collaborators Matthew supports us to become ever

more aware of how bias and misperception might get in the way of making our best conclusions—thereby showing us how we can become more accurate in our thinking.

A bonus comes at the end of each chapter, where Matthew not only summarizes the major points but offers activities that empower us even more, in the context of group discussions. I heartily recommend that you read this with others, preferably a group that includes different points of view.

Many of us don't have as much time as we would like to devote to our peace work. An advantage of the approach taken here is that a big focus is on *how* to do the work most effectively. In turn, that supports us to maximize the value of the time that we do have.

I found the book to be diversity friendly. Matthew shows ways that communication failures snarl conflict and make it more likely to become violent, but he doesn't say that "violence is simply about miscommunication." As he leads us through the field, he shows us multiple lenses through which we can view situations and offers multiple options for acting. His stories are especially vivid and likely to stick in the mind at moments when we need them.

His diversity friendliness supports unity because it suggests the variety of roles that can be played in transforming even the most bitter situations. For example, the late Quaker strategist Bill Moyer showed that successful social movements characteristically include four different roles. In confronting an environmental threat, say, the *advocates* focus on dialogue with the authorities while the *helpers* jump in to ameliorate the situation themselves by, for example, building windmills as an alternative source of power. A third role is the *organizers*, who like to build coalitions and pull people together in conferences and rallies. The fourth role is the *rebels*, who engage in nonviolent direct action to make it difficult for decision-makers to continue their injury to the environment and incentivize them to listen to the advocates.

Time and energy often get wasted by people criticizing a role different from their own and trying to get them to join their preferred role, instead of accepting the diversity as the reality and, at best, as a strength. Movements are more likely to solve the problem when people find ways to unite across lines of difference.

This book, by paying attention both to the individual and group levels of peace work, and even the group and mass levels, supports the big picture we need.

GEORGE LAKEY has been working for peace for over 60 years. He recently retired as a peace studies professor at Swarthmore College. His tenth book is *How We Win: A Guide to Nonviolent Direct Action Campaigning* (Melville House, 2018).

# About Quakers and the Author

The Religious Society of Friends (members are commonly called "Quakers" or "Friends," and I'll use both terms) has a history with peace and pacifism dating back to the 1650s. Friends are seekers after truth—a bold goal if there ever was one! I'm the Peace Program Coordinator of Canadian Friends Service Committee (CFSC), the peace and social justice agency of Quakers in Canada. When it was created in 1931, Arthur Dorland, among the founders of CFSC, wrote, "We trust that...in our united effort we may make a greater impact for good upon our day and generation."[1] This is still our hope.

For centuries, Quakers have been exploring the tough question of how to respond effectively to violence. Historian Robert Byrd explains that "Friends' primary interest has been in the underlying causes and forces at work in international affairs, or, in [early Quaker George] Fox's phrase, in 'taking away the occasions for war.'"[2] This book continues that way of looking at the issues.

In 1947 Quaker service agencies were awarded the Nobel Peace Prize for non-partisan medical support offered to all sides in war. (This later became a common approach used by groups like the Red Cross/Red Crescent.) In his awards speech, Norwegian leader Gunnar Jahn said, "The Quakers have shown us that it is possible to translate into action what lies deep in the hearts of many: compassion for others and the desire to help them..."[3] Bronnie Ware, a palliative care nurse, wrote that the single biggest regret people told her as they lay dying was not staying true to themselves.[4] I hope that the skills we'll be building in this book will help us discover practical ways to stay true to what lies deep in our hearts. We're not seeking in these pages to oppose violence or war. We're exploring to what extent, in any moment, we can stay true to ourselves and act on our peace aspirations.

When this book references Quakers and their practices, it's not out of some tribalism—a claim that Quakers are exceptional or have special access to the truth. In fact, Quakers believe just the opposite. We can all access inner wisdom and we need *each other* to help it flourish. The reason I make reference to Quakers is that those are the examples I know well, and they're examples that most people haven't heard of, so you probably aren't already sick of reading about them. I think Friends have some great stories they don't often tell, so I'm pleased to be sharing them. I hope they hint at the impacts a small group of people can have.

I'd like to express my deep gratitude to everyone I've learned from and bounced ideas back and forth with, and who supported the creation of this book—family, friends, and Friends. Significant contributions were made by Gianne Broughton, Trevor Chandler, Paul Dekar, Meg Gunsar, Barbara Heather, Keira Mann, Maggie Sager, Megan Schmidt, Bertha Small, and Linda Taffs.

Please know that this book was written and edited by white North Americans with their basic needs like food and shelter readily met. It's easy for us, with so many comforts, to talk about peace. But in the coming pages we'll discover the stories of remarkable people from many different walks of life using the ideas in this book. A cast of characters all around you is celebrating life with these skills right now.

# Introduction

What if there were something powerful you could do right now, today, that would impact not only your own life but your whole community? What if others were already using skills and knowledge that you'd never heard much about but that could be genuinely *transformative*?

Slobodan Milošević's rule saw mass unemployment, widespread corruption, ethnic cleansing, a million ethnically Albanian refugees, even the use of concentration camps. A 78-day, 3-billion-dollar military campaign led by the United States failed to impact Milošević much, if anything making him more aggressive. Then, incredible as it may sound, the Milošević dictatorship was toppled *without guns*. This is how Srđa Popović summarized the nonviolent work everyday citizens did to help bring down Milošević: "We won because we loved life more. We decided to love life."[1]

Imagine if you had the courage and skills to love life, whether living under a terrifying dictatorship or in a relatively peaceful and affluent country. Picture how you could use and spread these skills, what an impact they could make if they really caught on...

This is a book about thriving. There will never be a perfect moment for this book, nor a better one than right now. We'll explore the processes at play when hate arises, and learn all kinds of practical ways to counteract them. We'll see how fighting can get entrenched or can move in transformative and healing directions. For now, let's call that latter process "peace."

It has always been true, and certainly is today, that we're in a time of major change: cultural and political power shifts, skyrocketing inequality, climate change... We have increasingly powerful artificial intelligence, cyber warfare, even debates on new human rights to protect us from technologies like neural implants that monitor our thoughts or hijack our mental processes![2] The pace of change can be staggering, leaving us feeling vulnerable. This could contribute to division and violent unrest. Or it could produce a specific susceptibility to a very different type of infection.

In 2014 I had the chance to hear Quaker peace activists Dale Dewar and Bill Curry deliver a lecture examining war from a public health lens.[3] A shift in perspective like that can suddenly open fresh ideas, so I began to think that a further envisioning may be in order. I started to see a shimmering sense of what "peace" could be.

I read all sorts of peace books and blogs, and I felt something missing. Much of the work addressed our needs for security and justice. Less frequently authors acknowledged the roles of recognition and meaning in our lives. But a need was being ignored—stimulation! Without meeting it, there's always a price to pay.[4] Pictures of doves are lovely, but they can get pretty boring. Hearing about peace is alienating if it's too far removed from what's relevant and exciting. I don't want you to see a title like *Are We Done Fighting?* and imagine I'm going to argue that we should all just be friends! If peace is about forcing ourselves to be "good" in bland ways, it's weak. It can't just be the "high road" we're told we *should* take.

Sometimes we want to be contrarians, to cheer for the bad guy, to do what we're told not to. Peace thinkers often downplay this, overlooking the fact that for many, violence is exciting, even beautiful.[5] It's possible that many of us "are drawn to carnage, not repelled by it."[6] With this line of thinking my vision started to become clear— while thinking about violence as a form of infection I began to see that viruses, for example, can be at the same time horrible and yet, from another point of view, elegant. We have to marvel at the ways they've evolved to spread and replicate, often with terrifying results. Peace is actually powerful and exciting. It moves between us…like a virus. What incentives do hosts (folks like you and me) need to spread peace, to make it go viral?[7] We don't often hear about it, but this is exactly what people are doing all around the world. Sometimes it's as dramatic as overcoming the Milošević dictatorship, other times as simple as experiences at home or in the workplace. However it happens, this is an infection to celebrate!

What makes this book unique? Why another book on peace? Much of the study of peace and conflict has been abstract and intellectual. This kind of work isn't always easy to pick up and use. It's often focused on niches and directed at experts. Personally, I think it's a mistake to talk about peacebuilding in Colombia and not the United States. I wholeheartedly agree with the Quaker Council for European Affairs when they say "Peacebuilding is everybody's business"[8]—so this book aims to be practical and useful and to bridge artificial divides.

I think there's an obvious connection that's often lost when universities or the United Nations talk about peace. As valuable as these discussions can be, *they regularly forget the heart*. Simply put, I've witnessed that there's a central element of peacebuilding that too often gets overlooked—peace is built by people, and people aren't that reasonable. We're moved in surprising ways. This book explores the latest research from a range of fields like anthropology, behavioral economics, neuroscience, and social psychology. To my knowledge this is the first time these insights have been combined and related back to spreading peace. They can inform each other in fascinating ways!

My definition of peace will be vast and not technical. Peace happens at different levels, so whether you're looking for tips to understand yourself and your own feelings, improve your relationships with others, or work nonviolently for social change, I know this book will have something for you. It's an easy approach for everyone—from seasoned peace workers to folks with zero interest in violent conflicts. Whether you consider yourself on the political right or left, an optimist or pessimist, a realist or idealist, religious or atheistic, the following pages will be worth your time. This journey promises to be invigorating, empowering, and even infectious. Let's begin.

# Using This Book

This book may be interesting but, most importantly, it's designed for *action*! I've kept most chapters short, and each one has tips at the end for easy reference. There are also lots of examples and activities. Chapters are collected into sections based around key themes.

As with all stories, there's a simple way to tell it, and then there are many details. I've offered the details for those who want to really dig into how the peace virus evolves and transmits, but if that gets to be too much for you, feel free to skim and skip around—you don't have to read this book in order. If you want more reading, there are many references to explore.

Whatever the problem, there are countless ways of looking at it and seeking positive changes. This book will focus mostly on individual approaches, because those are relevant to all of us. That's not to discount the importance of institutions! If we have wise leaders creating peaceful conditions around us, peace can flourish even if many of us lack peace skills. There are great resources out there for folks building peace through influencing governments and corporations, but to make this book useful to all sorts of readers I chose not to make activism a main focus.

I really encourage using this book in a facilitated study and action group. Doing the exercises in a group will create an incredible chance to share the virus. If you're particularly lucky you might find time for a day or weekend-long retreat—a little peace-infection vacation! Many of the activities are deceptively simple. They're all tested and can be *powerful*, but this is the type of learning where you get as much back as you put in.

When doing the activities you might experience insights you would not have expected. Discovering your unacknowledged feelings or needs can't be predicted or controlled, so it could get scary or frustrating. You'll be asked to open to things that can be painful. Be ready to challenge yourself to the point of discomfort if you want to really grow. But it's not usually healthy to push past discomfort into full panic.[1] Listen to yourself, and discern when it may be time to take a break or sit out for an exercise.

Friend and experienced trainer George Lakey explains what can happen when a group really commits to a process like this. Everyone might start off in a friendly place but suddenly descend into conflict as the group "generates a storm when its members want to experience acceptance for the deeper layers of themselves, including differences that, up until then, they've been keeping under wraps." Lakey points out that the higher the stakes of what the group is trying to achieve, the more likely it is that emotional needs will assert themselves, taking group members by surprise. After enough effort, there may be a "breakthrough into community."[2] Be ready! It's also possible that none of this happens in your group, which is fine too.

If you can't do a retreat, I recommend picking a section of the book, reading it alone beforehand, and then meeting to discuss it and do the activities together. This can be enough for a rich hour or two, whatever your group can spare. While the activities are written for groups, most can be done by individuals too.

Make sure to name a facilitator who will lead the activities. Facilitators: don't worry—you don't need any prior experience. There's an appendix full of advice on the basics of facilitation. I encourage those who aren't facilitators not to read the activities beforehand. You'll gain more if you learn them by doing them.

Finally, a word about the findings we'll be looking at. The studies referenced in this book have their limitations. Many were done only on university students—not the most representative of groups! Some studies haven't been replicated enough to see that the findings really hold, and in some cases studies may have been conducted sloppily or even fraudulently.[3] A huge problem with most of the studies referenced is that they were often done in just one or a few cultures. I find this deeply frustrating, but that's the reality of the evidence I could find. Please keep that in mind. It means that some of what we'll learn won't apply everywhere. Also recall that statistics offer summaries. They tell us about *broad patterns*. Individuals can and do differ from these patterns. The studies discussed *do*, however, hint at useful insights that are expanded on with stories, examples, and thoughts from historical and modern-day peace workers. Each of these stories is, of course, far more complicated and nuanced than I have space for, so I hope that I've done the issues justice.

Political scientist Johan Galtung has explored how he sees the violence of different peoples as being rooted in distinct religious, political, and cultural structures and ideas. He notes, "Most important are the deep structures and cultures because they are unreflected [upon], even unknown."[4] The coming pages will offer chances for reflection, perhaps making the previously invisible come to life for you.

## Activity: Learning Contract or Journaling

1. If you'll be doing group work, this activity will help you create a shared "learning contract." If you're working alone, consider starting a journal to note down your reflections and to answer discussion questions.
2. Select a facilitator for the group. Facilitators: assign someone to take notes, or ask each person to write their response to each question on a single sheet of flipchart paper.
3. Go around in a circle, with each person stating their name and one reason they're here. Facilitators may need to instruct people to be brief as there will be lots of opportunities to talk further in future exercises.
4. Facilitators ask the group to go around again, explaining one thing they need in order to participate fully. For example, "I need to not be mocked for things I say," "I need someone to keep track of time because I have to leave right on time to pick up my

children," "I need people to speak loudly and slowly because I'm hard of hearing."

5. Facilitators ask the group to go around a third time, with each person stating one thing they will commit to bringing to this group learning. For example, "I will approach this with an open mind," "I will commit to be vulnerable with the group," "I will commit to talking about what I learn with X person."

6. Facilitators may need to suggest additional ground rules if they haven't come up already. For example, facilitators may cut in to keep the group on time, so there might not be time for every comment to be heard; nothing said may be shared externally without permission; anyone can leave at any time; photos or video may be taken only if everyone agrees.

7. Inviting everyone to speak in no particular order, facilitators ask, "Is there something you're sceptical about as we start reflecting on this book?"

8. Facilitators ask, "Do you have any other pressing needs, hopes, or expectations from this learning process?"

9. Facilitators check if everyone is OK with the stated needs and commitments. If not, discuss this further—what are the divergent needs, how can a consensus be reached? Once there's agreement, everyone signs the flipchart sheet or verbally agrees to this learning contract.

## Activity: Your Values and a Special Person

1. Facilitators let the group know that this will be done individually and no one will be asked to share what they wrote. Pass out paper and pens to those who need them.

2. Facilitators instruct the group, "Before we go further, spend a few moments reflecting on your values. Who are you when you're at your best? What person do you aspire to be? Pick a particular memory if you can think of a time when you behaved like that person. Please write your values down and keep them safe so you can refer to them easily when asked later." Give at least ten minutes for this, offering a two-minute warning to wrap up.

3. Facilitators now explain, "*Are We Done Fighting?* is a story, and we all know that the stories we remember most are the ones that are meaningful to us. Before we go any further, let's each think of someone we care about. As we read the book, let's imagine specific ways that the issues discussed are relevant to, and will have an impact on, the person we're thinking of. We can make our future discussions of the book more grounded by referring to how the issues it raises relate to challenges we ourselves, or the person we've just pictured, face."

## Activity: Your Strengths

Many of us start seeking change by identifying problems and looking for solutions. It can also be helpful to focus on what our particular strengths may be. Evidence suggests that focusing on and working with our personal strengths can help us achieve our goals.[5]

1. Facilitators divide everyone into small groups and ask them to take 15 minutes to each answer two questions: "What are your particular strengths?" and "How do you use your strengths to build peace?" Give a two-minute warning.

2. Facilitators gather the group together again to share what they were talking about.

# 1

# Peace and Power

*We'll start by exploring our sense of what peace is **not**. Toward the end of the book we'll return to the definition and try to decide what peace **is**.*
*In this first section we'll also look at divisiveness and forms of power. We'll clarify many mysterious and bizarre quirks about human attitudes and actions. As we do this, we'll find the gaps where the peace virus can spread. Skills developed in this section will primarily relate to understanding problems and proven tips for transformation.*

— 1 —

# What Peace is *Not*

*Fundamental to all else is the need that [humans]*
*should grow to understand and practise patience and tolerance,*
*and to substitute for the clumsy, uncertain, cruel tool of violence,*
*the methods of reason and co-operation.*[1]

— EMILY GREENE BALCH

EMILY GREEN BALCH was a Nobel Peace Prize winner with great
insights, yet the sentiment expressed here has its flaws. Thank-
fully, peace doesn't depend on our becoming reasonable! If we rest
our hope on reason, we're in impossibly deep waters. Reasonable-
ness and rationality are, it turns out, not at all what we may think.
This has huge implications for peace work, so let's see some examples of what I'm talking about.

Nowhere is cold logic more dependable than in the courtroom.
We're all supposed to be equal before the law, and a judge's ability to
think clearly and make carefully reasoned decisions is honed over
years. Yet research suggests that what should be irrelevant factors—
like how much sleep a judge got the night before—make a *big* difference to rulings. Researchers suspect that when judges don't get as
much sleep, they may be more irritable and have less mental energy
to make decisions, resulting in harsher rulings.[2] A different study
carefully controlled for many factors and concluded that parole decisions depend on how many cases a judge has seen since taking a
snack break. The authors suggest what may be going on is that "decision making is mentally taxing...if forced to keep deciding things,

3

people get tired and start looking for easy answers. In this case, the easy answer is to maintain the status quo by denying the prisoner's request."[3] Particularly when we're mentally tired, we make more reckless decisions or are more likely to not make a decision at all—doing nothing or accepting the default option presented to us even when we could have benefitted by picking differently![4]

Let's consider a case where a reasonable choice matters most—a life-and-death decision. You're told you have lung cancer. The doctor says in the exact same concerned tone, "You have a 70 percent chance of living if you have this surgery," or she says, "You have a 30 percent chance of dying if you have this surgery." What choice would you make? This was tested with patients in a hospital (they had a variety of conditions, not lung cancer) and with students and doctors. Every group—even the doctors, with all their years of medical training—were much more likely to choose surgery if it was explained to them in terms of how likely they were to live![5] The answers we arrive at depend on the framings we start off with.

Another example: Applicants arrive for a job interview. The interviewers are participating in a study. Before the interviews, researchers casually ask the interviewers to help them for a moment by holding their drink. Some of the interviewers get an ice-cold drink to hold, others a warm cup of coffee. The job applicants come in and answer the interview questions. People conduct interviews by rationally analyzing all the facts about each candidate, don't they? Actually, the applicants were secretly actors trained to say exactly the same things in each interview. Interviewers who'd heard the exact same answers liked the applicants a lot more if they'd held a cup of hot coffee instead of a cold drink! Interviewers who held coffee said applicants had warmer personalities, better skills, and were more hirable.[6] Sensations we're feeling get readily confused with decisions we've carefully reasoned out.

If a stranger asked you to volunteer to put a big ugly sign on your lawn, what would you say? A famous study found a way to increase people's likelihood of agreeing by 400%. First, people were asked to put a very small sign on the inside of their window for the same

Zawadi Nikuze

cause—safe driving. Having agreed to this, *self-perception* seemed to change. Now people understood themselves to be *the type of person who cares a lot about safe driving.* When asked to put up the big ugly sign, three-quarters of folks who'd agreed to the small sign now complied.[7]

What we're seeing is just a tiny bit of the wealth of evidence that we're actually surprisingly bad at determining why we do what we do. Yet we're very good at being convinced that we *do* know our motivations. Some of us might think that this is all very interesting but that we're too clever to be caught by such tricks, that our intellect will help us behave reasonably while *other people* don't. Research suggests this itself is just another bias. In fact, the smarter we are, the *more* likely we are to be affected by biases like the ones we've just seen.[8] But what does all this have to do with spreading peace?

Congolese peace worker Zawadi Nikuze, who's been in traumatizing conditions for decades but, incredibly, maintains a sense of optimism, advises, "Give what you have. [If you have] a good smile, give it to someone who is stressed who needs it…"[9] This might sound like a nice gesture but ultimately not much of one. How is a smile more than trivial? To be sure, being smiled at will make most of us feel better for a few moments and may not change our lives. But perhaps those moments are worth more than we'd imagine. It's even possible that what we do in those moments *will* change our lives for years to come.

As we saw with judges, decision making is hard work. To minimize the amount of work we have to do, we look for help from others and follow their lead. That may help explain why, for example, if the first online review for a product is positive, that increases the chances that other reviews will be positive by almost a third, and increases the overall rating by a quarter.[10] We even do this *with ourselves*. We regularly look to our past decisions as if they were made by someone whose lead we should follow. In order to be consistent and to save effort, we tend to do what we've already done, forgetting completely *why* we did it the first time.[11] Once we can look to our past and see that we made a decision to put up a sign about safe driving, we feel that we must care about safe driving and now we need to act consistently with that. We don't recall that right before being asked to put up the sign we were feeling good because someone smiled at us, or warm because we'd just held a cup of coffee. In other words—we don't understand the conditions that lead to our actions, but once we're going in one direction, we can easily get carried forward by following what we did before.

What was your mood last Wednesday at 1 pm? Did you have a warm cup of coffee or a cold drink in your hand? Had someone smiled at you recently? If you're like most people, you won't remember. But what you *will* remember is that on Wednesday you decided to put a sign in your window about safe driving. Since you made that choice, you'll be quite likely to follow your own lead further in that direction.

This means that a well-timed expression of care from Nikuze could actually help start a chain of events that changes our lives. If in the next moment we had to make a choice about a conflict, we might find ourselves pausing instead of escalating. Then the next time we're in a similar conflict, we'd recall that we're not *the type of person* who escalates conflicts, looking to what we did last time with zero memory of having felt good because of Nikuze's fleeting influence on us. This is just one of the ways that small acts can sometimes unlock significant changes—either for good or ill.

What I hope we're starting to see is that many of us are surprisingly uninformed about ourselves. This makes it tough to make decisions and to act based on our own interests. Here's a simple illustration of the challenge. Rank this list in terms of what will make you happiest:

1. Commuting to work
2. Watching TV
3. Surfing the internet
4. Doing hair, makeup, or other personal grooming
5. Shopping
6. Exercising
7. Preparing food

What did you think? Many of us will rank the list something like this: 2, 3, 5, 4, 7, 1, 6. Watching TV is obviously a fun activity, and preparing food tends to be a chore. Exercising is painful, and we do it for the results. We love spending long hours online chatting and playing games.

The actual findings are very different. Researchers used a phone app to check in with people at random during the day and have them answer a few questions to rate their happiness and say what they were doing. This information was collected from a diverse range of people. So what makes us happiest? Exercising, then preparing food, shopping, watching TV, grooming, commuting to work, and then surfing the internet.[12] What's striking is that most of us do these things, yet we *still* can't remember how happy each one actually makes us while doing it. When asked while *not* doing it, we get the order wrong.

So if we're not nearly as reasonable or informed as we think, and if we want to spread peace, what can we do? Many of us assume we need to spread information. We believe that if people had all the facts, they'd make more peaceful decisions. Some good-quality information is certainly valuable, but the proof that it's not usually enough is easily offered by author Dan Heath: "Are you doing something in life right now where you have all the information that you need to know it's not a good idea for you, and yet you keep doing it anyway?" From not eating balanced meals to staying up too late or other more dangerous choices, the honest answer for almost everyone is, "Yes!"[13] Having enough information and good intentions regularly fails us, and this insight is far from new. In the Bible we find Paul exclaiming with anguish, "I don't understand my own behavior—I don't do what I want to do; instead, I do the very thing I hate!"[14]

I think these points are crucial to understand, because if we're going to make peace infectious, it won't do to start with impossible premises about how peace spreads. We'll just squander our efforts. Our problem-solving tools need to respond to reality. Informing us that we're not being reasonable or cooperative enough is unlikely to change us. As folks ready to see positive changes, what we *can* do is go first, offering smiles if that's all we have, happily questioning our assumptions, and diving deeper into the constantly evolving understanding we gain. This is a challenge of self-discovery, skill building, and peacebuilding, all at once.

We've just dipped a toe into the river of questions we'll be looking at—how to feel inner peace, build more peaceful relationships (interpersonal peace), and support changes in the world around us (structural peace).[15] You may have noticed that in all this I'm not saying what peace *is*. That's deliberate. Together we're starting off where we are and testing our ideas as we move forward. Soon we'll do an activity to further outline what peace isn't. Here's one important distinction first—negative versus positive peace. Johan Galtung explains that negative peace comes from "the idea of a predictable social order, even if this order is brought about by means of force and the threat of force."[16] Negative peace is the mere lack of overt war and obvious violence. It is the appearance of stability. Many problems fester unaddressed just below the surface. Negative peace can go on our list of what peace isn't.

## Tips from This Chapter

1. There's a strong tendency to believe that we're more rational than we really are. Becoming aware of what motivates us can help our work for positive changes, making it more realistic and effective. Some tips offered in this book will also help address our biases— for instance, if you can, get a good night's sleep and take a snack break before making too many mentally taxing decisions!

2. Decision making is challenging, and we tend to look for short-cuts. For instance, we look to our past decisions, recalling our actions and forgetting what could have influenced us at the time. This suggests that we need to take great care in establishing any habit or pattern of behavior, no matter how seemingly minor, since it can escalate. (Agreeing to put up a small sign can make us feel inclined to put up a large one.)

3. Checking in with ourselves at random moments, we might see how happy we are. Is what we're doing with our time right now as fun as we imagined? Just because we can't see any obvious problems doesn't mean we're living peacefully. We may be caught up in negative peace.

## Activity: Group Ideas—What Peace is *Not*

1. Facilitators ask the group "What is *not* peace?" and write a list of the key ideas coming up. Facilitators encourage folks to speak from their own experiences, offering a story or anecdote if it helps clarify what they mean. A follow-up question could draw these responses out: "When you are *not* peaceful, how do you think or act?"

2. Facilitators ask what themes or clusters of ideas people notice emerging in the list.

3. Facilitators ask "Are there any assumptions coming through that you think need to be tested further? Are there any questions being raised that you would like to have answered?" In future activities the group will be reviewing these assumptions and questions, so facilitators need to write these down clearly and keep a copy.

## Example: Experience Changes Beliefs in Kenya

On a hot sunny day in Mtwapa a man is attacked by a mob. He's beaten senseless. The mob is about to set him on fire when police fight their way through and save him. Local religious leaders are there, screaming for ruthless violence against anyone who, like this man, is suspected of being gay.[17]

Imagine you're a gay Kenyan. You're shocked and outraged at what's happening, but how can you stand up to a whole culture? Where would you start? There's such an incredible risk if you speak out. Reeling from a wave of murders, one brave Kenyan civil society group meets to find its strength. Rather than condemn or confront the Christian and Muslim leaders provoking such hatred and violence, they adopt a surprising strategy—they befriend them. The group develops a 12-week program of sensitization, calling it Facing Fears.

Without mentioning homosexuality, the trainers invite religious leaders like Sheikh Ali Hussein to sessions to learn more about HIV/AIDS and patient care. Hussein, along with nearly a dozen other pastors and imams, agrees to join. He later recalls that he felt it was worth attending the sessions to learn how to stop the spread of AIDS in his community. The Facing Fears program opens with discussions of AIDS and the importance of, and right to, health care. After a few weeks, the trainers move to sessions about other rights.

> "The first lesson I picked up was that human beings have rights," says an Anglican pastor, "Thomas," who attended the program. He asked that his name be withheld out of fear of backlash from his superiors in the church. "What I don't like in a person does not warrant me to break that person's rights, period," he says.

After three months of sessions involving lively discussion and role-plays to broaden the participants' perspectives, trainers reveal the big secret—they're gay. The trainers then ask the religious leaders pointedly, "Do you still believe I should be beaten?" The leaders, stunned, say, "No, of course not, not you personally." The trainers explain that they're just the same as other gay people.

Hussein describes how before that moment in the training he felt, "We must be aggressive and kill them. [Homosexuals are] not worthy to live anywhere in the world." But having gotten to know actual gay people, his views changed: "The most important thing we learned is to listen before deciding... And one is supposed to be compassionate." Hussein still thinks homosexuality is "wrong," but he reconciles with a gay cousin he hasn't talked to for 20 years. Participants help recruit other religious leaders for a next round of training sessions.[18]

Similar programs have been used in the United States. First United Methodist Church minister Steve Clunn reports, "I went from ignorance and fear to a place of understanding because people had the courage to talk to me."[19]

— 2 —

# Us and Others

*As long as you cannot face yourself*
*and love even those ugly parts...*
*I will be left with the work of trying to love*
*what you cannot bear to witness.*

— ROD OWENS, a queer black man, asking that white people
stop trying to convince him they're not racist
and start paying honest attention to themselves.[1]

A UNIVERSITY STUDENT more than doubled the amount of money raised on campus by adding a simple phrase to the end of a fundraising pitch: "I'm a student too."[2] We have sympathy for people like us. This helps us cement bonds and cohesion in community. It also has devastating impacts when we see people as not part of "us." That's the process called othering or out-group bias. It's present in racism, sexism, homophobia, transphobia, anti-Semitism, Islamophobia... This bleak list could go on.

At an event welcoming Syrian refugees to Vancouver, a man rides up on a bike and pepper sprays the crowd.[3] What makes us act this way? We'll explore this difficult question in this and future chapters. It seems humans are remarkably good at othering. Even preschoolers describe teasing members of another group as more morally acceptable than teasing their own group.[4] The debate rages on about how early in life othering starts. Evidence from Germany and the US suggests that children might not show their parents' prejudices until about age six and aren't born assuming that the race of other children establishes anything about their character.[5] But by the time we're adults, if we see pictures of someone of a different race, many of us will experience more distress, anxiety, and aggression. In just *one-twentieth of a second* we can process a picture of an "other" differently than a picture of an "us"! This happens much faster than any careful thought or decision about the picture.[6]

When we think of prejudice we usually think of overt beliefs about why our group is superior to "others." Perhaps the pepper sprayer thought this way. But even when we explicitly find such prejudice repulsive, we can still maintain subtle biases that are *implicit*. As much as we might like to be, we're not blind to gender, skin color, or sexual orientation. If biased views are presented to us often enough, we may even learn to implicitly accept them *about ourselves*! Here's Theodore Johnson's description of testing his biases through an activity that flashes pictures together with negative and positive words, to see how long it takes us to respond. The test's purpose is to measure struggles to pair certain concepts (like positive qualities) with certain images (like dark-skinned people).

> Before I started the racial-bias assessment, a disclaimer explicitly warned me that those who are not prepared to receive uncomfortable news should not proceed. I was too intrigued to turn back, but it turns out I was unprepared for the outcome.
>
> According to the Implicit Association Test, I have a "strong automatic preference for European Americans compared to African Americans." That's a sterile way of saying that I'm biased against black people. For most people, such a designation would probably be unsettling.... But for me, it caused a mini-existential crisis.
>
> Why? Because I'm black.[7]

The Implicit Association Test has been criticized because, for instance, if the same person takes it at different times their results tend to vary. But the overall reality of implicit bias has been quite thoroughly documented.[8] There *are* people who don't show signs of implicit bias. However, these individuals may have a bias of their own. One study of racial bias-free individuals found that they all seemed to see neutral objects around them as positive (a chair? That's a good thing!)[9] For the rest of us, here are a few examples of what can happen:

> Show subjects slides about some obscure country; afterward, they will have more negative attitudes toward the place if, between slides, pictures of faces with expressions of fear appeared at subliminal speeds. Sitting near smelly garbage makes people more socially conservative about outgroup issues (e.g., attitudes toward gay marriage among heterosexuals). Christians express more negative attitudes toward non-Christians if they've just walked past a church.[10]

Much of this comes down to feeling uncomfortable, even threatened. It's quite possible that the pepper sprayer felt that somehow newly arrived Syrian refugees represented a threat. Threat detection is critically important for survival, but we're easily mistaken. The opposite of seeing neutral things as positive, some of us are extra sensitive to imagining that most changes in the world around us are threats.[11] Evidence suggests that when we're prejudiced, we often experience "others" not just as challenging to understand but as a danger to "us." Like the difference we saw between framing an operation in terms of chances of living or of dying, there's an important difference between perceiving someone as challenging, or as a threat:

> Challenges incite a sequence of physiological responses that send more blood to our muscles and brains, enhancing our physical and cognitive performance. Threats, on the other hand, set off a physiological response that restricts our blood flow and releases the hormone cortisol, which breaks down muscle tissue and halts digestive processes so that the body can quickly muster the energy it needs to confront the threat. Over time, these responses wear down muscles, including the heart, and damage the immune system.[12]

This means that our prejudices can literally kill us, increasing our risks of serious health problems associated with chronic stress—from cancer to Type II diabetes!

The example above—that smelling garbage can make heterosexuals feel less supportive of gay marriage—highlights the important and related role that disgust plays. From an evolutionary perspective it makes sense that we'd be motivated to stay away from things that can make us sick, like rotting food. This is highly useful. But somehow, many of us are unwittingly projecting ancient fears of sickness onto people or situations that have no potential to make us sick. This may be why bigoted language is often related to disgust—labeling groups "dirty," "filthy," "cockroaches"…

The more squeamish we are, regardless of our income, education levels, and other key factors, the more readily bothered we will be by, for instance, seeing an unflushed toilet. And the more readily we're distressed by the unflushed toilet, the more likely we are to want to keep things the way they are, and to feel threatened by the unfamiliar.[13] We saw how sensations like warmth from holding a cup of coffee influence our decisions, and the same is true of disgust. When we're feeling disgusted, we're more likely to say that lying on our resume is a terrible thing to do, whereas if we're feeling clean after just washing our hands, we're more likely to say it's no big deal.[14]

Those of us with fewer physiological signs of distress (like sweating and rapid blinking) when we see disturbing images are less likely to support wars and are more open to receiving refugees to our countries.[15] How disgusted and threatened we feel by different situations isn't just something we're born with and experience throughout our lives though. For instance, experiencing trauma can make us less accepting of refugees, perhaps because we're newly fearful and attuned to what can go wrong in life.[16] Evidence suggests that feeling frightened makes us temporarily more focused on protecting ourselves (and so less welcoming of Syrian refugees, for instance). The opposite is also true. When people in one study were asked to imagining having a superpower that gave them complete physical safety, they were temporarily more open to accepting refugees.[17]

So the pepper sprayer may have been feeling a sense of threat, fear, and disgust—all unpleasant sensations all of us are familiar with. I think that, without condoning terrible actions in any way, the research findings just discussed can give us cause to understand each other a bit better. Looking at the world around us, it's easy to find reasons to feel safe and cared for or to feel disgusted and under threat. Within limits, both make a lot of sense. When taken to extremes, they can lead to hate crimes like pepper spraying a group of strangers who pose no threat to us whatsoever.

When we're feeling distressed or not doing well in life, for whatever reasons, we often look for simple explanations as to why. Sociologist René Girard says, "Everywhere and always, when human beings either cannot or dare not take their anger out on the thing that has caused it, they unconsciously search for substitutes, and more often than not they find them."[18] Imagining that Syrian refugees are doing well and getting free handouts while causing problems for "us" may feel comforting. Neuroscientist Robert Sapolsky calls this type of thinking "a horrifyingly effective stress-reduction mechanism." He sees it as a displacement of pain, which helps us feel better.[19] (I'd add—in a limited sense and in the immediate term!) And there's another bias that contributes to such scapegoating too.

When a camera is focused on the suspect during a police interrogation, people watching the video are *twice as likely* to rate the suspect as guilty as when, *in the exact same interaction*, the camera is focused on both the suspect and the police interrogator.[20] The information that sticks out to us (like whoever's face is on camera) just naturally feels important and influential. It seems like the *cause* of what we're witnessing. So, if we're feeling angry and unsure about our future, we may look around and disproportionately notice a particular group—Syrian refugees—simply because they stand out to us as different. Then it's an easy step for us to create a story about how Syrians are the *cause* of our bad situation.[21] International trade agreements are remote and tough to comprehend, so they just don't *feel* like they're impacting our career prospects the same way a Syrian family next door is. Our perceived social status and power play a large role here. When we have power in experiments, we're far more likely to make stereotyped judgments about "others" and less likely to pay attention to them as unique individuals.[22]

As much as we might feel disgust and distress around "others," many of us decide that our own group is particularly likeable and trustworthy.[23] We see ourselves as the farthest thing from disgusting. In one example, Canadians who voted for different political parties were asked to look at yearbook photos of random people and guess which party they vote for. The result? Regardless of our political leanings, we assume that attractive people vote for the same party we do![24] Evidence from Japan, Hong Kong, and South Korea suggests that over-rating our own group isn't universal. One theory is that collectivist cultures, while still showing prejudices about "others," don't inflate the positive qualities of "us" as much as individualist cultures do.[25]

So, what can we do to reduce our biases against "others" if some are implicit and can play out in the brain in fractions of a second? It's important to point out that experiencing people as "others" can be the result of focusing on any number of characteristics, from their holding different religious or political views to their having particular personal traits. Our brains seem to track relevant information about who we think of as "other," whether they're from another race or another team.[26] So prejudice is *heavily* dependent on the stories we tell ourselves—which makes it vulnerable to a positive infection.

For example, participants in one study were asked to think about "others" as *individuals* by imagining what types of vegetables they like. This shift in thinking seemed to reduce anxiety when seeing pictures of "others." So, if we think of "others" as people, seeking to imagine their perspectives, our biases soften.[27] Similarly we can "try to consciously identify what qualities and goals [we] might have in common."[28] Other evidence suggests that we like people far more when we believe they like us.[29] So one way to reduce our discomfort is to consciously assume that people like us!

Later we'll look in detail at beliefs, but for now it's worth pointing out that it's often possible to identify examples that conform to stereotypes. ("Look how badly that woman is driving. Women are such bad drivers!") We can notice that this is happening and then be deliberate in looking for examples that *don't* conform. ("Oh, that was a stereotyped thought. Let's see who else is on the road... Actually those other women are driving OK. And that man is driving badly. Some *people* are just bad drivers.")

In other cases there's actual evidence to back up stereotypes—for example, that people of color are more likely to be poor. Canadian census data listed poverty rates as 22% among racialized groups compared to 9% for white Canadians.[30] When we find this out we can try to notice our immediate thoughts to get a hint of our biases. Maybe we think, "They must be lazy." Zooming out to take a bigger view, we might discover many factors that make a stereotype come true, showing us that our initial ideas about laziness were off base.

We read how contact between people was used in a creative way by gay rights activists in Kenya to reduce prejudice. For at least a century Quakers have been among the strong proponents of this approach. Pierre Cérésole and other Quakers in Europe in 1919 tried to reduce prejudices and hostilities after war by establishing programs where "young people from many countries had an opportunity to know each other through the comradeship of shared constructive, voluntary service."[31] The idea is that members of groups that have been in conflict work alongside each other on common projects— volunteering to build a community center, for example. What does the evidence say about this work?

An analysis of 515 studies involving people from 38 countries shows that contact can indeed help to reduce prejudice but not always. In a minority of cases contact makes matters worse—so the details are important![32] Keys to successful contact are "having the support of relevant authorities, sharing common goals, a sense of cooperation, and equal status."[33] It's also important that programs be prolonged and not short one-offs. A leading theory says this is largely because continual contact reduces the sense of distress and unfamiliarity when we see an "other," turning them from some*thing* we're unsure about and feel threatened by into some*one* whose presence is comfortable and predictable.[34] An emotional involvement like a friendship or romance with a member of an out-group can be an even more powerful way to overcome the prejudices we might have learned.[35]

Again, context matters, and there are times when social conditions deeply strain meaningful possibilities for friendship and dialogue. After programs help them make friends, "young Palestinians return to a reality of unchanged occupation. Young Israelis return to their schools, and later complete military service." This deep divide has led many Palestinians to feel "betrayal, anger, and hurt as Israeli friends that they'd met at camps joined the military and took up positions enforcing Israel's occupation. Rather than building relationship, trust was broken and people were pushed apart."[36] When deep structural problems remain, contact could do more harm than good.

Physical contact might not always be necessary in countering prejudices. Simply seeing "others" portrayed in the media seems to help,[37] again perhaps because this makes "others" seem more normal and less threatening. Obviously, this effect depends on the quality of the portrayal—stereotyped portrayals won't reduce stereotyped and prejudiced ideas.[38]

Some media try to counter prejudice in one-dimensional ways ("Look at this beautiful African village where everyone is good and hard working and always smiling"). While apparently positive, these images, used by nonprofits and even programs designed to *address* racism, may still be increasing it, "especially if they depict the 'out' group as wholly good and undifferentiated," researcher Emile Bruneau has found. To counteract this, he highlights the importance of not just painting "others" as one homogeneous group, but allowing human uniqueness to shine through[39]—as we've seen, effective messages help us imagine "others" in detailed ways—like what vegetables this specific person prefers!

Another technique that works is getting into a better mood! A basic instruction like asking someone to smile has been shown to reduce implicit bias, as has asking participants to listen to a 10-minute guided meditation. What's particularly interesting about these findings is that neither the instruction to smile nor the meditation said anything about biases.[40] It appears that when we're feeling good it's just tougher to also feel as threatened and ready to pepper spray people.

This may last only for as long as our good mood does, but other research shows that our brains physically change as we build inner peace (a topic we'll return to later). This is one of many exciting recent findings about neuroplasticity. It used to be commonly taught that at a certain point in early adulthood our brains were fully developed and the best we could do was just maintain them as they slowly declined. Today it's understood that use continually changes the brain. For instance, the insula—brain structures important in tracking our internal experiences and in constructing our feelings—have been found to get physically thicker (due to increased density of neural networks) when we spend enough time consciously working to use them. What's more, this also increases our abilities to experience empathy and compassion *for others*![41] So paying careful attention to our own feelings, learning to know and label them as precisely as we can, over time seems to help us find more caring feelings for other people.

This is all a reminder that we don't live in a world of absolutes. Most of us carry around some very positive aspirations and values, as well as some very unsavory thoughts and impulses. It might not be too useful to think of ourselves as "good" or "evil" people but as people with sexist, ableist, or otherwise biased views to varying degrees, degrees that change based in part on our environment and mood.

## Tips from This Chapter

1. There's no one criterion we use to decide someone is an "other"— they can be as diverse as being on a different sports team, holding different religious or political views, or having any number of personal characteristics.
2. Even if we reject explicit prejudices, most of us still have implicit biases. Knowing this, we can check in with ourselves when interacting with members of an "out-group." If we notice that we're

feeling uncomfortable or threatened, this could be a sign of implicit bias at play.

3. In particular in individualist cultures, our biases tend to hold both that our group is more trustworthy and admirable than we might actually be and that "others" are more threatening and disgusting.

4. What we notice most seems to us to be most causal of whatever problem we have. We may blame it on whoever stands out to us because of being different. Important causes that aren't as easy to notice just don't feel as influential.

5. When we're in positions of power, we have higher chances of being impulsive and biased.

6. We can use the following techniques to overcome the pitfalls of "us" and "others":

   a. Thinking of those around us as unique individuals. When we think of other people as individuals and not just members of a group, especially when we seek to imagine their unique individual perspectives, our biases soften.

   b. Consciously assuming that people in "out-groups" are friendly and that they like us.

   c. Consciously identifying what qualities and goals we have in common with someone from an "out-group," overcoming the tendency to think of "them" as different from "us."

   d. Noticing ourselves having prejudiced ideas, and looking for the real-world evidence that contradicts them, or discovering the factors that make stereotypes come true in some instances.

   e. Working to notice and reject any portrayal, even apparently positive, that shows groups of people as being all the same.

   f. Trying to get into a better mood (which has been shown to reduce prejudice).

   g. Paying attention to our own feelings (which has been shown over time to boost empathy and compassion for others).

7. It can be particularly transformative for all involved to have prolonged contact with "out-groups" in a way that includes sharing common goals, a sense of cooperation, and equal status.

## Activity: Transforming Bias

Facilitators ask each member of the group to pick one or more tips from the chapter Us and Others and to report back to the group after at least one week of testing it out. Facilitators ask, "What tip did you pick? What successes and challenges did you experience with it?"

# Power-over

*There are obvious variations between being powerless and*
*powerful, but many of the problems mirror each other.*
*In both cases, people are caught in the same*
*unhealthy social systems.*

— RACHEL MACNAIR[1]

WHAT DO YOU think of when you hear the word "power"?
Maybe it's pleasing images of athletes, superheroes, or poli-
ticians you admire. Perhaps it's characters you're disgusted by—
greedy and heartless CEOs, authoritarian rulers, criminal gangs...
Right now, what's your feeling of power or powerlessness? Where
does it come from? How much does it change moment to moment?
The next two chapters will present some concepts about power that
I hope will be useful for the rest of the book.

If you're like me, you grew up with a sense that, ultimately, power
means the ability to use violence, and without it, we're powerless.
From this perspective flows a faith in what's been called power-over.
Here's one helpful description of it:

> Power-over comes from the consciousness I have termed es-
> trangement: the view of the world as made up of atomized,
> nonliving parts, mechanically interacting, valued not for
> what they inherently are but only in relation to some outside
> standard.... We live embedded in systems of power-over and
> are indoctrinated into them, often from birth. In its clearest
> form, power-over is the power of the prison guard, of the gun,

power that is ultimately backed by [violent] force. Power-over enables one individual or group to make the decisions that affect others, and to enforce control.[2]

An important point raised here is that power-over seems to rely on conceptual divisions. If we experience others (including other species) and ourselves as intertwined, doing damage to them would be hurting ourselves. But in power-over abstractions "us" and "others" are two different camps. We win when they lose, and vice versa. We're separating the world into opposites—good vs. evil, right vs. wrong, truth vs. lies. At its simplest, power-over relies on this binary logic—either you're a one or a zero. Either or. Conceptual divisions are extremely useful—we're using them right now to divide up and discuss different types of power—but these divisions can become too entrenched. We can forget that they're *our own concepts*.

Quaker educator Parker Palmer explains: "Without binary logic, we would have neither computers nor many of the gifts of modern science. But for all the power it has given us in science and technology, either-or thinking has also given us a fragmented sense of reality that destroys the wholeness and wonder of life."[3] This is a profound issue. For thousands of years philosophers in places like India and China have described far-reaching problems with conceptualizing the world into hard and fast divisions.[4] Either-or thinking doesn't need to be violent, but violence and all forms of abuse *can readily arise from it*. This isn't to say that generating abstract concepts and judgments is inherently dangerous. But getting hung up on our judgments and becoming rigid about them and removed from the wholeness of the world—that can be! If this type of power-over approach were to be drawn in a diagram, its dynamic might be "all-under-one." We see the one as most righteous, worthy, and significant. That one can be any "us," any identity concept we believe in and hold (deliberately or implicitly) superior—one nation, one religious group, one gender...

Power-over is informing everything from national security strategies to ideas about childrearing and about managing employees.

It's simple—we think threatening to harm others will force them to stop doing what we don't want them to do and that by rewarding them we can make them do what we want. Our power-over mentality assumes that we know best, that *we* should have more power than *others*, and that if we didn't have this physical, violent, or emotionally coercive power over them, we'd be subjected to *their* power over *us!* A point of tension is immediately obvious—we can't *all* know best and *all* have power-over. Some of us are bound to lose out.

Let's assume for a moment that we're the winners and gain power-over. That very feeling can quickly corrupt us. Recall last chapter how we saw that it's when we think we're high status that we're particularly likely to hold prejudices. That's not the only bad behavior promoted by power-over. Winning a competition significantly increases our likelihood of being dishonest in later unrelated activities. This dishonesty happens when we feel we've *beaten others* but not when we feel we've been successful in relation to a personal goal.[5] It's when we look around and decide we're better than other people that we're ready to dominate them more and more.

Particularly as the *violent* power at our disposal increases, so does a drive to crush people. Social psychologist Morton Deutch was one of the first to show in the lab that "the introduction of weapons into negotiation situations heightens conflict by tempting the participants to use those weapons to press for advantage, and that negotiations increasingly become zero sum, with both sides aiming for complete victory and the complete defeat of the other side."[6] *Either* I win pure power over you *or* I lose completely to your power over me, there's no other way. In spite of the damage, this kind of battle for dominance can still be fun for some of us. You might have heard that bullies have low self-esteem and are insecure. The evidence doesn't back this up, suggesting instead that most bullies feel pretty good about bullying and don't lack self-confidence when doing it.[7]

Many of us are probably thinking, "I don't like bullying, but doesn't power over others work?" That depends on what we mean by "work." There's no clear line where simple pressure becomes violence, but there are certainly ways to press for something successfully and without doing major harm. In the lab, mild punishments can increase honesty. What's most important seems to be that punishments are probable, not how severe they are.[8] Whether or not punishment changes how we act is influenced by such factors as whether the punishment is seeking to bring our actions in line with accepted social norms (in which case punishments are more effective), whether it's being administered by just one person or by many, and how much it costs us to comply.[9] We all have experiences that back this up. There are many actions we take so we won't get punished, even if only by an unspoken negative judgment, but not every punishment works to deter us.

Most of us don't have philosophical problems with fines for overdue library books. The library fine may be a mild form of power-over, but the harms created are minimal and there's a straightforward purpose behind them. They could be seen as creating accountability to a collective aspiration (that libraries have books to continue to lend out). Trying to deter some behavior through power-over can be profoundly ineffective though. Gerry Williams was given tickets amounting to over $65,000 while homeless in Toronto. The tickets were for non-criminal violations associated with his living on the street—jaywalking, loitering, littering, and trespassing to sleep in various places.[10] Clearly, continually issuing Williams tickets did nothing to change his behavior. It's fairly obvious why: threats didn't address the issues causing Williams to sleep on the street. The belief that he could be deterred through power-over rests on flawed "common sense" about motivation. Much power-over is this way— abstract and removed from the real situation it tries to impact. It's caught in narrow binary logic—either you're sleeping in the right place, or we'll punish you to make you sleep in the right place.

Some might see this and think that the punishments were just too lax. As Friend Ray Cunnington puts it, "If a smack on the wrist doesn't produce the right result there are always those who advocate something more serious."[11] This is taken to the extreme with nuclear weapons being imagined as a threat to others that's so severe that it keeps us safe. Winston Churchill sounded enraptured with the grim glory of nuclear power-over when he quipped, "Safety will be the sturdy child of terror, and survival the twin brother of annihilation."[12] The power-over that nukes convey is still said by NATO to be "the supreme guarantee of our security."[13] In this bleak view peace can at best be negative, an eternal stalemate protected through keeping inconceivably brutal violence close at hand.

One weakness in the deterrence argument is that there's no good evidence for it. The US and USSR did not go to war prior to their becoming nuclear powers, and they haven't gone to war since, but there's no compelling reason to think that nukes helped ease tensions. (We already saw that adding weapons does just the opposite in lab experiments.) There have also been many wars where nonnuclear states *did* fight nuclear ones, apparently undeterred. In fact, a study of 348 territorial disputes shows that nuclear states are no more successful in coercion than other states.[14]

Still, the threat of violence sounds like a good motivator. Maybe it doesn't work for nuclear nations, but wouldn't threatening the lives of everyday citizens stop them from committing murder? It seems not. An examination of murder rates in countries the year before they abolished the death penalty, and the year after, found that the rates decreased more often than they went up.[15] Many factors are at play, but I couldn't find evidence that without power-over threats like the death penalty more of us become murderers. Again, we may be misunderstanding what motivates us when we assume that threats will stop murders. (Do most murderers sit down and calmly do a cost-benefit analysis to see if the death penalty is just too big a risk? We'll explore this issue of security in detail in a later chapter.) Scaring us seems effective as a persuasion strategy when we're already scared and are being asked to do something minor. It also works to get us not to make a decision.[16]

A common approach used by parents and caregivers seeking to shape behavior is hitting children. According to a detailed analysis of 88 studies covering 62 years of data, this has one strong association that could be considered positive by many parents—it seems to lead to increased immediate compliance on the part of the child. That's what violent power-over can often do. This immediate compliance may come at a great cost though, as hitting children is also associated with negative impacts, including increases in child aggression, deterioration of the relationship with the parent and, later in life, increases in criminal and antisocial behavior and mental health problems. These effects are not seen in every child, and other factors, like how often the child was hit, how severely, and the quality of the relationship between the parent and child overall, can mitigate against some of the worst impacts of physical punishment.[17] Still, this example may illustrate a point that's true more generally.

Immediate reactions—like the compliance of a child to the demands of a parent—can make it *appear* that power-over "works." Yet quick changes may not last, and the underlying issues that caused the original behavior haven't been addressed. The child might do it again as soon as a parent's back is turned. Violence can have long-term unintended consequences that undermine the apparent gains—relationships suffer, meaning in this case that the child might be *less* compliant and more aggressive in the future. And the stress and pain that's generated when we use power-over doesn't just disappear. Any form of punishment that increases chronic stress can have long term costs, like harming children's development.[18]

Perhaps we continue to use punishments even when we know they often fail because they can feel immediately satisfying and we don't know what else to do. In schools, suspensions persist with no evidence that they improve students' behavior and plenty that they harm grades.[19] So here's a helpful distinction: "Discipline is not the same as punishment."[20] It's a common mistake to think that not using power-over means doing nothing—letting kids run amok and be disrespectful, letting people walk all over us. Yet many parents have found that violent force isn't necessary to maintain discipline, and conversely that children may not learn discipline from being hit. (Toward the end of the book we'll see an inspiring example of a classroom that shares power with children.)

Another place we use power-over is at work. Author Daniel Pink has collected data on rewards and punishments from both real-world work places and lab experiments. He explains that rewards and punishments work best in getting us to do routine or narrowly focused tasks. Even then, it helps to explain to us *why* the task matters and to let us do it our own way. Where external ("extrinsic") motivators fail us, though, is that they can actually *crush* our motivation, make us *less creative* and more focused on the short term, and lead us to *worse performance* in many domains. A robust body of evidence has replicated these findings for decades, and they've been shown in multiple cultures. Rewards and punishments are just inherently limited.[21]

Power-over in the workplace has been linked to major negative impacts as well.[22] Multiple large-scale studies in various countries and contexts have found a range of problems created among employees. These include worse health during employment and even increased long-term health risks decades after leaving the job (the effects of chronic stress again).[23] On the other hand, more compassionate leaders have been found to build teams that prove more effective and resilient.[24] Employees seem to be more productive when they report feeling that their managers care about them *as people*.[25]

The idea that, whether as children or adults, fear of being punished forces us to learn our lesson and perform better has also been challenged by neuroscience. When we're generating emotions like fear, anger, or sadness, we aren't in an optimal condition to pick up new complex behaviors or to make our best decisions.[26] Instead, we tend to stick to current habits.[27] On the other hand, psychologist Shawn Achor has documented how when we're in positive moods we perform significantly better in all kinds of work, and we learn and adapt better to the pressures around us.[28] This may explain why, in spite of what we might intuit, punishing someone seems generally less effective than rewarding them. In lab experiments we respond faster and more consistently when moving toward a rewarding goal than when trying to avoid an unpleasant one.[29]

Power-over lies along a spectrum, so it's important that we not think only about the extremes. Because power-over is so common, we might not see its subtler forms at all:

> At one end of the spectrum, we decimate humanity in overt ways, including mass incarceration, human trafficking, slavery and genocide. At the other end, this process is more covert—expressed through habits and relationships that subtly manifest beliefs like "You are worthless," "I am better than you," and "Your voice doesn't matter." We do this when we talk over other people, for example, when we stereotype them, and when we say that we are listening and then proceed to act in ways that ignore their views completely.[30]

We regularly use power-over but actually it's only one kind of power, and in many ways it's fragile. If we're resorting to heavier forms of power-over, like violence, we're likely feeling afraid, vulnerable, or unhappy that something we think *should* be happening isn't.[31] Maybe we're stuck in abstract ideas about what we're entitled to or how the world ought to be. As soon as others refuse to comply, even when we threaten them, our power-over can falter. What are other types of power?

## Tips from This Chapter

1. Punishments and rewards offer one source of power. This is often based on abstract ideas and standards, the conceptual division of everything into discrete parts to perceive in isolation and to then manipulate and control. Power-over can often rest on simplified binary logic—either-or thinking. A power-over model of life can be described as "all-under-one" and can easily promote zero-sum thinking where we win only when others lose.

2. The evidence shows that punishments can improve certain behaviors in certain circumstances. One factor that's important appears to be the consistency of the punishment, not its severity. On the other hand, even serious punishments are regularly

ineffective at producing behavior change. There's no evidence that nuclear deterrence works or that the death penalty decreases murders. Physical violence against children can lead to immediate compliance but also harmful long-term impacts (though not in every child). Power-over in work environments is associated with many negative outcomes for employees, some of which can be long lasting.

3. Power-over can feel immediately satisfying and can produce immediate results but often with unexpected long-term negative consequences. The underlying causes of a behavior we're trying to change are rarely dealt with when we use power-over. Feeling distressed and anxious actually blocks learning, whereas positive moods boost it, which may be why rewards seem to work better than punishments in many cases (although they also have their limitations).

— 4 —

# Power-with
# and Power-from-within

*Through widening circles of identification,
we vastly extend the boundaries of our self-interest,
and enhance our joy and meaning in life.*

— JOANNA MACY and MOLLY YOUNG BROWN[1]

WE OFTEN HEAR about the value of tolerance. Would you like it if someone found you tolerable? It sounds better than being actively attacked, but it's a low bar. Douglas White, former chief of the Snuneymuxw Nation, has offered a more encouraging vision to strive for. Speaking about Canada he explains, "I think about what I want for my children and grandchildren. What I want for them is to be loved and love other people in this country. Not to tolerate them, not to go to our respective corners and stop hurting each other, but to be wrapped up and engaged in each other's lives."[2]

I think White is beautifully describing what's been called power-with. Recall a time when you were happy. It could be a recent moment or one long ago. Think about where you were and who you were with. Now I'm going to read your mind. I think you're thinking about a connection with other people or the natural world. Chances are I'm right because, for most of us at least, there's no experience of deep happiness in which we're disconnected from others (whether people, pets, or mountains). This suggests that we are now, and always will be, dependent on others—folks beyond our control—no matter how much power-over we might come to enjoy.

If we think about it, any time we impact another living being, we're expressing our power. If we smile at someone and their mood changes momentarily, that was both of our powers at work, as Zawadi Nikuze explained in Chapter One. So we don't need to think of power as always backed by violent force! Power-with moves us from the straightforward either-or to a messy mixture. We aren't so certain, so fixated about our concepts. We're no longer anxiously trying to be superior to others so we can get our way; we're curious and looking for ways to succeed together.

Let's explore two interesting studies about this. You might think you could guess who'd support going to war if you knew what political party they voted for or their level of religiosity. But a study done in the US found that support for war was best predicted by another factor—whether or not we believe that some people are *evil*.[3] This is either-or thinking at play. Some people are just zeros against our ones, and the way to deal with them is violent power-over. The second example is this: in experiments where we're forced to memorize random information so our minds are already taxed, we're more likely to rate others as "pure evil" and skip the nuance.[4]

Complex thinking seems to take more mental effort, while collapsing the spectrum of reality down into simple and pure categories—ones and zeros—is less demanding. Psychologist Peter Coleman's lab has tested how arguments transform or become further entrenched. Coleman brings together individuals with strongly opposing beliefs (in favor of abortion versus opposed to it, for instance) to have one-on-one conversations. Sometimes the conversations go terribly. Other times, although their beliefs don't change after an hour in the lab, participants leave feeling that being there was worthwhile. In these latter instances, peoples' experiences are *more complex*. The folks who don't do well descend into a mood of distress and negativity and stay there. Those who find some value in the conversation are able to feel and hold contradictions simultaneously. They feel *good and bad* about the conversation.

They have some respect for the person they're talking to even as the words they're hearing are deeply challenging. They go beyond the either-or of power-over and somewhere into the messiness of power-with. It's not feeling purely good that predicts that they're satisfied with the conversation; it's spending time feeling *both* good *and* challenged.

Remember the decision to have surgery being much more popular when we're told our likelihood of living? Similarly, Coleman found that how information is framed makes a big difference in how tough conversations go, whether they stay complex or become simplistic and entrenched.[5] This isn't just relevant in the lab. Scientists examining speeches and debates have found interesting evidence that politicians speak in less complex ways as they become more unyielding and likely to go to war, and conversely peace agreements coincide with increased complexity.[6]

It's easy to think *either* you can see the world in a complex way *or* you can't, but that may not be so. One way to increase complexity in our thinking is to bring to mind our own inner struggles, the fact that we're never purely one way or another. Are you the exact same person when you're around your family as when you're with close friends? These two versions of you likely have certain conflicting aspects. We long to be wild and adventuresome but want security and to be comfortable. We want more free time but also to have more hobbies. Recalling our tendencies to behave in conflicting ways, and how much we change depending on the situation, helps us reduce the imagined distance between "us" and "others" we disagree with.[7] Certain training programs also claim to be successful in increasing complex thinking, with the result of making us less supportive of violence[8] and more conciliatory.[9]

Power-with seems to require a readiness to stay with some discomfort. If we feel too threatened, disgusted, afraid that we don't have enough power, that others are pure evil, that the next moment might be bad for us, we'll start looking for power-over. Paradoxically, the loneliness, fear, and uncertainty we feel seems to mostly *increase* when we do. The more we retreat out of the world and into our abstract ideas about what *should* happen, the more desperate and unsettled we might feel. When we build power-with, we typically *feel better*. This is a sort of enlightened self-interest, acknowledging that power-over isn't our actual goal—happiness is, and for happiness to thrive, we need healthy relationships. I believe it's largely because power-with so often *feels better* over the long-term that the peace virus continues to replicate despite the fact that complex thinking is more demanding and having power-over can seem more immediately appealing.

Power-with is each of us expressing ourselves within a community, without seeking to take over or to be subsumed. This is a continual balancing act. After all, "within a group, influence can too easily become authority."[10] Where power-over has all the answers, power-with shares the act of questioning and exploring. Where power-over drives in a specific direction to take everything else with it, power-with coevolves and adapts. So power-with isn't something we sit down and experience on our own in the library. We build it together. It can be challenging, but *it may add years to our lives!* Studies have now shown that, at any age or income level, social isolation has very serious damaging effects.[11] We need other people, and not just to dominate, manipulate, or repress them. In the previous chapter we asked the question of whether or not power-over works. So, let's now ask: what's the evidence that power-with "works"?

Psychologist Dacher Keltner has studied youth and adults in multiple environments and found that people who demonstrate five particular qualities (enthusiasm, kindness, focus, calmness, and openness) are considered powerful by those around them. The evidence suggests that for a short time, demanding or aggressive power-over can work.[12] But those who are willing to manipulate and backstab to get power don't tend to hold onto it. It's when our actions are seen as fair *by our group* that we're respected and granted leadership status.[13] This means that gauging and helping serve others' needs and interests *is powerful*. Skills like getting along with others and making friendships can be thought of as "master skills that affect all aspects of life."[14]

So, we can build our power with others. But how would this work in challenging cases? Perhaps the most disturbing crime of all is pedophilia. Various psychological and criminal justice responses have been tested—and they haven't done well. Even with tough power-over, overall rates of re-offending in Canada are 14% after five years and 24% after 15.[15]

Groups of volunteers, many of them Mennonites, and some Quakers, wondered about a different approach—power with sex offenders. Believing that "no one is disposable,"[16] Circles of Support and Accountability was created to connect volunteers with convicted child molesters on their release from prison. Rather than using shame to prevent re-offending, the Circles build friendships. They mostly just sit together and talk.

Many of the former offenders interviewed said they felt like they'd become real friends with these volunteers. Circles make an effort to reduce the stigma and isolation and to connect former offenders with a sense of community. Importantly, they also *hold them accountable* for their commitments and doing the hard work of rebuilding their lives. (Power-with doesn't mean not speaking up when someone breaks their commitments!) This program, based largely around treating former child molesters like human beings, seems to have had significant success. The evaluators admit some challenges with the data available, but it appears that there's a 5.6% rate of reoffending after five years. More studies are in order, but if these findings hold, a drop in reoffending over the first five years from 14% to 5.6% is worth taking seriously! This may be an illustration of how, even in an incredibly difficult situation where professional psychologists struggle, a low-cost dose of genuine power-with can have a transformative impact. The program requires getting over the binary logic of treating former child molesters as pure evil, and that's not easy—a fact that may be reflected in Circles' struggling to recruit and retain enough volunteers.[17]

Of course, we don't need to develop the close friendships that form in a Circle in order to use power-with. Basic respect is often enough! But power-with isn't at its richest and most infectious until we're able to feel close enough to really speak our truth. If we're not free to make mistakes without being shunned, we'll have strong incentives to be defensive and justify whatever missteps we may have made, perhaps remembering them in self-serving ways while denying all evidence to the contrary.

Brian Goldman describes his experience with misjudgments that cost lives. Goldman, a doctor, misdiagnosed a patient who later died. The profound sense of shame that followed didn't help him talk about what happened—or help other doctors to not repeat the mistake. "The unhealthy shame says not that what you did was bad, but that *you* are bad... That's the kind of system we have. It's a system in which the perception is that there are two kinds of physicians—those who make mistakes and those who don't." There's that either-or thinking again. Denial of reality though—that doctors make mistakes every day—means that the problem becomes entrenched: "It's estimated that between 9,000 and 24,000 Canadians each year die in hospital of preventable medical errors—and this is probably a gross underestimate..."[18] This culture of power-over through shaming isn't universal, so specific environments—like hospitals or schools or even whole countries—can shift.[19] Power-with types of thinking can be applied by institutions, not just individuals.

What about when we're not being listened to and power-with looks like it's failing? We may feel that some caring "tough love" is in order—say in the case of a family member with a devastating heroin addiction. A study examined the results when we threaten to disown family members unless they enter rehab. The families involved felt this was the only way to get through to their loved ones. This is classic power-over—deciding a course of action without consulting the recipient of the decision, and threatening a heavy punishment for non-compliance. Another group of families in the study was taught skills to help "nurture the addict's own motivation." The result? "More than twice as many families succeeded in getting their loved ones into treatment (64 percent) with the gentler approach." Similarly, with alcoholics going to counseling, studies have found that, "counselor empathy—not confrontation—is connected with recovery."[20]

Notice that these outcomes are far from perfect. Only 64% of families using power-with got their loved-ones to check into rehab; 5.6% of sex offenders had reoffended within five years even though they had a Circle of Support and Accountability. Power-with often fails, but *it seems to generally do better than power-over*. Whether as children or adults, as doctors caring for patients, or former sex offenders trying to rebuild our lives, being helped to honestly understand what's happening and to tap into our own power for action seems more successful than being punished or told what we ought to do.

This brings us to the last type of power I'll mention, what's been called transformational power, personal power, power-from-within, or even soul-force. Early Quaker George Fox once said, "After ye see yourselves, power comes."[21] The open and creative power-from-within, a power aligned with what's really happening in a situation, with the raw truth, reveals opportunities for reintegration, for shedding our estrangement. This may seem farfetched or unclear, in particular because we're so used to the narrative that superior physical force "wins." What is power-from-within? Where does it come from?

Power-from-within might be called our own potential, or inner capacity, to act in peaceful ways. It connects to our sense of morality (but not an abstract morality). All of us have had an experience of suddenly helping someone without seeking a reward, or of making art, dancing, or engaging in pure play that felt healing and uplifting. (If you're wondering why I'm connecting power to activities with no obvious usefulness like playing, Johan Huizinga and others have studied play and found it central in the development of culture—from design, to business, to politics—so what we're talking about is anything but frivolous.[22]) As soon as someone makes our play or our generosity into a transaction, perhaps with a paycheck or a positive review, the original joy starts to fade. It can be quickly replaced by new rules and feelings of mechanically acting for an abstract

Erdem Gündüz and others in Istanbul's Taksim Square, 2013.

result, a future incentive outside of the action itself. Power-from-within, on the other hand, tends to arise in the moment.

In Turkey in 2013 a protest style that would appeal to Quakers suddenly spread. Performance artist Erdem Gündüz stood *silently*. With his hands in his pockets, Gündüz defied orders to leave a square in Istanbul that had been the focal point of violent clashes. After eight hours of silent witness, Gündüz had been joined by a crowd of more than 300. The protest was eventually broken up and several people were arrested, but this was not the end. Twitter helped transmit the viral idea of the standing man (#duranadam in Turkish), and the next day similar actions broke out all over Turkey.[23] Gündüz was not seeking to be intimidating, but he was clearly not willing to acquiesce to power-over, the command to leave the square. Perhaps his action caught on because it conveyed a powerful and direct experience. Seeing an image of Gündüz, we can start to feel the stirrings of our own power-from-within, resonating with his. (Evidence about this will be explored in a future chapter.)

What did #duranadam protests accomplish? Does power-from-within "work"? It's important to say that #duranadam was just one small part of wider social change campaigns in Turkey, so isolating the impact is difficult. Generally, of the three types of power we've looked at, power-from-within is the trickiest to define and study, so this is a good point to take a brief detour into questions of causality.

Some would argue that the #duranadam protests accomplished nothing, because they didn't change the human rights situation in Turkey. Some might say they made conditions worse, perhaps making the Turkish government more authoritarian. It can be helpful to think in such simple ways in some circumstances, but as we're seeing, simple answers often fail to describe the richness of the conflicts we face. As Columbia University puts it, "Four hundred years of analytic, linear, cause-and-effect science has left our understanding of social conflict dynamics largely decontextualized, short term and piecemeal."[24]

Science is beginning to understand what many cultures have expressed forever—we're embedded in webs of interrelation. Everything is significant. Conditions impact each other in ways so rich they may be impossible to know beforehand. New properties *emerge* that could not have been predicted, because no part of the system had those properties on its own.[25] In other words, we can't simply engage in a #duranadam protest and understand what the consequences will be. I don't see this as an excuse for a lack of strategy, but it is a sobering reality about seeking change in complex systems. So we don't know what the #duranadam protests accomplished, but we can be sure that any sense they "did nothing" is naively simplistic and out of step with reality. They definitely impacted on-going social change movements, as well as efforts to counter those movements.

Actions may seem to have failed for a long time before their impacts become clearer. Power-with—because it's building people up—has a good likelihood of producing positive changes in the future, exactly when power-over, if it creates pain and resentment, may cause unintended negative consequences. Parker Palmer recounts a story told to him by John Lewis, who was very active in the civil rights movement in the US. In 1961, Lewis and a friend were attacked and badly beaten with baseball bats while waiting at a bus station in South Carolina. They'd been trained in the skills of non-violence, and their power-from-within motivated them not to fight back. Lewis went on to a career in politics.

> In 2009, forty-eight years after this event, a white man about John Lewis's age walked into his office on Capitol Hill, accompanied by his middle-aged son. "Mr. Lewis," he said, "my name is Elwin Wilson. I'm one of the men who beat you in that bus station back in 1961. I want to atone for the terrible thing I did, so I've come to seek your forgiveness. Will you forgive me?"
>
> Lewis said, "I forgave him, we embraced, he and his son and I wept, and then we talked."[26]

Sometimes the peace virus can be very slow in working its way to our hearts. That's why power-from-within is so crucial—some personal faith (even if derived from secular moral values) can provide great reserves of energy for the long-term work of seeking healing and balance in destructive and ever uncertain situations.

The purpose of the previous two chapters hasn't been to establish a rock-solid formula for deciding whether or not an action is power-over, power-with, power-from-within, or any other type of power. I hope instead we're seeing that categories tend to be a bit malleable and imperfect. Undoubtedly, we can think of examples that sit somewhere between power-over and power-with, or that aren't quite power-from-within. But to the extent that these ideas help us clarify the dynamics at play in our lives, they're worth considering.

## Tips from This Chapter

1. Power-with requires the flexibility of uncertainty as we build ways forward together with others. Part of the reason this style of power flourishes around the world is that it often feels better. We don't have to fight to prove our supremacy over others, and we can be ready to give without ignoring our own needs. This requires significant honesty, trust, and openness, and it's

particularly when we become powerful leaders that we may forget these qualities that got us there.

2. When we engage in a both-and rather than either-or style of thinking we tend to find more rewarding ways to be in conflict and are less inclined to support dangerously simplified solutions to problems. We can be trained to think in more complex ways, such as remembering our own inner conflicts, to help us feel closer to "others" with whom we disagree.

3. Helping people to find their own power has been proven in various circumstances to be more effective than telling them what they should do.

4. Power-from-within moves us to respond in the moment in sincere, heart-felt ways that can transform dysfunctional situations. It's an inner source of inspiration that pushes many of us to be at our best.

5. Change resulting from power-with and power-from-within is often slower to arrive but—because these powers involve building people up—the long-term effects are more likely to be positive.

## Activity: Walk Around

1. Facilitators ask the group to clear out a space big enough for everyone to comfortably move around the room. If someone is not able to walk, facilitators invite them to pay attention to the activity and be ready to speak about what they witnessed or to visualize participating and share about what they visualized.

2. Facilitators invite participants to move however they want through the room, paying attention to their bodies as much as they're able. After a few minutes, facilitators instruct people to move very slowly. Facilitators keep changing instructions every minute or two: to move very hurriedly; to walk with little steps; to walk with big steps; to choose a particular body part and let it lead; to walk like a man; to walk like a woman; to walk peacefully; to walk like someone who is weak; to walk like someone who is very powerful.

3. Facilitators invite everyone to sit in a circle, and get a few people's responses to each question before moving on to the next one:
   a. "What stood out for you?"
   b. "How did it feel in your body to walk in these different ways?"
   c. "What was most familiar and what was least familiar?"
   d. "Did you notice any connections between your body and your mood?"
   e. "How do you embody power (or not)?"[27]

## Activity: Find your Power-from-within

1. Facilitators ask everyone to arrange themselves in a big circle and have a seat.
2. Facilitators say, "Please close your eyes. Try to notice any tensions or fear you're carrying. Locate them within your body." Pause to let this happen.
3. Now facilitators offer the following suggestions, "Can you now, just for a moment, let yourself relax a bit? Imagine what might be different for you if you believed that peaceful paths were always possible, if you thought before reacting to anything that happened, expected the best, cared for others, and respected yourself.[28] Please imagine for a few moments letting go of your anxieties and feeling power-from-within, a power that moves you to make positive changes in your life and in the world."
4. Facilitators pause for a few minutes and then tell the group that they're going to go around the circle with each person answering the question: "What's hard or painful about your identity?" Facilitators say something like, "You can pass on answering the question if you wish, but I'd encourage you to try. Be as specific as possible. The designers of this question say it helps us discover what we most want to share and then we get to hear ourselves share it."[29]
5. After the go-around, facilitators take responses popcorn style to the final question: "Recalling some recent interactions, can you think of ways you use power-over, power-with, or power-from-within?"

# Process and Change

*We had an unusually long and troublesome agenda,*
*promising to keep us at it until well into the night. The only*
*thing to do...was to alter the time of our opening [silence].*
*We would simply have to take more time... And we did.*
*After a few minutes, there were some restless rustlings;*
*but we went on for surely no less than twenty minutes—long*
*enough for the restless impatience to "get on with it" to fall away*
*as we began to come to our center individually and as a group.*
*I have rarely attended a meeting for business conducted with*
*more peace, order, love and even dispatch. From the place of quiet*
*we had come to, many of the difficulties fell away...*

— PATRICIA LORING[1]

THINK OF A TIME when you had a particularly delicious meal. Recall the smell, the environment you were in, the way you sat down to eat with anticipation. Now imagine if you'd had the meal while standing, about to rush out the door to an appointment. Clearly, process matters. Yet many of us, in our eagerness to get things done and meet obligations, are ready to make compromises, cut corners, tell some lies, use power-over when it suits us and we know best anyway. Our intentions are good, so getting our intended result is all that matters.

Sometimes we do just need to make quick decisions and implement them. There's certainly a place for that. But there's also something important about *how* we achieve a result. While it may be tempting to force our way forward, as we discussed with hitting children, the conditions (violence) that brought about an apparently positive result (compliance from the child) could lead to future problems. Pushing too hard for a change—especially by using violence—can be counter-productive, causing a backlash.[2]

One of the big reasons we use shortcuts like power-over is that we don't believe conditions can change without them. Or we may go further and say that, quite simply, people don't change. You've almost certainly heard someone express that idea: "You can't teach an old dog new tricks." It's the idea we saw in the last chapter—some people are just evil. It's as if our behaviors are as fixed as our eye color. Is this true? In fact, change can sometimes surprise us, even when we think it isn't happening.

Daniel Aires began dreaming of a career as a soldier when he was 10. He joined the Canadian Armed Forces at 16. One day he was given a book about peace issues.

> I remember reading the book and being absolutely enraged. How could anyone be so peaceful? How could they live their life where everyone is their brother and everyone is their sister?...I'm thinking, "This is complete lunacy!" And I took the book and I threw it in the bottom of the vehicle and drove around and it got all full of gunpowder and gasoline and I read it again, and again, and again and it wore a hole in my side pocket. I had it on me all the time. And within six months I was out of the military.[3]

Somehow what seemed impossible happened, and a single book changed Aires' life. But he had to go *through a months-long invisible process* first. Most of us underestimate the likelihood of such changes. A major study found that the average person surveyed thinks their personality is far more constant than it actually is. "People, it seems, regard the present as a watershed moment at which they have finally become the person they will be for the rest of their lives." But the study found that this just isn't true. Most of us are closer to Aires, changing our beliefs in many ways as we age.[4]

Once, while watching a nature documentary, I was mesmerized by scenes of brilliantly colored moss. In real time the moss seemed to my eye to do next to nothing. But as the camera sped up time, I was treated to a brand-new understanding of the moss—there was so much change happening; I'd just imagined there wasn't because of its pace! The same may be true for each of us. Researchers recently did a careful review of 207 studies of therapeutic tools that help people think and act differently. They discovered that major personality traits—our emotional stability, our degree of extraversion—can change in just a matter of months.[5] We're simply not doomed to always be the person we are today.

What might be the impact of believing that our abilities are largely determined by our genes and there isn't much we can do about it? Research suggests this idea makes us more rigid and less comfortable admitting mistakes.[6] Remember Brian Goldman, who couldn't talk about his misdiagnosis that led to the death of a patient, for fear of being labeled a bad *person*? If we believe our genes define us, we can readily see our mistakes as expressions of *our inherent and unchanging qualities*.

In one recent study a group of students—some Jewish Israeli and some Palestinian—were taught how much people can change. They performed more cohesively and successfully on a number of tasks than a group taught strategies for coping with stress. Not only did the students who believed people can change cooperate far more, they also had more positive feelings about each other. Researchers explained what seemed to be happening: "When you think people have fixed traits your job is to just figure them out and go from there. If you think people can develop and change, you don't tend to make blanket judgments." Importantly, these effects were seen by telling the students *factual information* about people in general, not discussing details about Israel/Palestine.[7]

The effects of believing in change have been documented elsewhere as well. Teens in the US were given a brief training where they watched videos of adults explaining how much they'd changed since they were in high school, and they saw scientific findings that backed the stories up. This fresh perspective—believing that people can change—made demonstrable impacts on how calm the teens were under social stress and even improved their academic achievements over the course of a school year.[8] In other words, the fact of believing we can change significantly contributes to our wellbeing! And we all *do* change, so this is really just about *correcting a false belief* that says we're more fixed than we really are.

Geneticists confirm that DNA is not our destiny, just a contributing factor,[9] and neuroscience is revealing how malleable our brains are, as we've already touched on. Even in old age we are quite literally, to some degree, reshaping our own brains! The thoughts we think, the ways we focus, and the habits we keep, all impact our brains' wiring. When we repeatedly pair emotions, ideas, or behaviors together in time, associated neurons can wire together, and when we don't, they can wire apart.[10] Our brains' plasticity is both a great opportunity and a threat. Eternal change leaves us vulnerable to the peace virus, or to becoming trapped in new negative beliefs and obsessions. So, peace must be *continually* built.

Fundamentally, neuroplasticity tells us that whatever we practice enough, whether empathy and peaceful actions or aggression and hate, becomes easier and more automatic over time. This doesn't mean that just any change is possible, and certainly not that we can achieve anything by simply wishing for it. What it does tell us is that invisible changes are happening right now, whether we harness them consciously or not.

For centuries, Quaker agencies have had a lot of faith in the transformative power we can uncover in slow quiet processes. Friend Jane Orion Smith explains that this is all about trust. By showing consistently that they're reliable, don't have a hidden agenda, and follow through, these Quaker groups build relationships of trust and help people uncover their own power for change.[11] This often happens when Friends play the role of convener, taking great pains to establish environments where people meet as equals—eating, talking informally and off-the-record, and, as much as possible, not feeling the pressures of specific expectations or agendas. This happens at Quaker houses in places like Washington, Brussels, New York, and Geneva. For instance, in cozy settings near the United Nations, Friends play the role of "community-builders within the diplomatic community."[12]

Community building can't be rushed or forced by conveners. Conversations must happen organically and authentically. To feel a sense of power with another person, we need the space and time to arrive at conclusions for ourselves. In this process, we may grow to understand each other and to feel less threatened and more familiar. (We've seen how important this can be.) Of course, we often start off certain of a solution to the issues before us, but that won't make other people feel good about our proposals! Studies have found that when we put effort into a choice, we like and care about it more. Something about going through the *process* seems to make us decide that what we choose is more valuable.[13]

One of the particular quirks of Friends is their readiness to patiently pursue slow processes that appear to be making no progress. As Michael Bartlet, who worked as a liaison with British Parliament on behalf of Quakers, explains, this engagement is about understanding the realities of politics "without being overwhelmed by them."[14] Rachel Brett, former staff of the Quaker United Nations Office in Geneva, relates that for over 50 years Friends were among the very few voices in the wilderness calling for the formal recognition of the right to conscientious objection to military service. Quakers have long felt that at any time we can experience our deep connection to each other—our radical equality—and find it impossible to kill anyone. After an experience like this, even a soldier may become a conscientious objector. There was little evidence that anyone within the UN took this seriously. But Friends continued to raise conscientious objection as a human right year after year, decade after decade.

Finally, there was a breakthrough. The UN Human Rights Committee ruled conclusively that the International Covenant on Civil and Political Rights—specifically article 18 on the right to freedom of thought, conscience, and religion—applied. The UN then published *Conscientious Objection to War*[15] and followed it up with a guide detailing conscientious objection as a legitimate and protected ground for a refugee claim.[16] There was finally recognition of many of the issues groups like Quakers had been persistently naming.[17] *Much* more needs to be done to see that governments follow these standards, but there's also no question that conscientious objectors are treated far better in many countries today than ever before. It's been a painfully slow process, but to the extent that Brett and others did help this change happen, it happened in large part because she saw and treated people not as representatives of governments or the UN, but as *human beings* to slowly work with until the issue of conscientious objection "clicked" for them.

## Tips from This Chapter

1. How we get to a positive result matters. Sometimes the conditions for change aren't there yet. Shortcuts can be appealing, but they may just lead to further problems. The peace virus can demand patience and perseverance, and the way we live it out makes a difference to the results we get.

2. The evidence is clear that all of us are changing to a surprising degree all the time. This means that we're ever-vulnerable to a positive infection but also that peace must be continually built. We benefit when we're aware of the power each of us has to change.

## Activity: Meeting an Unsympathetic Politician

1. Before the session, facilitators choose a contentious issue that members of the group are likely to be familiar with. It could be any issue making headlines: environment, labor, criminal justice... Facilitators or another assigned member of the group research and print copies of a few key arguments being made both for and against a proposed course of action.

2. When the group meets, facilitators choose someone to play the role of a politician who's already made public statements committing to a course of action. Three to five other members of the

group are a delegation meeting with the politician for the first time, with the hope of changing her/his mind. The rest of the group watches.

3. After the role-play, facilitators explain that the role-play participants will have a chance to discuss their experience, but first those who were watching will give their reactions. Facilitators ask the watchers, "What did you see? What seemed to be effective or ineffective? What was the overall dynamic?" After this discussion, facilitators ask the actors how the role-play felt and what came up for them.

2

# Communication Skills

*Too often, we communicate merely to solidify
our positions. So much of what is not peace flows
from broken connections, misunderstood information,
opposing views of the same events, and verbal violence.
In this section we'll examine communication from
a peace perspective. These skills are deeply practical
and essential in spreading the peace virus.*

# Firm Belief

*People may use their intelligence*
*not to draw more accurate conclusions*
*but to find fault in data they are unhappy with.*

— TARI SHAROT[1]

VERY FEW OF US get up in the morning and decide to be un-ethical or irrational or to act on false beliefs. But how do we know we're not? Whoever we are, the chances are above average that we think we're above average.[2] We even think we're more likely to win the lottery if we pick the numbers ourselves instead of having them randomly assigned.[3] While obviously wrong, such optimism and self-assuredness can be admirable and beneficial, to a point. As much as our confidence makes us resilient in the face of life's hardships, it can also make us tough to talk to. We all have beliefs; they're different for each of us; and we tend to be certain about them. (This overconfidence is not universal of course—culture and personality make a difference.[4])

At a shallow level we could call them ideas, frames, or scripts. They're the stories and thought patterns informing us of who we are and what matters. At a deeper level we can call them worldviews. Largely unconscious, they give rise to our cultural expressions—our values, our art, our identities. Worldviews offer us meaning. If we're talking with someone who makes no sense to us, it could be that they have a worldview we can't understand. Perhaps they experi-ence some feature of the world as fundamentally important, and we don't even *notice* it. If we have a collectivist worldview and are talking to an individualist, she might keep coming back to the importance of "self-sufficiency," a concept that means nothing to us because we find it obvious that people depend on their communities. The best way to understand this is to go somewhere particularly strange to you and make an on-going effort to engage with people rather than staying in your cultural bubble. When I've done this I've always been shocked by how many beliefs I take for granted. Just how much our culture influences our perception of reality is a fascinating question for further study. We already know that our beliefs can play a major role in how our eyes take in images, how we experience pain and healing, and even how our bodies process the food we eat.[5]

Many wars are at one level battles over worldviews, struggles for control of meaning.[6] One group seeks power-over by establishing the dominant way of being in the world, defining the boundaries of what can and can't be believed, and therefore done. Imposition of a worldview is among the most damaging expressions of power-over, a core tactic of colonizers. It moves the conflict into the minds of people now struggling between opposing senses of meaning. Canada's residential schools did this. They sought to eradicate existing diverse Indigenous worldviews, replacing them with a foreign one in a process Canada's Truth and Reconciliation Commissioners called "cultural genocide."[7] Canada failed to destroy Indigenous worldviews, but it did leave many Indigenous people with what Blackfoot academic Leroy Little Bear calls "jagged worldviews"— an internal fragmentation where the pieces of different incompatible views collide. Healing the jagged worldviews can be a long and painful process.[8]

Much of the harm we cause is from taking assumptions embedded in our worldview as universal and obvious. To do anything else is a major challenge, since we largely accept our worldview without even noticing its implicit assumptions. When we feel as if our worldview is the full and universal truth, anyone with a different one is just wrong, and we can readily wind up in a struggle for power-over them. It *is* possible to have healthy cross-cultural conflicts though, and the skills we'll be building can help.

Firstly, let's acknowledge the miraculous achievement of having a worldview at all. All of us are flooded by *staggering* amounts of information, which we weave into a world that appears coherent. This is truly incredible. But to do it, we don't just take everything in. Instead, study after study finds that we notice and remember things that fit with our beliefs.[9] For instance, two of us can watch the exact same political satire show and both decide it expresses our own ideologies—*opposing* ideologies![10]

Once we believe, we tend to seek only information that agrees with us and reject information that doesn't. That's called confirmation bias. It maintains and strengthens our beliefs over time. Psychologists asked a simple question to a group of people: "Is Yin an extrovert?" A second group was asked "Is Yin an introvert?" Each group, when meeting Yin, decided to ask questions that would confirm yes, she was an extrovert, or, yes, an introvert. That meant, however, that both groups were getting evidence only for what they wanted to find. In the end, the two groups both reported yes—confirming Yin as an extrovert and an introvert! In order to more accurately do this task, the groups would have had to look for evidence that *contradicted* what they wanted to find.[11]

We filter down vast amounts of information to form our beliefs, and then what we believe shapes our experiences and memories, which shape our future beliefs in an ongoing feedback loop. It's easy to see how this process can readily drive us apart! The internet facilitates it, since, if we don't browse anonymously, search engines and social media sites build up profiles on us and show us information associated with our habits and beliefs. In other words, they show us things the algorithms think we want to see, content that agrees with and seems to confirm our beliefs.[12]

We feel good in these information bubbles because seeing only what confirms our opinions makes us happy. In fact, when we hear something that agrees with our beliefs we get a pleasurable rush of dopamine, the same chemical that gives us chills when we hear a piece of beautiful music.[13] At the same time that it's pleasing to have our beliefs confirmed, it can be deeply disturbing to have them questioned. You can probably recall the sense of tension from a time when you had a disagreement with someone. Perhaps your heart rate increased, your chest or face started to feel hot or constricted, and your mind raced for the next thing to say to prove your point.

Of course, we're not always stubborn, information might change our minds about how to fix our computer if we're not that bothered to admit we have no clue how computers work. But many beliefs are closer to home—they're part of our *identity*. Studies find that when confronted with factual information that challenges these beliefs many of us show brain activity associated with processing threats and ruminating about who we are. Having a belief challenged can throw our whole understanding of ourselves into flux. Those whose brains show the most distress and rumination hold most stubbornly to beliefs in the face of contrary evidence. In other words, as researcher Jonas Kaplan puts it, "…when we feel threatened, anxious or emotional, then we are less likely to change our minds."[14] (This agrees with what we've seen about learning new behaviors too!)

As obvious as Kaplan's point sounds, very bright people keep trying to change beliefs through debate, a process our schools and business meetings often encourage. It's not that debate never works, but is it an optimal way to change beliefs? The metaphors we use here are instructive. We stick to our guns, defend our position, fire back, and shoot down our opponent. We slam, burn, destroy, or even eviscerate them. This colorful language might not be as far from the truth as it sounds. Hearing a word like "excruciating" is enough to trigger areas of our brain that process physical pain.[15] Our brains also anticipate coming pain by reacting *as if we were feeling pain already*.[16] So we don't need to be physically hit to feel like we have been. When we're "attacked" verbally, even when we just know we're about to be, we experience social pain that can be remarkably *intense and long lasting*.[17] And when we're in this anxious state, we're likely to hold firm to our current beliefs, gripping them like a protective shield that tells us who we are.

The peace virus can be an uncomfortable sort of infection at times, precisely because it puts us in the position of challenging firm beliefs and exposing inconsistencies. Now that you know this, try seeing what happens if you simply acknowledge any discomfort as it arises while reading this book. Not running away from our anxiety can be liberating. We create the space to openly recognize more of ourselves. Research suggests that a good way to overcome confirmation bias is to remain curious. (Curiosity is also "associated with less defensive reactions to stress and less aggressive reactions to provocation."[18])

What about when we're not curious though? The fact that it's less taxing to maintain our beliefs than to change them helps explain a frustrating reality: beliefs have incredibly long shelf-lives, whatever the evidence against them. The idea that the earth is flat has never gone away and may actually be gaining in popularity.[19] Maybe that's just an extreme example, but a 2014 study in the US found that more than half of the population believed in at least one such conspiracy theory. (Education level made no difference to the readiness to believe.)[20]

It's easy to be dismissive about the absurd beliefs of "others," but it's worth empathizing with the challenges we all face. Knowing what to believe is tough! We don't have time to look into everything, so we take a lot on faith. Of course, the danger is that many people want us to believe their version of the truth, and there are powerful groups spreading misleading views, such as when the tobacco industry hired PR firms to create an apparent lack of consensus on the health risks of smoking—likely delaying life-saving public policies for decades.[21]

The challenge is this: if I told you the earth weighs $6 \times 10^{24}$ kilograms, how would you have any way of knowing if I'm right or not, aside from looking it up and deciding what seems credible based on what you already believe? It's the same process you'd use to decide most facts, like whether or not the earth is flat. So the information we access makes all the difference—and most of us think the information "others" get is worse than *our* information. For instance, a study done in the former Soviet Union and the US found that both sides thought the other was being deceived by its government, while they had a better understanding of the real world.[22] We know that a goldfish has a three-second memory and that it's not good to go swimming right after we eat, because we'll get cramps. But both of these statements are false.[23] What other inaccurate beliefs do many of us hold and spread?

The challenge of finding credible information has always been with us, and technology is adding to it. We can create reasonably convincing audio and video of celebrities saying things they never said.[24] Opaque artificial intelligence recommending what we should watch may systematically amplify divisive and inaccurate click-bait.[25] Just 1,600 accounts issuing hateful tweets for a year can get their messages viewed 10 *billion times*![26] Of course, many of those views may themselves be from bots programmed to boost polarizing content. Organizations in at least 28 countries have used bots and other techniques to run coordinated social media manipulation campaigns.[27] These are a few of the disturbing trends we're facing. Questions about who to believe get even messier when we move from issues with clear-cut answers to ones shaded by perspective. Acknowledging these major challenges in deciding what to trust can help us empathize a bit with those caught up in bizarre or hateful ideas.

Just because there's information and arguments that seem to support a belief doesn't mean that's why we believe it. How often are people around us being murdered? This is a question just like how much the earth weighs—we can't know and so we'd have to rely on the best available data. Instead of looking up violent crime rates, most of us will get a sense based on what we've been exposed to— TV. Writing in 1995, one US film critic noted, "About 350 characters appear each night on prime-time TV, but studies show an average of seven of these people are murdered every night. If this rate applied in reality, then in just 50 days everyone in the United States would be killed and the last left could turn off the TV."[28]

Over time, enough of us might believe in such an inflated murder rate that we'd call for our governments to get tough on crime to keep us safe. The opposite process is also possible, we could go into an information bubble that ignores murders and then call for misguided policies based on a false sense of safety. In either case, our beliefs have significant impacts.

You've likely heard about how at Halloween sick individuals put razorblades in children's candy. Many parents are terrified of this, to the point that California and New Jersey enacted special laws to deal with candy tamperers. But a careful review by two sociologists found that there was never a single reported incident of a razorblade in candy. It was an urban legend![29]

Unfortunately, simply having heard a piece of information makes us *much* more likely to believe it. (This is one of many "mere exposure" effects.) We can't quite place the source of our knowledge, but it's easier for us to process something familiar, so this makes it seem credible. Researchers had participants in a study read news stories, some real and some fake. Five weeks later, this group was much more likely to consider the fake stories true and plausible than were people reading the stories for the first time. Many of the people who'd read the fake stories at the lab five weeks before had also invented memories of having heard the information elsewhere.[30]

It's disturbingly possible to get us to invent such memories, and memory is also biased by factors like our mood—when we're sad, we remember more negative information, and when we're happy, we remember more positives.[31] We might even, perhaps with no awareness of it, generate a false or exaggerated memory that serves us. When asked what percentage of the total housework they do, couples each tend to say they do far more than the other remembers them doing. When the total from the two answers is added up, it's way over 100%.[32] We could assume that one partner is lying or that both are, but it seems likely that they're remembering in self-serving ways, recalling the work they did and maybe exaggerating it, while not remembering as much of what their partner did. This is a mild example, but false memories of abuse have ruined lives, leading to accusations of horrific crimes that never happened.[33]

Memory is also highly susceptible to the influence of those around us. In one study participants watched a movie and then answered questions about it. Before the questions, some people were shown fake answers and told they were given by other respondents. The answers were all wrong. When participants believed that multiple people had all given the same (wrong) answer, 70% of the time *they too* gave these wrong answers. Afterward the trick was revealed—no one had actually provided those answers, they were made up. Participants now answered the questions again. Half *continued* to remember false information about the movie![34] The peace implications of all this are obvious. Facts might be manipulated by any group trying to hide its violence, and repeating a lie enough times is indeed an effective way to make it seem true. Even the collective memories of entire groups can be shifted over time.[35]

Perhaps most surprisingly, sticking with the belief that we've been exposed to before is common, *even when we have enough information to know better*. Cleverly designed studies have found that those with a lot of knowledge about a topic *still* tend to rely on false information that feels familiar, instead of thinking things through![36] How can we explain this? As we've seen before, it's simply more mentally draining to think carefully than to go with what feels comfortable and recognizable.[37]

This all presents major hurdles for healthy interactions with each other. Once we believe something, we tend to just repeat it, which isn't real communication. A piece of advice written to women receiving hateful online comments explains this point well: "The majority of online comments are people rehearsing their worldview and personal identity. It's about them, not you...people are being asked to think about things they previously took for granted, and their brains are on high alert to shoot down new demands that need processing."[38]

So now we've seen many reasons for humility and for not feeling too convinced about our beliefs. But this doesn't mean we need to accept that there's no way to know anything, or that everyone's beliefs are equally true. Some beliefs are simply inaccurate. Let's look at how we might talk to a friend expressing one.

We're going through our email and see an article forwarded by our aunt: *Thousands of Charity Workers Earn Big Salaries: Report*. That's outrageous! How dare people who depend on donations made in good faith get paid fat salaries? And it's not just one or two people, but *thousands*! We picture armies of charity workers in fancy boardrooms smoking cigars and, feeling angry, write a witty line about it as we share the article on social media.

If we read the article, we might notice that it mentions there are around one million people working for registered charities in Canada, while data analyzed by The Canadian Press found that some six thousand of them earned more than $120,000 per year.[39] That's 0.6%. Imagine if the headline read *Less than 1% of Charity Workers Earn $120,000 or More: Report*. Would this information change our reaction?

There's the further question of what's a fair salary. Looking into the details we may find it less straightforward than it appears, with further issues to consider. In the end, if we saw all the data about the compensation of charity employees, we'd almost certainly find that some are over-compensated, some under-compensated (an issue not mentioned in the article), and others somewhere in the middle. This is very different from the initial image we formed. There aren't nearly as many cigars being smoked, and frankly, it's a lot less exciting. We don't get to be as outraged, and that righteous outrage felt good. We were the heroes, and there was a clear villain. Many issues are this way! The more we look into the messy details, the less like pure binary ones versus zeros they become.

Let's say we just glanced at the article, didn't explore the details, and then a few months later we're speaking to a friend and the topic of charities comes up. We might say something like, "I don't trust them. Almost all of the employees are over-paid." This belief is inaccurate and arose from misremembering a confusing and sensational headline.

What would be an ideal response from our friend if she knew a lot about the charity sector in Canada? Research suggests it's not what most of us would think. We'd likely discuss the false belief in detail, discrediting it point by point. Our friend might explain what's commonly said about the over-compensation of charity staff and their luxurious lifestyles and how that's true in only a few cases and is inaccurate overall. While trying to politely tell us we're misinformed, she actually repeats key elements of the belief we're familiar with—that charity employees are not trustworthy and are over-paid. Our feeling of familiarity, although the facts are being discredited, actually makes it *harder* for us to understand and accept that our belief is inaccurate.

Our friend might do better to correct our misinformation with new information, making it as vivid and easy to picture as possible, and raising it in a way that encourages a back-and-forth discussion. Last chapter we saw how we value ideas more when we put effort into reaching them. Engaging us helps us modify our beliefs more than being told why we're wrong.[40] Perhaps our friend could say that there are more than 80,000 charities in Canada and many are run by volunteers. Of the charities that can afford staff, many don't pay that well. She could ask us to think of examples and pause to give us space to imagine them. We might remember a small local food bank. She could continue with questions about this so the idea develops further.

Perhaps this will work, particularly if we don't feel that passion-ate about charity salaries. But what if we're very confident? A series of experiments in the US found that participants had firm beliefs about nearly any issue from how teachers should be paid to impos-ing sanctions on Iran. People from across the political spectrum were consistently very confident. After explaining "I'm strongly opposed to sanctions on Iran," or "I'm strongly in favor of sanctions on Iran," participants were asked another question. What would you ask if you wanted people to tone down their certainty?

Most of us would think to ask: "Why?" We'd listen to what was said and then present counter-evidence. This study asked people to simply *explain the details*. That's it. So: "How would sanctions on Iran work?" not, "Why do you support sanctions on Iran?" What happened? People quickly faltered. When we try to explain, it becomes obvious to us that the *mechanisms* at play are not as straightforward as we thought. When asked to re-rate their confidence after trying to explain the mechanics, people were significantly more neutral. Importantly, this *did not happen* when participants were asked to explain the *reasons* for their beliefs. Why? Well, as we've seen, we can readily come up with arguments to support whatever we want to believe. Our arguments may sound ludicrous to others, but they sound believable enough to us. What helps instead is realizing for ourselves how little we understand the details of what we're talking about. Once participants noticed how little they knew about the workings of the issue, their behavior also changed. They were less likely to donate to organizations that advocated the positions they'd started off feeling so convinced about.[41]

This would be another approach to the conversation about charities. Our friend might ask, "How does compensation in Canadian charities work?" We might respond, "I don't know; I just know people get paid way too much." But she could ask more about the details. "I'm really curious about this question. How many people work in charities? What's the average salary? How much do people make compared to other industries?" (We've just complained, not offered a solution. If we had—"No one should get paid more than $40,000 if they work for a charity!"—then she could ask for details about how this would work.) Hearing ourselves trying to answer these questions and floundering, we might realize just how little we know about the mechanics of the charitable sector in Canada. It would be important that our friend listen attentively and not offer any contradictory evidence, at least not before letting us realize for ourselves that we lack information and can't justify being so certain.

It's possible none of our friends' questions will impact us. Particularly when we don't care about the *results* of our beliefs but hold them on *principle*, explaining the mechanisms at play doesn't seem to make us less certain.[42] We might decide the US should impose sanctions on Iran not because we understand what effects sanctions have but because Iran is evil. In this case, as we saw with the abortion debate, it can be helpful to frame beliefs differently to generate more complex thinking. Rather than debate whether or not Iran is evil, we can ask about the possible *consequences* of sanctions on Iran. If the US did that, what would happen? What specifically would it cause? This very act of being asked questions, especially if it happens in a spirit of curiosity and care, might encourage us to become more inquisitive ourselves, perhaps shifting our views just a little. Remember Daniel Aires reading a book that enraged him for months and then suddenly changed his life? Who knows what changes might be building from these conversations.

Megan Phelps-Roper grew up in a family that took her, by age five, to stand with everyone she loved and trusted, holding signs with messages like "Gays are worthy of death." As you might guess, the world was an epic battle between "good" and "evil," between "us" and "others." Every time her church was criticized for its hateful beliefs, the members felt a surge of justification, strengthening their identities as righteous outsiders. This continual battle gave Phelps-Roper a purpose in life. (A quest for significance is a common draw for many members of hate groups.[43])

When the peace virus began to infect her, it was via an unlikely source—Twitter. She says that while many on the platform were angry and disrespectful, soon she started having civil conversations with various people who had a genuine curiosity, one that she shared. They were reaching out to each other with a question, "How had the other come to such outrageous conclusions about the world?" The line between friend and foe started to blur after months of continual virtual contact (another example of contact powerfully increasing our feeling that the "other" is familiar and no longer a threat). Respectful discussions online opened her to the knowledge that, as she puts it, "People on the other side were not the demons I'd been led to believe." She eventually escaped her hateful community and was welcomed and helped by some of the very people she'd recently been wishing death upon!

From her experience, Phelps-Roper offers an incredibly valuable tip. When addressing firm beliefs it helps if we assume the other person thinks *their intentions are ultimately good*. Her hate, she firmly believed, was noble. She was fighting for the right cause—harming some people, yes, but to serve a higher good.[44] Assuming others are just *trying* to be "bad people" gives us an excuse to disengage, writing them off. But for Phelps-Roper, the change didn't come from being written off or from being debated with facts or pressured to admit she was a bad person. It came with continual engagement *over years* (again, the slow process). The peace virus spread because people persisted in asking her important questions, presenting their beliefs, and also taking the conversation momentarily to safer topics when it was getting too heated.

Shifting Phelps-Roper's understanding demanded tenderness. People didn't have to agree with her, but they did need to recognize her struggles and her power-from-within, her capacity to see a new truth. Both sides had to move beyond either-or thinking to build power-with. When we're very fixed in our moral stance though, our certainty can be a dangerous impediment. Researchers call this "the dark side of moral conviction."[45] Having a clear ethical position can actually make us feel like part of a team, an "us." Then we stop trying to engage with "others" like Phelps-Roper. Luckily, simply being trained to recognize that not only are "others" ideologically motivated but *we are too*, can make us significantly gentler about our moral judgments! This finding fits nicely with what we've already seen about our capacity to learn to think in more complex ways. It might work because once we have the details of this particular bias explained to us, we can readily notice that we indeed have an ideology[46]—it's not as tricky to accept as that we invented a false memory!

Imagine playing a game against your cousin, but you get to decide all the rules as the game goes on. What's more, you can continually change what matters and what doesn't. Sound like a sweat deal? The fact is that, although our beliefs and moral convictions are generally firm, much of the time *we don't behave consistently with them.* Instead, we find ways to rationalize whatever we're doing. This works because of inconsistent rules—*ambiguity.* We change what we pay attention to and what we ignore, and this lets us believe that our actions are consistent when they aren't. Sociologist Stanley Cohen thoroughly documented how this process of denial plays out all over the world. For Cohen, "Denial may be neither a matter of telling the truth nor intentionally telling a lie. There seem to be states of mind, or even whole cultures, in which we know and don't know at the same time."[47] Even when it seems only reasonable that we should know we're causing great harm, we can find ways to not know it, to believe in our own good intent. An example is the bullies we discussed before—they know they're harming other children, but they think those children provoked the harm and ultimately deserve it, so the bullies feel they're acting to restore *fairness in the world.*[48]

Studies of these mechanisms have found that once we've established *for ourselves* that we're honest, we're *more* likely to cheat on a later test—but only if there are easy ways to rationalize the cheating.[49] We know we're being dishonest, but we're able to not look at it that way because we've established that we're honest people. Behavioral economist Dan Ariely has studied this in many cultures, and his conclusion is that only a tiny handful of people will cheat as much as they can get away with—even when they get to shred their own tests and pay themselves for how many answers they claim to have gotten right! So the vast majority of us aren't acting out of a rational selfish interest to get as much money as we possibly can even if there's no way we'll get caught. However *almost everyone* will cheat a bit on Ariely's tests if the conditions allow. (You might not be surprised to learn that Canadians believed they'd cheat less than folks in the US. Actually people in many different countries all had similar patterns of cheating.[50])

Ariely found that the more creative a person is, and the more symbolic distance there is between the act of cheating and the pay off from it, the more people are likely to cheat. This is all about beliefs. It's likely that the creative among us can simply come up with better stories to rationalize why cheating is reasonable.[51] ("It's only fair for me to say I got that question right because I would've known the answer if they'd worded it properly.")

There are many sinister examples of rationalization and other techniques of denial. Roy Baumeister has studied what's known about the psychology of murderers and torturers and concludes that almost none do what they do for the pleasure of hurting others. What's *far* more common is to find ways to feel justified, even seeing *themselves as victims*.[52] A firm belief that what we're doing is somehow creating justice leads us to accept committing horrible acts.

One takeaway is that whether stopping ourselves from cheating a bit on a test or justifying murder, if we want to act consistently with our moral values, it helps to be as clear as possible about *what that means*. Make the rules of the game explicit and stick to them. This is why I invited you to write your values down. (If you forget what you wrote, now's a good time to re-read it!) Recalling our values gives us a brief break from our rationalizing stories, helping us reorient ourselves. Studies have shown that when we affirm our values, it buffers us against stress, maybe making us feel a little less caught up in our present worries as we remember our higher aspirations.[53] It's important not to push this into the dark side of moral conviction where we know for sure it's "us" versus "others" and we're right, but we can benefit from remembering our pro-social values like honesty and treating others the way we want to be treated. It can also really help if we make these commitments public.

Restaurant owner Gordon Sinclair found that 30% of the time when people made a reservation they didn't show up and they didn't call to cancel. When making the reservation receptionists would always say, "Please call if you have to change your plans," but many didn't. It's likely these were folks who, if asked, would say they value being trustworthy, but that's not what they were thinking about in the moment of not calling the restaurant. They were thinking about the other things they needed to get done or the effort it takes to make the call. They were able to rationalize not calling, while still believing they're the type of person who's trustworthy.

One day, Sinclair decided to test a different approach, instructing the receptionists to ask, "Will you please call if you have a change to your plans?" and wait for a response. With this new strategy, the no-show-no-call rate dropped from 30% to 10%.[54] The simple act of hearing ourselves say something out loud might help us to remember it and go along with it.

We need ways to recall what acting consistently with our beliefs and values looks like. The effects of this might not last long, so frequent reminders are useful. Studies show that committing to ethical behavior immediately before having the chance to cheat makes a significant difference. For example, there's an incentive to report on a certain insurance form that we've driven less so we'll get better rates. Moving the signature line from the bottom to the top of the form (right before having the chance to fudge the numbers) caused reported driving to increase by 2,400 miles.[55]

There's also evidence that helping us see how our beliefs aren't applied the same ways to ourselves as to others can make it tougher for us to rationalize. Researchers asked thousands of participants in the US questions like this:

On June 17, 2015, Dylann Roof entered the Emanuel African Methodist Episcopal Church, and during a prayer service killed nine African American parishioners. Roof cited his White identity as a motivation for the attacks. How responsible do you think you are for the acts of Dylann Roof? How responsible do you think White Americans are for the acts of Dylann Roof?

Later questions included, "Muniba is a Muslim who owns a small bakery in Southern France. How responsible do you think Muniba is for the Paris attacks [in 2015]?" After answering these questions, collective blaming of all Muslims for violence by groups like Daesh dropped by half. People showed less support for anti-Muslim policies and less willingness to sign an anti-Muslim petition. This effect has been replicated in Spain and found to last at least a month. The researchers also tried showing people videos including factual information about Muslims and rants explaining why it's inaccurate to portray all Muslims as violent. As you might be able to predict by now, those videos didn't change people's beliefs.[56]

Let's look at one last clever experiment that offers a related practical tip. Participants were asked to answer a slew of bland logic questions ("A shop sells apples, none of the apples are organic, what can you say for sure about whether fruits are organic in this shop?") and explain why they chose their answers. Next, people were given the chance to evaluate their answers and change them. Very few did. They reported feeling strongly that the answers they'd given were correct.

Now the participants were asked to evaluate someone else's answers. Half were secretly given their own answers again. Some figured out they were looking at their own answers, but those who didn't figure it out and thought they were looking at what someone else had said were critical of the answers *more than half the time!* Remember, these were answers they'd previously given and then had the chance to change but were very confident about. When rejecting their own arguments (believing them to be someone else's), people were correct more often than not.[57]

This is a simple and valuable trick. Do a role reversal. If our belief was someone else's, would we find any flaws in it? If we had to argue for a belief we dislike, what arguments would we make? If someone else was treating us the way we're treating them, how might it feel? Of course, we can't know someone else's mind or speak for them, but this trick can help us identify rationalization or gaps in our thinking.

Along similar lines, Quakers have several practices that can help with testing and modifying beliefs. They sit together beginning in silence and listening for truth within. (Many of us rarely make time to settle ourselves and listen, but this practice can be rich in cutting through the chatter of initial certainties.) They also have the longstanding practice of "Clearness Committees." This is when a group of people we trust, folks with different opinions and life experiences, volunteer to help us test important beliefs or issues arising in our lives. Rather than telling us what to do, a Clearness Committee listens and asks questions. It's common that everyone involved enjoys the process, because everyone learns something.[58] Members of the Committee ideally strike a balance between being supportive and asking questions that help us discover our irrational thinking or unaddressed problems. What's particularly important is that they not try to push their own agendas or beliefs.[59] The Clearness Committee is seeking *together* for a way forward. In other words, the process is not about any one person having the answer, and not about our asking for approval or permission.[60] We can really benefit from this type of power-with in a supportive community.

All this talk about biases and false beliefs can be disheartening. Yet biases are playing crucial roles in our lives right now, so they're worth knowing about! We may never eliminate them, but through awareness and the practical tips we're learning, we can gain new powers of insight and action. Since many of us are blocking the peace virus with firm beliefs, we'll be exploring some of these beliefs in coming chapters, encouraging reflection, discussion, and techniques to see if the beliefs hold true or if we're carrying them around out of convention or mere exposure.

## Tips from This Chapter

1. Worldviews impact us dramatically, yet their influence can be difficult to understand since they can feel so normal and universal.

2. We have a tendency to seek only information that confirms what we already believe, because it makes us feel good. The internet can help us create information bubbles around ourselves. It's worth actively seeking out perspectives different from our own. When we want to believe a fact, we might search it with words like "myth" or "debunked" to see what other evidence comes up, being careful to investigate the credibility of the sources.

3. Words and social isolation can hurt as much as physical injury, and when we're feeling anxious or threatened we're most likely to stick to our beliefs in the face of contradicting evidence. This means that aggressive communication or debate isn't optimal for shifting beliefs. Instead, we might try asking for details about *how* a proposed course of action would work, not the reason *why* it is the right thing to do. To encourage complex thinking, we can try to keep framing beliefs in terms of their results and not in abstract moral terms. It's worth listening carefully without offering any contradictory evidence, at least at first. Engaging in a back-and-forth conversation, not just hearing the evidence, is proven to increase the chances that our beliefs will shift. When offering countering evidence, it's good to avoid too much detail about the familiar false belief and instead go into detail about the new belief.

4. Rising anger or defensiveness are signals not to ignore. Questions to ask could be "What is this? Where does it come from? Why is this feeling so intense?" If our beliefs are being challenged, this will create discomfort, and that's OK. Without suppressing or ignoring the discomfort, can we find any signs of our biases at play?

5. We're likely to believe in things simply because we've been exposed to them. We may even invent memories about where our beliefs came from. Being aware of this, we can ask ourselves, "How do I know what I'm saying is true? What's the source?"

6. Feeling righteous outrage can be really enjoyable—it makes us feel like part of a team opposing a clear villain. Yet for many issues, we feel this clearly only when we don't understand the details. The more we investigate, the less pure and straightforward the situation becomes. We generally notice, eventually, that everyone involved believes their intentions are good. Evidence shows this is overwhelmingly the case, even among murderers.

7. We often behave inconsistently with our values because of ambiguity. We interpret situations to make what we did seem fair. We may be most likely to engage in harmful behaviors when

we're most firmly convinced that what we're doing is moral. Reminding ourselves of our pro-social values can help us overcome the tendency to rationalize. This works particularly well if we commit to another course of action publicly.

8. Rather than pointing out logical inconsistencies in someone's beliefs, we can ask the questions that will cause them to first think about and hear themselves offer an answer ("I don't think all white people are responsible for the hateful murders committed by Dylann Roof") and then see that their standards aren't being applied similarly in other situations (collectively blaming all Muslims for hateful murders committed by Daesh).

9. Believing that our own arguments are being made by someone else increases our likelihood of thinking logically and critically about them. When we need to reach a decision or figure out if our position is fair, imagining that it was someone else's position or decision can help. What critiques would we offer that person? When we need to engage with an argument that we find troubling, we can imagine that it was our sincerely held belief. This way, we might be able to better connect with the person we're talking to.

10. Sitting silently with our beliefs or testing important questions with a group of people can offer helpful opportunities for new perspectives and support in understanding ourselves.

## Activity: Decision Making

Amazingly, the types of questions in this activity—relying on simple shifts in perspective away from our existing beliefs—have been tested and shown to greatly help decision making.[61]

1. Facilitators pass out pens and paper and ask everyone to think of a decision they need to make but struggle with. People jot down for three minutes, using point form or full sentences, what the decision is and what makes it difficult. Let people know when there's one minute left.

2. Facilitators ask people to imagine that the option they're leaning

towards will turn out terribly. Group members have two minutes to write in response to this question: "Where could you look right now to find evidence that your preferred option will actually be a disaster?"

3. Facilitators explain there's one final question to write about for three minutes: "What would you tell your best friend to do if she were in this situation?"

4. When the writing time is done, facilitators divide people into small groups to discuss their responses together, asking each other, "Did writing help generate new ideas or perspectives?"

5. When the conversations seem to be winding down, facilitators ask, "How can taking new perspectives help us to think about or discuss peace?"

## Activity: Our Position

1. Facilitators explain that this activity will help us explore the beliefs present in the group. For each question, everyone is invited to move to a place in the room that represents their belief. The spectrum is from "No/Never" on the left side of the room to "Yes/Always" on the right side (facilitators move to these spots to show where they are). The group needs an even number, so facilitators can participate, or not, to make the numbers work.

2. Facilitators read off the first question and then ask group members to move into position: "Is it ever right to break the law?" If group members all clump in one area, go on to the next question. If there's a wide spread between people, ask everyone to find someone who's as far away from them as possible. Each person will be given one minute to state not the evidence but rather what they think is the key *belief* or *value* that led them to stand where they did. Facilitators time this and tell people when to switch speakers.

3. This process repeats with other questions. Facilitators might think of questions that would be particularly interesting for the group or use ones from this list: Will there be a major political

upheaval in this country in your lifetime? Are you generally optimistic? Can you predict a person's personality if you know what they were like as a child? Do we have the capacity to know universal truths about our world? Is it important to engage with oppressive groups? Is the world getting safer? Is technology mostly beneficial?

4. Facilitators debrief this exercise with questions like, "What stood out for you?" "Was anyone having a conversation they'd like to share?" "Did anyone learn something about themselves through their conversations?" "Did anyone learn something about the group?"

# Treating Emotions with Care

*As we go deeper into ourselves we shall eventually reach*
*a still, quiet center. At this point two things happen*
*simultaneously. Each of us is aware of our unique value*
*as an individual human being, and each of us*
*is aware of our utter interdependence on one another.*

— George Gorman[1]

W E'VE STARTED to see our interdependence and malleability, how much the people and situations around us shape what we think and do. This is bad news in the sense that we can be manipulated toward violence but good news in that we're ever-changing, with the constant potential to become more peaceful as individuals and communities. You may notice that at times this book moves you on a non-rational level. If we didn't have the emotional conviction and trust that peace can be built, we wouldn't try. Clearly, being passionate *matters*. But being too passionate can get us in trouble. We'll explore instances of both.

In the previous chapter we looked at how to talk to people who hold difficult or inaccurate beliefs. Building from there, we can ask a question running throughout this book—how can we inspire peaceful changes in those around us? Once we're in conversation and trying to propose a change, what do we need to offer to have the greatest chance of being infectious? Here's what studies recommend:

1. Define the audience.
2. Have a realistic goal, and be as precise as possible about what achieving it will mean. (Remember this important point: "What looks like resistance to change is often a lack of clarity.")
3. Create an *emotional* desire for that change.
4. Make the change as easy as possible.

How would this work? Author Dan Heath offers a good example. Doctors and nurses know they should wash their hands between interactions with different patients. Do they just use their reason and all wash their hands consistently? Unfortunately not. So how can hospitals save lives through getting doctors and nurses to wash their hands?

We know the audience—doctors and nurses. And we know the goal—washing hands every single time. In this case our audience is highly likely to have consistent beliefs—in other words, we don't need to use the techniques from the previous chapter because doctors already know the dangers of germs. What else do we know about our audience? What could possibly be keeping them from just washing their hands? Well, they're likely very busy and stressed, and they often see a great many patients. They need to wash their hands dozens of times a day. With important things to get done, so much hand washing could feel like a bureaucratic chore. Also, the hand washing technique itself is complicated, and the little details (motions like washing around each finger individually) could be forgotten.

Hospitals that have been successful use this knowledge in a few ways. First, they carefully illustrate the procedure to ensure clarity. Next, they periodically bring in family members to speak to nurses and doctors about losing loved ones because of preventable infections transmitted in hospitals. This is a powerful way to reconnect the medical professionals with their emotions, helping them *feel* how important hand washing really is. Finally, making hand washing as easy as possible means hospitals must be designed with sinks and disinfectant *everywhere*. Doctors are smart people. They know how infections spread, but still, evidence shows that hearing directly from people who've lost family members *changes doctors' behaviors*.[2]

Why was Martin Luther King, Jr. so successful in spreading messages that profoundly challenged many people? Why are other leaders with similar messages not as successful? What's happening when we feel deeply attuned to a story? Fascinatingly, we actually *replicate* what's going on in a speaker when we feel a strong resonant relationship with them.[3] Called "emotional contagion," the phenomenon is familiar to many of us. We seem to have an innate tendency to pick up on and frequently to *mirror* each others' states of being.[4] This helps explain why someone with an emotional message can spread it, becoming a driver of mass scale change. Of course, what worked for MLK has worked for charismatic warlords too.

There's another downside to such powerful resonance with individuals like MLK. We might get too fixated on remarkable leaders and feel that we can never live up to them. They might make the peace virus seem too demanding. So let's remember to enjoy uplifting emotions from resonant leaders, but also remember that peace isn't just for heroes. Its hosts are everyday people.

In 2011, decades of negative peace in Syria turned into full-scale war. Canadian Friends Service Committee wrote about the situation and possible nonviolent responses. We made an urgent call on Canada to do more to support Syrian refugees. No one contacted us about Syrian refugees, although by 2013 there were already more than a million who desperately needed assistance.[5] Then in September 2015 we experienced a major spike in interest. That month, news media had shared a heartrending photo of a single dead Syrian—three-year old Alan Kurdi.

There may be other factors at play, but this appears to show the power of a single story—one that *spreads an emotion*. That emotion moved rapidly and encouraged people, and later the Canadian government, to make support for Syrian refugees a major point of discussion. If news outlets had decided to include detailed information about the other 10 plus people who died alongside Alan

Kurdi when his boat capsized, would the story have generated even more sadness, outrage, and desire for action? It's highly unlikely. Evidence from behavioral studies and neuroscience suggests that the public would—illogically enough—have been *less* interested.[6] Strong emotions are generated when we see a single person in need and feel that we could do something. On the other hand, when we're asked to think about masses of people or to do math, we feel less motivated to help.[7]

We can use this knowledge to encourage positive behaviors, but empathy also has a downside. When we empathize with someone, it can make us more aggressive—even toward *random people* who we know had nothing to do with the crime we've just heard about.[8] So empathy doesn't always help us make good choices. Alan Kurdi's tragic story spoke of the plight of millions of Syrian refugees, but there are times when powerful stories aren't representative and our eagerness to be supportive can lead us astray.

A man once told me how being regularly beaten as a child had taught him to be a good person. He said proudly that he later thanked his father. This was a passionate and moving story, and I was getting swept up in the man's eloquent words about how useful it is to hit children. I cannot discount his experience—it matters— but that doesn't mean that it should shape policy for everyone. In fact, he's an outlier. We've already looked at the evidence, and it doesn't show benefits to hitting children. An 80-year-old heavy drinker could tell us her story of how great it feels to drink and how she's been binge drinking for decades and never had liver problems, but that wouldn't disprove the fact that alcohol abuse often causes liver disease. It's possible to find an outlier with a resonant story about why *any* public policy is good or bad.

Emotionally resonant stories about violence and wars are often shared in ways that conceal important information. The general narrative is that hatred and grievances cause wars. Yet according to scholars like economist Paul Collier, the situation is more complicated. "The objective factors that might contribute to grievance, such as income and asset inequality, ethnic and religious divisions, and political repression, do not seem to increase the risks of [armed] conflict."[9] We might just empathize, after hearing powerful stories about hatred between two ethnic groups, and assume that war must be caused by such ethnic or religious strife. But picture a case of two drunk men on the sidewalk in front of a bar, punching each other. When asked later why they did it, one explains that the other started it with an insult, and the other says, "He hit me first. I was just defending myself." They may each have a story that makes us empathize, believing we've understood the conflict. But a more important cause—drunkenness—goes unnamed.[10]

Since our emotions are so powerful, emotional manipulation can be a key tool of power-over. We've talked about the power of shame already and how social pain hurts as much as being hit. We can go even further though, for instance, by gaslighting—a process of getting others to question their grip on reality. Last chapter we saw how our beliefs can be deeply altered, for instance, through mere exposure to false information leading us to generate false memories. Gaslighting exploits this, consciously or unconsciously wearing people down through continual lying, denying things for which there is proof, and otherwise confusing and isolating the target.[11]

When used by national security or military forces, such manipulation is called terms like "psyops" or "psychological warfare." The roots of this kind of war are ancient. In India the *Arthaśāstra*, a text begun some 2,200 years ago, advocates the use of propaganda, rumors, and secret agents to sow misinformation and destroy one's enemies. The book also encourages spreading false information among one's own troops to boost morale.[12] Canada has been using psychological warfare to systematically manage and manipulate emotions since at least 1918.[13] In recent years this has become more targeted and powerful. A few companies now control the information accessed by billions of people—a level of influence that would have sounded like science fiction until very recently. These companies have largely been free to set their own rules on how they'll use customers' data and which third parties they'll sell it to. So companies can acquire a staggering variety of data about us and, taken together, it can be used to build a psychological profile and create emotionally powerful messaging. This is a step beyond what advertisers have already been doing for decades with mass messaging, because now it's targeted.

Campaigns trying to convince voters in Britain to leave the European Union were apparently "using 40–50,000 different variants of ad[s] every day that were continuously measuring responses and then adapting and evolving based on that response."[14] A major goal of these ads and other coordinated messages on social media was to push emotional triggers to shape voting behavior. We can't know if it worked, but a real-world study of over three million people found that psychologically targeted ads increased clicks by up to 40% and purchases by up to 50%.[15] We might remain totally unaware of this process as it's happening, yet across the various websites we visit, we could be exposed to a barrage of content designed to influence a person with our tastes and beliefs.[16]

To protect ourselves, we can use privacy software and try to be conscious of what we share. We can also become more in tune with our emotions. If we notice after reading a few articles or seeing ads online that we're feeling angry or nervous, we can check in with ourselves. Is what we've seen worth researching further? Is this content presenting useful information? What are the content creators trying to achieve?

By no means is big data all bad. The same technologies that can increase our feelings of anxiety and hate might in very different contexts help save lives. For example, in Canada an Indigenous-led campaign using Facebook delivered targeted advertising to isolated Indigenous towns with high suicide rates. The campaign shared interviews where Indigenous youth explained what they do when they're angry or hurt, and what they can do for friends feeling that way.[17] Campaigns like this one and countless others use emotional content and technology in caring and constructive ways.

Amazingly, computers can even help us generate healthier emotions. When we're distressed, our brains become particularly vigilant to whatever frightens us, meaning *we notice it more.* Our anxious and biased brains may actually focus overly on the very fears we want to avoid. We simply keep noticing and being pulled into them. Surprisingly simple software has been effective in calming these states of mind and reducing our biased negativity and prejudices. In one program, the computer flashes two pictures at once, with a cross on one picture. We simply click the picture where the cross is. The trick is that the cross always appears over a benign picture like a mushroom, while the other picture is threatening, like a snarling dog. Twenty minutes of this task a few times a week rewires our neuroplastic brains to be less intensely focused on what frightens us. This in turn has been shown to reduce some of our cognitive biases.[18] (This aligns well with findings we saw at the end of the chapter Us and Others.)

There's one other important area to consider when thinking about emotions and peace—gender. We won't go into great detail here, not because it's not an important topic but because it's so important that a wealth of excellent writing is readily available. Depending on our culture and upbringing the binary logic of power-over might make us equate female with weak, emotional, empathetic, caring, and illogical, and male with the polar opposites. In this over-simplified view, these opposites can't intermingle, they must battle for supremacy. We know how this goes already—such battles readily denigrate the pains experienced by "others" as fake or irrelevant and elevate those experienced by "us." Let's not collapse our thinking in such simplistic ways. Life is demanding on *everyone* and there are often creative ways for *everyone* to get their needs met. Also, when we accept the notion of a battle for supremacy, we tend to take on a view with major flaws. Apparently cold and calculating men are *heavily* influenced by emotions and irrational biases, and neuroscience hasn't found either a "female brain" hardwired to be emotional or a "male brain" that's more rational.[19]

Gender plays a *huge* role in most violence. It's not that women and non-binary folks aren't also violent and can't choose to support structural violence—they are and they do. Still, unquestionably, the face of violent force in the world is a male one. Biology does appear to play a role in this,[20] but that's far from the whole picture. Studies of men around the world "reveal a diversity that is impossible to reconcile with a biologically fixed master pattern of masculinity."[21] So the idea that "boys will be boys" just doesn't hold. Masculinity has very creative and constructive, as well as violent and awful, manifestations. It's complicated, and it's shifting all the time. Even the same men behave very differently in different moments. For instance, studies in the US found that when men think about their roles as fathers they appear to feel more nurturing, *see themselves differently*, and *show less aversion to women and gay people*.[22]

Men often feel pushed to be tough, protect others, take decisive action, defend their honor, enforce justice, and not admit to being in pain.[23] Men are pressured to take heavy risks—whether dangerous driving or risky deals in the corporate world.[24] Many end up in a constant inner war to shut off parts of themselves, and they use similar power-over in their relationships with other people. It's easy to see how this can generate violent and sexist ideas, producing narrow frames everywhere from the schoolyard to the war room.[25] This can be damaging *for everyone*. An analysis of 78 studies involving almost twenty thousand participants identifies the harm *to men themselves*. Particularly detrimental are the beliefs that men need to shut themselves off emotionally from others and that being a man means hating people seen to be weak.[26] (We've already looked at some possible reasons why, such as the health costs of social isolation and chronic stress.)

I think that, in many parts of the world, efforts to address harmful gender dynamics are having positive impacts. One area that's improved—but where much remains to be done—is the involvement of women in peace processes. Women peacebuilders are "an important source of community stability and vitality,"[27] and including women significantly increases the chances of reaching a lasting peace agreement.[28] Social change movements also need to take a clear stand on gender issues and actively work to engage women. One study of 104 groups in the Middle East seeking social change over a 24-year period found that the biggest predictor of whether or not a movement adopted violent tactics was not what we might expect—factors like whether it was left- or right-wing, religious or secular, or the levels of government violence the movement faced. *The biggest predictor for a movement staying nonviolent was its commitment to gender equality.*[29] Yet the importance of women in conflict transformation remains massively downplayed. One recent study found that just *six percent* of media coverage about issues of peace and security made women central to the story.[30]

Let's wrap up by considering how masculinity can shift. Much important work has been done to break down the belief that being a "real man" means having power over everyone else. Feeling our feelings, rather than fighting them, can be empowering. Friend Bruce Dienes explains how he's successfully helped men get there. His approach is an interesting complement to the four steps for encouraging behavior change that started this chapter. His four stages may be of interest when working with groups on other peace issues too. The stages-of-engagement model uses four questions that men will ask (consciously or unconsciously) when the issue of ending violence against women arises. In order to successfully engage men, Dienes says he's found that these questions need to be answered satisfactorily, ideally using experiential learning exercises, in this order:

*Sensitization stage*

1. **What are the issues?** (People at the top of a power imbalance don't need to know the lived experience of the ones below them. Men are typically unaware of the challenges faced by women and girls.)

*Motivation stage*

2. **Why should I care?** (Or "What does this have to do with me?" Men often run from "women's issues" so this needs to be clearly identified as a men's issue too, and not just in the traditional "protector role." How does this impact men's lives?)

*Empowerment stage*

3. **What can I do?** (Men often feel helpless to do anything, as the issues are so overwhelming. Introducing them to small wins and achievable goals is crucial at this stage, e.g., see *Just the Tip* exercise in the workshop series *Man to Man*, developed by the Fredericton Sexual Assault Crisis Centre.[31])

*Sustainability stage*

4. **Who will help?** (Doing this in isolation is not sustainable. Importantly, it needs to be other men keeping one another on track in this work, while remaining accountable to women's organizations.)[32]

## Tips from This Chapter

1. In order to motivate change, research recommends that we define the audience, have a realistic goal with clarity about what achieving it will mean, create an emotional desire for the change, and make the change as easy to make as possible.

2. A simple and focused story is most helpful in allowing us to open our hearts and take action. To help illustrate peace issues we care about, we can use personal stories or ones we know well with a single protagonist.

3. Emotions are contagious. We can literally recreate emotions similar to those we perceive around us.

4. We need to be careful about acting after we empathize with someone whose experiences may be valid but not widely shared. We can resonate with a person's message, but we also need to do our research.

5. We're being increasingly targeted with personalized emotional appeals, some benevolent and others not. It can help to protect our data, and to check with ourselves if things we see online are feeling emotionally manipulative. We can stop and ask what the content creators might be trying to achieve.

6. The face of violence in the world is a male one. Biology plays

a role, but masculinity has a vast range of expressions around the world, and men have different roles, some more constructive and some more violent, in different moments. Men can learn to block themselves from connecting with certain emotions and needs. When that happens, everyone suffers. Involving women and men in decision making and peacebuilding processes is vital for social change, as is a commitment to gender equality.

7. When working with groups to address issues like male violence, consider incorporating all of the following questions and corresponding stages: What are the issues? (Sensitization stage); Why should I care? (Motivation stage); What can I do? (Empowerment stage); and Who will help? (Sustainability stage).

## Activity: Making Connections

1. Facilitators split people into groups of three to five, making sure everyone has a blank sheet of paper and a pen.

2. Facilitators ask each person to write for three minutes, listing five challenging feelings or situations they regularly experience. If possible, these can be single words. People will need to share what they write. Facilitators let everyone know when one minute remains.

3. Facilitators ask the group to find one word that seems to be common—for instance "isolation."

4. Facilitators give groups a sheet of flipchart paper. Groups pick one writer, who puts the word "isolation" in the center of the page inside a bubble. Everyone lists issues associated with isolation, and these are written in other bubbles connected to the first. Once five or so words have been listed, facilitators stop people and say that's enough for now. The group then comes up with issues associated with all of the new bubbles, expanding outward. Repeat this until the sheet is full.

5. Come back together in the big group and discuss the connections. Is a focus emerging? Do the words center around inner, interpersonal, or structural peace issues?

6. Optional—if the group is feeling inspired to take action, a discussion could now happen about which of the issues the group could hope to change and how.[33] A broad idea-generating conversation like this takes time and a group ready to commit to frustration and confusion—see the appendix The Basics of Facilitation for more about this.

# Communication

*At the root of every tantrum*
*and power struggle are unmet needs.*

— MARSHALL ROSENBERG[1]

W HEN I WATCH movies I'm often frustrated by the lack of communication. If characters talked openly with each other, I'm sure most of their conflicts could be addressed. What happens instead is gossip and snappy back-and-forth exchanges that avoid naming key issues, leaving much to be guessed and read between the lines. This makes for good drama, but it's not that functional in real life. Given how important communication is to *everything we do*, it's incredible that an ineffective style that doesn't help us get our needs met is the one so many of us learn.

A big part of the problem is this: "When two people meet to discussion *one* subject, they are really discussing *two* subjects, which are the two people's viewpoints."[2] We regularly assume we're having a conversation about the same one subject when we're not. Often, we don't even know how muddled we are. Have you ever had the experience of believing you've been understood, and then being surprised when the person acts in ways that show they didn't get what you were talking about at all?

One challenge is that so little of our communication depends on what we're actually saying. When we watch lectures, whether the sound is off or on, whether we watch for seven seconds or

17 minutes, we rate the speakers *very similarly* in areas like their intelligence and credibility.[3] Think about that. Seven seconds of body language will lead you to a similar conclusion as someone watching a full lecture and listening intently to all the nuanced and carefully crafted points!

We also struggle with communication because our experiences are so *obvious* to us that we can't imagine how different they are from those of other people. What is your experience right now? Whatever it is, it's a unique state that you alone know.

Elizabeth Newton got her PhD studying a simple game with a surprising result. In the game, people are assigned one of two roles. The first person picks a famous song like *Happy Birthday to You* and taps it out on a table. The second person is assigned to listen and guess what song they're hearing. Before starting, the person doing the tapping predicts how likely the listener is to guess the song. Put yourself in the shoes of someone playing this game. How likely do you think a listener would be to guess that you're tapping *Happy Birthday to You* on a table? Newton found a fair bit of confidence—tappers predict the songs will be guessed about 50% of the time. In reality the success rate is 2.5%. Why such a massive difference? "When a tapper taps, *she is hearing the song in her head….* Meanwhile, the listeners can't hear that tune—all they can hear is a bunch of disconnected taps, like a kind of bizarre Morse code."[4] When we know something, it's incredibly difficult to imagine not knowing it. This game is a poignant illustration of the ongoing challenge of communication.

Before we decide to give up on being understood, let's recall what we saw last chapter—the contagious power of some communicators. What does it look like when we're really tuned in with each other during a conversation?

> The more listeners understand what a speaker is saying, the more closely their brain responses mirror the speaker's brain responses. What's more, while normally there was a slight delay in a listener's response matching up with the speaker's,

in cases of extremely high comprehension, the delay nearly disappeared. In listeners who scored highest on comprehension, brain responses sometimes preceded the speaker's.

In other words, this study found that when we understand clearly what someone's talking about, we might piece it together in our own brains *before it's even said!*[5]

When we're speaking to someone with very different beliefs, this type of resonance is probably lacking. One way to build it is to use concepts that the other party uses. So if we're talking to someone who values tradition, framing the exact same information *in terms of tradition* can make our ideas resonate. This is just what recent studies in the UK, US, and Germany found. Participants who cared a lot about tradition were more open to policies like strict gun control when they were framed in the language of nostalgia for the past rather than as new innovations.[6] I think often our positions aren't as far apart as they appear. Connecting with someone by speaking to what they value can make all the difference between a constructive dialogue and a divisive shouting match. And we find out someone's values when we ask questions and listen. People randomly assigned in online chats to ask more questions were better able to guess things about their conversation partners, and their partners rated them as more likeable.[7]

Sometimes even when we share values and ask questions that build a sense of understanding, we get taken by surprise. We're sailing along in resonant agreement, but then we express a belief that seems like common sense and find that our friend has a totally different take. Typically, we start such a disagreement by expressing *our views* in response to what our friend says. This may be a blunder. Instead, we could first *validate* our friend, both verbally and with attentive and understanding (rather than frustrated or dismissive) body language. Each of us needs to feel heard *before* we can hear criticism. To show we're listening, we might say something like, "I think this is a really important issue, so I'm glad you brought it up."[8] Next we might acknowledge points of agreement. Perhaps, even if we strongly disagree, we still learned something from our friend's view and can acknowledge it.[9] This creates as much of a shared starting place as possible. Such shifts can take a conversation out of the war-like dynamics of attack and defense. In disagreements we get distracted, thinking of what to say next instead of listening. Sometimes we put words in others' mouths. But it's powerful to pause and really imagine the perspective we're opposed to. Trying to express it in our own words has been shown to make us more understanding, but only when we feel *accountable* to our friend to make sure we're communicating what she said *accurately*.[10] So when she expresses something we disagree with, to start a conversation about it we can't just pick a way to caricature her opinion and make it sound as dumb as possible. To stop having two different conversations about our two different views, to meld these into one coherent discussion, it will help to listen and reflect back in our own words what was expressed. This isn't a complicated technique, but it can make a great difference in achieving clarity, overcoming the gulf between what the tapper thinks is obvious and what the listener is actually picking up.

Have you ever been ready to launch into a heated argument only to find the other person unexpectedly pleasant? As much as you try to hold on to it, that righteous momentum can just slip away. It's very demanding to keep up a "belligerent approach that's not reciprocated."[11] This is one of the best ways to shift to a healthier conversation, and it's often done with humor. When we laugh *together* we feel closer, diffusing tension, even deflating our exaggerated sense of importance. But when it's directed at people to isolate or belittle them, trivializing real concerns and needs, humor becomes power-over. It seems to come very easily to us to give orders like "Get a sense of humor" if people don't laugh at our demeaning joke, but feelings don't tend to work that way—changing on external command—so this communication style usually won't help. Instead, a useful approach is "humor but not humiliation"—make jokes to poke fun at situations, not to alienate people.[12]

Psychologist Marshall Rosenberg spent his career studying and developing ways to communicate effectively. He called the results nonviolent communication.[13] Rosenberg suggested that most of us are using language in confusing ways, often while trying to get others to do what we want. Yet most of us also like to feel in control and to resist orders, so we feel resentful of so many people telling us what to do. Our demands are a good way to get pushback. (Signs at a hotel pool saying, "Don't You *Dare* Litter" caused *increased* littering.[14])

Even if we tell someone in a friendly way what they *should* do and they comply, they likely aren't acting out of joy or response to their own needs. They might feel put upon. We get what we want in the short term, but strained relationships and bitterness could follow. Statements like "You should..." express the isolated and abstract ideas of power-over. We're describing an outside standard, a judgment not necessarily connected to what's happening right now.

To bring the focus back to the moment, we can use a discovery made by many religions and philosophers and more recently used in therapies like cognitive behavioral therapy: *no one is causing our feelings.* When we say, "You're making me angry," we're using a convenient shorthand, but it's not quite accurate. Of course others provide stimuli, but *we* weave these together and generate our feelings. We all know this is true because the same events don't always *make us* feel the same way, and they certainly don't make everyone around us feel the same. If someone cuts us off in traffic one day we might feel a violent rage, another day just a mild annoyance, another a sense of relief that we've been reminded to slow down and not rush the way this person is.

The stimulus—what others do or communicate—is not in our control, but we *are* very much sculpting our experiences, even if they seem automatic. "An emotion is your brain's creation of what your bodily sensations mean, in relation to what is going on around you in the world," neuroscientist Lisa Feldman Barrett contends. We've already seen examples of this—when we touch a hot cup, then shake hands with an interview candidate, our brains interpret that to mean that we feel warmly *toward that person.* When we smell some garbage and are asked how immoral it is to lie on our resume, we interpret the sensation of disgust in our body as relating not to the smell, but to the immorality of lying. "Emotions are not reactions to the world. You are not a passive receiver of sensory input but an active constructor of your emotions."[15]

We might know we're having an unpleasant feeling about being cut off in traffic, but there are countless concepts we might use to describe our feeling to ourselves. Studies have shown that folks who are able to distinguish between their feelings more precisely, using larger and more refined vocabularies to label and understand their emotions, are more flexible in regulating their emotions, deal with stress better, and are less aggressive when someone hurts them.[16] This realization can liberate us to communicate in richer ways. We might stop looking to external standards and judgments about what's happening and start speaking more accurately and precisely *for ourselves*. We could try stating only what actually occurred and how we're *feeling*, keeping the responsibility for our feeling with us. This frees us too from the impossible burden of trying to *make* other people happy. Since we don't generate emotions in anyone else, all we can do is act well, not cause someone else to respond how we might like. Once we're attending to and communicating our own feelings, we then begin to discover and express our *needs*.

It can seem like we know our needs pretty well. Many of us are buying things for ourselves all the time. Apparent desires ("I want *that!*") aren't the same as needs though. Needs aren't future plans or what we want other people to do. "I need you to clean up around here" is basically the same as "You should clean up around here." It's a command. We've already decided by ourselves what's right and what *should* happen; we're only communicating to make the other person do it. We've jumped ahead, never stating what we need: "I need a creative and stimulating environment to live in." In conversation, we might find that cleaning the place would indeed serve our need, but maybe we'd find other ways to serve it that we didn't think of. It's the conversation that helps us both to understand each others' needs and *then* decide how to meet them. And if cleaning up is the agreed way forward, it might no longer feel like such an arbitrary command.

Let's take another example: we send a message to a friend and don't hear back. The next day we notice that we're angry. This emotion tells us important information about our needs and about our ideas. Our feeling angry tells us that we're generating certain judgments—that our friend is heartless, an idiot, and we deserve better. Now we can, and often do, try communicating these judgments, but that rarely goes well. Our friend is unlikely to hear and agree with us. What we know and are certain is true isn't what he knows. We're having two different conversations about our two perspectives. We could follow approaches from the movies—lying, seeking revenge, blowing up in anger about something unrelated, or speaking in veiled ways and hoping we can manipulate him to start texting more often—but these might not get our need met, and even if they do, our friendship could suffer.

Rather than focusing on our abstract judgments about what type of person he is (the power-over categorizations we like to make), we could state what we see, our feeling, and our need. In this case we might have an unmet need for respect. Noticing this need is empowering. Accepting the vulnerability of having needs will often create a very different dynamic of communication. We're no longer meeting our friend by telling him what to do and getting pushback. We're not blaming or even politely stating solutions before our friend has understood what we think is happening. Now we're finding and expressing our need, making room for him to join us in the conversation, sharing what his needs are. Needs are universal— love, belonging, safety—so bringing the conversation to this level can really shift it. We might discover that we both have valid needs, ones we hadn't considered. The dynamic can go from "me versus you" to "me and you versus a situation to transform."

So to recap, if we can say just what we see ("I sent you a message and didn't get a reply," not "You never answer your texts; you're a bad person, and you drive me crazy"), how we feel ("I'm feeling annoyed"), and what our need is ("I need respect"), we can explore what can be done *together*. What does a need for respect look like? As soon as we can hear someone's need and express it in our own words, our perspective is transformed. We can hear the song that's being tapped.

If our friend doesn't use this communication style, we can listen for his need and ask about it. So if he says, "You're so demanding! I was going to respond, you know?" we could say, "I'm trying to understand what you need. What would you say your need is?" If we get nothing but more judgments about us—which is likely—we could offer a guess. "I'm just guessing, and I might be wrong, but would you say you need more free time? You're feeling tired trying to get so many things done?" If this is wrong, it can still move the discussion from competing judgments about who's being reasonable to the needs that aren't being met.

Once we've identified what we see, what we feel, and what our need is, we can make a request. (Many times in conversation—in particular in arguments—we start to ramble or repeat ourselves, hoping our views will be understood when in fact we haven't made a clear request.) When we do: "Can you please respond to my messages the same day?" our friend might say, "No." Many problems happen when we don't know how to say no, so while it can be tough to say and to hear, it's actually better than getting a yes that would lead to resentment every time he texts. His no, like all responses, expresses needs. Underlying the no might be, "I can't respond to messages quickly anymore because I've realized I'm happier when I reduce my screen time," or "I need to feel more independent and can't communicate with you that often." Asking questions can help us understand why we got the response we did.

This communication process sticks to observations and to truths. Isn't too much truth dangerous though? Isn't it better to hide our thoughts and speak in safer or more polite ways? There are times when truth can be too dangerous or too hurtful, but recall again the important distinction between *observation* (which is a truth—what we see) and *evaluation* (our judgments about the mean-

ing of what we see). Most often it's the latter that can be problematic. When we feel the urge to offer a critical evaluation or to tell a
half-truth or a lie, even just by omitting something important, it's
worth exploring our motivations and needs. Perhaps not speaking
our truth will help us or others, but maybe it'll cause problems. We
might be feeling pressure to put on a mask, to present ourselves a
certain way that seems safer or easier, but there could be costs to
these apparently harmless choices. (We'll return to these issues in
the chapter Who Benefits?)

Of course, plenty of conversations are honest enough and feel
truly fulfilling without using nonviolent communication, and
sometimes our abstract evaluations and judgments are fascinating
topics to chat about. If we get too rigid in using techniques like nonviolent communication, the flow of our conversations could suffer.
We could start to sound inauthentic and awkward. Where nonviolent communication can be particularly helpful though, is during
conflicts.

Shifts in communication aren't easy and will take practice.
We've experienced combative language all our lives. On top of that,
for many of us, needs are uncomfortable. Maybe we were raised to
be good by not fidgeting, not complaining, not making noise. As
we internalized this, we might have learned to silence signals from
our bodies, to inhibit certain feelings, to dampen awareness of our
needs. We want to be good, not *needy*. So, we disconnect from ourselves a bit, becoming fragmented.

At some level we might decide our needs are unreasonable or too
scary to express. Perhaps we feel guilty for having needs in a world
where people have less than we do. We might even take pleasure
in denying ourselves our needs, a type of power-over relationship
with ourselves. (We'll look at research on this in a later chapter.)
Whatever the reasons, we often expect that others will pick up on
the needs *we can't bring ourselves to identify and state*, and we fault
them if they don't.

These are just some of the complicated processes going on
below the surface in conversations. Many—like physicist David

Bohm—have noticed that we lack a way to uncover these processes and seek deeper understanding together. This would entail a tricky shift—not being stuck on our own thoughts and beliefs and being genuinely *happy* when errors in our logic are pointed out because *everyone* benefits when we move together toward better thinking.

A dialogue process as described by Bohm is based on acknowledging and questioning assumptions. Where did our beliefs come from, and why are we so identified with them? Are they serving us? To explore this we sit together in a circle with a small group with no agenda, no leader, and no specific goals. We're not trying to be persuasive. We're not agreeing or disagreeing with anything said. The group is simply considering what each opinion *means*, while suspending further judgments for now. In the end, the group may participate together in coming to a *shared sense of meaning*—while still recognizing each of the various distinct assumptions present. This isn't easy—it takes paying close attention to notice an assumption and to not hold onto it! Bohm readily acknowledges that this process can be frustrating and may not work if conditions like trust within the group are lacking.[17] It isn't always going to be practical, but in the right circumstances, such a dialogue could be richly rewarding.

The method has some similarities to a Quaker meeting, with important differences too. Both express the idea that truth can be found through multiple people sharing their slivers of experience and understanding (a power-with way of communicating), not that one person's ideas must prevail over everyone else's as in rhetoric and debate (power-over ways of communicating). Both are heavily focused on creating an opportunity to get deeper unity (Bohm uses the word "coherence"), where everyone has their own unique views but simultaneously understands the view of the group. Various Quakers have told me their experiences of feeling that a meeting— a group of Friends gathered together—had decided on a course of action that they *never* would have personally chosen but that the rightness of that action was somehow clear as well, because of the deep unity the meeting had reached. When used in a business meeting, the Quaker decision making process holds that every group member brings something uniquely valuable, so people will be listened to in a way that doesn't just seek resolution based on what the majority thinks. For this to work, members need to come to the meeting informed about the issues and disciplined enough to respect the process.

For many of us such alien modes of communication might seem to contain a paradox. How can we both want to get our own way and genuinely participate in a group that decides to go a different way? It sounds like trying to be two people at once. But accepting these tensions may just be part of the process of healing artificially created divides, moving from fragmentation toward wholeness through "embracing everything or thinking the world together again."[18] It takes trust that others know things too, even though we might not be able to see it. If in our certainty—our firm beliefs and judgments—we've skipped something, if our uniquely biased categorizations are a bit off, we may be missing a key piece of the puzzle that is the real situation before us. We might be filtering out a perspective that can give us new clarity.

For the rest of this book you'll have regular chances to practice the skills of listening and speaking via an exercise called concentric circles. For some this will be a novel and challenging way of approaching something familiar. For others it may seem quite straightforward. In any case, these skills are one thing to know about and something else entirely to make your default mode of communication, *especially when tempers flare!* Using techniques like nonviolent communication won't put an end to painful conflict. Hearing other peoples' needs can still be daunting, and not everyone can be engaged with. Especially online some folks are "trolling," trying to create confusion and discomfort, not to have conversations. But we regularly do have opportunities to deepen our communication and have more rewarding interactions if we want to.

## Tips from This Chapter

1. When we know something, it's incredibly hard to remember how it felt to not know it. Our knowledge and beliefs aren't necessarily

shared, though, so being clear and precise in conversation can make a big difference.

2. When approaching a disagreement it can help to listen, validate the person so they know they've been heard, acknowledge points of agreement, acknowledge anything we've learned from the person, and ask questions for clarification.

3. What has actually been said, and what are we just assuming? Careful listening means not putting words in others' mouths. Clarifying assumptions is often enough to show us that an apparent conflict isn't at all what we'd thought. This can be done by reflecting back what we think we've heard to make sure it's what the speaker intended.

4. Framing the exact same information in terms of the values of the person we're speaking with can help that information to be understood and engaged with very differently.

5. When it pokes fun at situations, rather than trying to demean particular people, humor can be valuable at bridging divides.

6. Emotions are heavily dependent on how we interpret what's happening both inside us and outside. They give us important information about the stories we're telling ourselves. They're not something another person is *making* us feel.

7. We regularly speak in judgments, assigning blame, and deciding by ourselves what the solutions are to the various problems we've defined. This is a poor strategy for getting our needs met. Our judgments and solutions might not make sense to other people, and even if people do what we tell them to, they may resent it. Someone using nonviolent communication would explain only what they observe happening (without adding evaluations of what that means), what their feeling is, what their need is, and after some discussion, what they would request of the other person.

8. Asking questions, we can move beyond the judgments of the person we're communicating with to identify their needs. In this process, open-ended and bigger questions can support more enriching communication. Needs are universal, so moving a con-

versation there can shift the dynamic from "me versus you" to "me and you versus a situation to transform."

9. When we feel the urge to conceal information or to lie, it can give us valuable insights. Sometimes we need to protect ourselves by not telling the whole truth, and sometimes telling the truth would just be a way to attack people. In other cases we could find a conflict positively transformed if we speak plainly.

10. When we have time we can sit with a group, listening receptively and discussing thoughts and experiences without trying to prove a point or judge the points others are making. Is deeper coherence forming?

## Activity: Rewording a Conflict

1. Facilitators split the group into pairs and hand out copies of this script, one per person. The pairs each decide on their characters and read through the script once together.

   A knock at the door.

   Person A: "I'm busy right now, can you get the door?"

   Person B: "I guess so, but I deserve to put my feet up. Why don't you do it?"

   Person A: "I'm *busy!* You should listen better."

   Person B: "Oh, I can see you're in one of your moods again."

   Person A: "What's *that* supposed to mean?"

   Person B: "Why are you always so aggressive? Do you think I'm supposed to always do things like get the door?"

   Person A: "I'm not trying to be aggressive; I'm just not feeling great. I have a headache and it's been a long day."

   Person B: "You've got to do a better job of telling me when you're not feeling well."

   Person A: "I know I should. You've told me. You make me feel like I'm a monster sometimes. You know, other people don't have big debates about who's going to answer the door!"

   Person B: "Fine, you win, I'll get the door."

2. Facilitators write the following questions on flipchart paper and ask each group to take 15 minutes to discuss their responses:

    a. How effective is this conversation?

    b. What are the assessments or judgments being made?

    c. What assumptions might be present?

    d. What could the needs be?

    e. How might you change each sentence to enhance the communication?

3. Facilitators look to see when the pairs are winding down and give a two-minute warning. The group comes back together, and one person from each pair shares their responses. After hearing what each pair did, facilitators ask the group:

    a. What similarities and differences did you notice?

    b. What might be the long-term impact of interactions like this one as it happened originally?

    c. What could it mean to make the changes we made?

    d. Does this activity generate any insights or stories anyone would like to share?

## Activity: Concentric Circles

This activity will be used at various points throughout the rest of the book. The overall structure of concentric circles each time it's done is as follows:

1. Everyone in the group moves their chairs to form two circles: a smaller one on the inside facing out and a bigger one on the outside facing in. Enough space is left that people can comfortably sit facing each other. There needs to be an even number of people, so facilitators can either participate or not, whatever makes the numbers work. In either case, someone needs to be timekeeper, because some of us are chatty!

2. Facilitators read off the questions, and people choose which one to speak to, choosing only one.

3. The person sitting on the outside is first speaker. Speakers have the freedom to express themselves without being interrupted or attacked. Speakers practice being clear and precise with their words. Speakers are encouraged not to focus on blaming, judging, or punishing others.

4. The person sitting on the inside is a listener. Their role is to engage in active listening. This means, when asked by facilitators, repeating back what they've heard the speaker say, without offering judgments. The listener may ask questions for clarification only if necessary and not to cut the speaker off or challenge what they're saying. The listener can practice engaged body language, eye contact, and demonstrating to the speaker that they're present to what's being said. Many of us like to jump in to offer advice or solutions to peoples' problems, but this isn't always welcome; so this exercise will help listeners practice not taking control of conversations or trying to fix the issues raised.

5. After five minutes, the timekeeper says the time's up. The listener provides a very brief summary of what they heard. Summarizing is an important skill—it means choosing key points without putting words in the speakers' mouth. The speaker can use this as an opportunity to discover how their message was heard and if there are areas that were unclear.

6. Facilitators read off the questions again with the two roles of speaker and listener reversed. Again, speakers choose just one of the questions they wish to speak to.

7. At the end, facilitators allow people to share with the group their insights and experiences by asking, "Would anyone like to share how that was? What came up for you?"

## Questions for This First Concentric Circles Activity

1. Recall a time when you felt particularly powerful. Why do you think you felt that power?

2. When you speak the truth, even in a situation where you don't stand to gain by it, how does it feel and what are the results?

3. When you seek to attack with your words, how does that feel, and what are the results?

# Conflict

*This is a common fear among Friends, and I am sure
many of you share it with me... We do not want to hurt—and
so we do not share our differences of thought, word or experience
in the open, loving way which would help all of us to grow.*

— Betty Polster[1]

CONFLICT IS BOUND to run through all relationships in differing flavors. We feel like reading, and our partner wants to chat. We want to go to an art gallery, and our friend wants to go to a movie. We will never live in a world where everyone agrees or shares the same desires. And that doesn't need to result in hatred. Conflict is healthy and beneficial *if* it's navigated in healthy ways.

Previously we imagined the case of two drunk men punching each other. Their being drunk was obviously an important cause of the conflict. But we could go further and ask why they were so drunk. Exploring that could lead us to blame their upbringing, their stressful work environments, a culture that associates masculinity with heavy drinking, the alcohol companies with their alluring advertising, or even self-medication for chemical imbalances in the brain. We could examine what stories the men told themselves that encouraged the fight, what their unmet needs were, and on and on. Remember the activity Making Connections? The dense networks of causes and effects that we can think of (and as we've seen, someone with a different worldview could readily think of others we'd never notice) can be overwhelming. A conflict doesn't happen just because of the last thing we did. We could think about a minute earlier and recall a further factor that contributed, and a minute before that another factor still. In transforming conflicts—where do we begin?

Trying to address every issue is impossible, while trying to figure out what the "primary cause" is and focusing there has its own drawbacks. Here's an example of that sort of thinking, taken from a book on violence: "The emotion of shame is the primary or ultimate cause of all violence..."[2] If we believe that, then we could best prevent future outbursts of drunken fighting if we help both men process and overcome their shame. But one thorough literature review found 57 causes being named by different authors as *the primary cause* of entrenched conflicts![3] So as tempting as it is to look for the one main cause (remember how power-over thinking tends to follow this all-under-one dynamic), it's often more helpful to "keep it complex." (As we've seen, this is more associated with power-with.) It's going to be tough to start in 57 places, but we can remember that just because we think we know the obvious starting place, that doesn't mean we're right or that others will agree: "Most positions are one-sided or premature solutions to a half-understood problem."[4] Instead of assuming we understand, we can try communicating to identify important factors at play, paying attention in particular to ones we could address. In complex conflicts we may *never* agree on what the main causes are, but as long as everyone agrees the situation *is* problematic, we can often still find new ways forward and test them out.[5] I think having a conflict analysis tool can help. There are many tools, but let's look at just one:

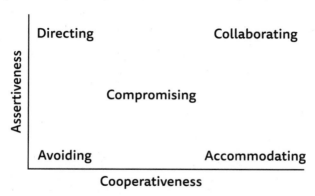

On the y-axis is assertiveness—how much we care about getting our own way. On the x-axis is cooperativeness—how much we value our relationships.[6]

- If we don't really care about relationships but care a lot about achieving the result we want, our style will be competing or directing. This style is the most closely related to power-over.
- A collaborating or consensus approach means not giving up on our desired outcome, but also caring about the relationship and getting along with the other party. This style means we're willing to spend the time to understand the conflict, the different viewpoints and needs involved, and the possible ways forward. It means not being hung up on anyone's initial proposal. This style is most closely related to power-with.
- If we don't care much about the result, and we don't care much about the relationship, our style will be avoiding.
- If we don't care much about getting our way, but we do care a lot about relationships, we'll be accommodating, a type of self-sacrifice.
- Finally, compromise is somewhere in the middle. The idea here is finding an easy enough solution where everyone is somewhat satisfied. This style can also be an example of power-with.

It's important to know that *none of these is "the right way" to engage*. As we keep seeing, the peace virus isn't prescriptive—it evolves in ever-new directions depending on the moment. If you're on the bus and about to get off at the next stop as a woman sits down beside you blasting her music, avoidance may make a lot of sense. You don't have time and energy to launch into cooperation in every conflict. It's a process that can be slow and requires willingness from all parties. When your child is about to touch the stove, you won't come up with a compromise where he can hold his hand close to the burner but not on it, and you won't accommodate him by just watching. It makes sense to use a directing style, physically moving him away from the stove.

Depending on the problem, it may be tempting to reach a compromise. But that also means that no one is fully satisfied. In

particular when we're tired or impatient, we're ready to just compromise—to win a bit and also lose a bit. This may seem like the
mature route, but it could have been possible for all parties to win in
unexpected ways if we'd thought about the options further instead
of compromising too soon. Another problem with believing compromise is the best path is that it ignores the specifics of the conflict.
Author Walter Wink gives an example. In the Philippines, small
landowners would find their land encroached on by powerful landowners with massive holdings. The two would be called to attend
meetings with local government officials, who discussed the conflict as if it was a breakdown in communication and then encouraged compromise and reconciliation. But the underlying injustice
hadn't been addressed, and the power imbalances were ignored.[7]

It's equally mistaken to think that by not engaging, or by sacrificing our needs, we're automatically being good and helpful to
others. Accommodation and avoidance can be very appropriate in
situations where we genuinely aren't too committed to our original
goals, but many of us actually adopt them with resentment, as we
saw last chapter. Our desire not to cause trouble can create trouble
instead. The problem gets particularly pronounced any time a group
tries to present itself as free of conflict or to promote values like tolerance without openly addressing the frictions of conflicting needs.
One chilling example is offered by author Miriam Toews, in this case
speaking about her Mennonite community, which "shuns" someone
for serious transgressions.

> It involves a complete denial of the individual's existence. It is
> a method of conflict avoidance that maintains the righteous-
> ness of the community while preventing any resolution or
> possibility of justice. It is murder without killing and it cre-
> ates deep-seated wells of rage that find no release.[8]

This is negative peace—violence that appears tranquil by avoiding reality. It's the denial we saw in the chapter Firm Belief. It happens too when people or governments say they're tolerant and let
conflicts come to light but don't actually engage with them. After
we speak our piece we might feel better for a while, but not if the

conflict situation remains the same. When we don't want to address conflict, or to examine the processes underlying it, the results can be awful! This is why it's helpful not to see conflict as negative or something to "resolve" as quickly as possible. Dealing with a conflict process half-heartedly doesn't end it; it simply changes the conflict's trajectory. This is a danger in popular approaches like "conflict management," which may be too rigid and limiting in framing and addressing the issues.[9] Of course, there are very different scales of conflict (it's possible to neatly resolve which restaurant to go to for lunch!), but for larger issues, ones that go on for years or that turn violent, it can be helpful to think that the energy generated may never be "resolved," simply transformed. Tensions that build over years won't disappear, but they can continue in healthier directions. If new dynamics play out, the energy that was once destructive could become creative and nourishing.

Whatever style we choose, exploring the beliefs and assumptions present, paying attention to the process, treating emotions with care, and using the communication skills we've learned, are all fundamental. No matter the conflict, we all want to be heard and to have our feelings and needs respected. Even when we're trying to work together in constructive ways, we can tend to focus on a solution too early and get stuck there, so it's helpful to keep reminding ourselves to think together of several ways forward before making a choice.

We just looked at an analytical tool, but this isn't necessarily "the best way" to be in conflict. In many cultures conflicts are successfully transformed without ever being abstractly analyzed and broken down. Instead, stories, proverbs, and teachings, in particular from elders, offer advice and wisdom to reorient people who've lost their way.[10] Conflicts are transformed by communities, not just the individuals involved. Shared rituals and ceremonies tap into transformative power-from-within, creating space for deep shifts of old conflict patterns.[11] These patterns are understood, experienced, and redirected through dance, music, theater, and other arts.[12] A central focus is changing hearts—helping parties to recall the society's values, to feel, and to *embody* new relationships with each other. However we approach them, conflicts are always present and always changing—offering continual opportunities for peaceful transformation. We'll learn much more about this in the pages to come.

## Tips from This Chapter

1. Conflicts are normal and will never go away. Even when we feel we understand the primary cause of a conflict, there's often more going on. Others could have different insights, so it's helpful to listen and decide together where to focus. Depending on the scale of the conflict, it may be a mistake to push for neat "resolutions" too quickly. Instead, when deciding our approach, we can consider how much relationships matter and how much getting our way matters. No one approach is right for every situation.

2. In particular if we're tired, there's a tendency to adopt a partial win/partial lose compromise. But thinking together of a few possible solutions before deciding on one can often reveal ways where everyone wins.

3. There can be major costs to sacrificing our needs or keeping quiet about injustices, so it's important not to think that compromise, accommodation, or avoidance are necessarily the moral choices.

4. It can be helpful to think of long-lasting conflicts in particular as generating energy that can be transformed in new directions, but that won't just be "resolved" and vanish.

5. Conflicts don't need to be logically analyzed. Any process that can transform their dynamics, such as recalling our power-from-within and being reminded of our values and our place in society, may be just what we need. Involving full communities through rituals and ceremonies is used all over the world to successfully transform conflicts.

## Activity: What Would You Need?

1. Facilitators pass out paper and pens and explain that everyone will be asked to write down their immediate responses to two scenarios. There will be five minutes for each.

2. Facilitators read off the first scenario: "Imagine that someone physically threatened you and then later stole from you and vandalized your property. List what your emotions might be and what you'd need from others to process the harm you experienced." Facilitators give a two-minute warning.

3. Now facilitators read out the second scenario: "Imagine that you've harmed someone—you've threatened them, stolen from them, and vandalized their property. List what your emotions might be and what you'd need from others to address the harm you've caused." Facilitators give a two-minute warning.

4. Facilitators ask members of the group to read their responses or post their lists on the wall and browse around, reading each others' lists.

5. Facilitators ask the group for any reflections. People are usually surprised to see how similar the two lists are. They reveal common needs. Facilitators, if no one in the group raises it, make sure to draw attention to the similarities (and any differences) between the lists. This exercise shows how related our needs are, even when we seem divided.[13] Facilitators can also ask how the needs listed relate to the values people wrote in the exercise Your Values and a Special Person. We often find that they're similar— we value what we need and need what we value.[14]

## Example: Who Gets Recognized?

After a well-received lecture one evening, there's a question-and-answer period. The moderator recognizes people to ask questions, and runners deliver microphones. The discussion is rich, and everyone feels energized. Afterward, amid many smiles and happy conversations, a woman of color approaches and says she wanted to ask a question but she wasn't recognized by the moderator (a white woman) while white man after white man got recognized instead.

The moderator explains that bright lights were shining toward the stage, so she was having trouble seeing anyone sitting in the higher rows, as this woman had been. Almost everyone picked was from the lower rows because they were easiest to see. The woman repeats that no, she was ignored because of her gender and race. The moderator says that she's sorry the woman feels that, but it's not what happened. She makes sure the woman did get to ask her question now, and then explains the incident to the event organizers so they're aware. A day passes and it appears all is now well.

On the next day, the organizers of the event publish a prominent apology, saying the moderator (not using her name) recognized a disproportionate number of white men at a time when women and people of color were seeking to be recognized. The moderator is not told about the apology or asked for her input before it's published. When the moderator reaches out, the organizers say they're sorry they didn't contact her but felt it was important to apologize right away and not make excuses or try to explain what happened. They say they decided the impact felt by the woman who wasn't recognized was what mattered most.

The moderator is upset that the apology didn't offer context. A great many people, including many white men, weren't recognized to ask questions, because there wasn't time. The apology didn't make this clear. It also failed to note that at least one woman of color and several white women *did* get recognized. This was a very white crowd, so the woman who wasn't recognized might have been the only person of color seeking to ask a question who wasn't able to. Omitting these facts in the apology gave a sense of a clear incident when what happened was more ambiguous. The moderator's employer then engages in a long back and forth with the organizers, seeking an apology.

### Analysis

Let's start by recalling the tip from the chapter Firm Belief—we have no reason to think that anyone involved in this conflict has anything but good intentions. No one is seeking to deliberately harm others. As is so common, we could make assumptions, but in fact, there's a lot we don't know. For example, we don't know what the woman of color's history with racist exclusion is, but sadly, it's likely she's experienced it. We don't know the extent to which the moderator does or doesn't have the implicit biases discussed in Chapter Two. We don't know the histories of the event organizers and how they perceive their roles.

When a conflict involves many people, it helps to define clearly what our roles will be. Among the event organizers, who will decide what process to follow? Who will communicate with the moderator and the woman who raised the complaint? Confusion about roles can mean no one follows up, fueling further misunderstandings and spin-off conflicts.

Recalling what we've learned about communication, let's recognize what happened, the feelings present, and the needs. It seems the woman felt ignored and devalued, and her need is for respect. Was she allowed to make a request in this case, and was her request for a published apology, or did the organizers just assume that would be a good way of addressing her needs? The moderator likely feels attacked and misunderstood, and perhaps needs her personal integrity to be recognized. She has requested an apology from the organizers, but they're tied up in a long process of discussion with her employer about it, which is proving painful for everyone. The event organizers might feel pressure to get this right and need to be seen as caring and committed to racial justice. They have particular powers here and have not made any requests; they've simply made decisions (a directive approach). Here we're just guessing, and it's important to establish the feelings, needs, and requests of each party not through guesses but in conversation. When we do come to understand each others' feelings and needs, we can get a sense of how much we have in common. The importance of status in the community and feeling respected are shared by all in this conflict.

Acknowledging and honoring feelings means making sure to label them as such, and not as anything less or anything more. We can't challenge the way someone feels; that's their personal experience. Feelings matter and aren't to be ignored or minimized. At the same time, our judgments and feelings need to be kept distinct from objective facts. Our tendency to confuse these can escalate conflicts.

Speaking to what we know to be true means using statements like, "I feel…," "From my perspective…"

As with many conflicts, what happened is unclear and subject to different interpretations. There's agreement from everyone that more men than women were recognized to ask questions. The rest is contested. The event organizers were in the challenging position of deciding they needed to honor the woman's feelings right away, but in doing so, they stated something they didn't know was true. It *might* have been true, but it's also possible that the woman's feeling of being ignored based on her race was inaccurate and another variable—distance from the stage or some other factor—more accurately explained who was recognized. (If this is what happened, it's called omitted-variable bias—when one or more factors we didn't consider better explain what happened than the factors we did consider. It's a common mistake to watch out for.)

What we choose not to say matters as much as what we do say. Honoring one perspective by silencing another will usually create further conflict. Again, we can benefit from pausing and reminding ourselves to be precise about saying what's known, rather than what's assumed. So, "During the question period, time constraints meant many people weren't able to ask their questions. While some women and people of color were recognized to ask their questions, at least one person felt that too many white men were recognized while she was ignored because of her race and gender. The event organizers apologize for the feelings of hurt experienced." As a general rule, it's worth saying only what we actually know.

If an apology like this was to be issued, the *process* of getting there mattered as much as the apology. To avoid further damage, we'd do well to slow down even though there's a strong urge to get excited and speed up. Taking what appeared to be a quick route generated further tensions that made the conflict take *more* time and energy instead. As it widened, with the moderator's employer and more members of the event organizing team getting involved, further misunderstandings from different judgments being stated as facts increased the divides, generating further conflict. This is very typical of conflict processes, which expand each time underlying needs remain unnamed and unmet. As the conflict progresses, the desire to stop listening and start using power-over increases. Continuously picking spots to interpret unclear actions and messages in the most positive light possible, and to make caring gestures, can really help. It's easy to see from this simple example how conflicts among well-meaning folks can become entrenched and how they can be transformed.

# 3

# Violence and Interpersonal Peace

*We've been exploring the roots of violence,*
*but what is violence? What are its impacts?*
*This section considers violence more deeply,*
*revealing entry points where peace can flourish.*
*Skills developed here will relate to deeper reflection*
*and choosing our responses deliberately.*

# Seeing Violence

*Life eats life.*

— JOSEPH CAMPBELL[1]

JOSEPH CAMPBELL studied spiritual traditions from around the world and found that the violence inherent in life is one of the uncomfortable truths they all grapple with. Life eats life. Our world is perpetually destructive and creative. Can peace be consistent with such a violent world, or is it a total fantasy?

In his article "On Staying Sane in a Suicidal Culture," Dahr Jamail describes his personal struggles with post-traumatic stress disorder after working as a war correspondent in Iraq: "I was unable to go any deeper emotionally than my rage and numbness. I stood precariously atop my self-righteous anger about what I was writing, for it was the cork in the bottle of my bottomless grief from what I'd witnessed." How often do our firm beliefs and hard-line moral convictions cover our pain and fears in a world in which life eats life? One day, Jamail went to meet a stranger for tea, eco-philosopher Joanna Macy. "After quietly pouring our mugs full, she looked me straight in the eyes and said, slowly, 'You've seen so much.' My own grief beginning to be witnessed, tears welled in my eyes immediately, as they did in hers."[2]

Acknowledgement—*seeing and being seen*—is an ancient and deeply powerful experience. Having a complete stranger just sit with you while you do something painful reduces the pain you

Marina Abramović performing *The Artist is Present*

experience compared to doing it alone.[3] In her 2010 performance artwork *The Artist is Present*, Marina Abramović spent a grueling eight to ten hours a day in silence, looking into the eyes of strangers. Many who participated were moved to tears.[4]

Quakers often describe the feeling of entering into silence together as an experience of coming home. Perhaps they're finding a deeper experience of themselves because of this new openness in the presence of others. I expect I'm not unique in having discovered that it's much easier to be critical of someone behind their back than when I'm sitting with them. I often seem to understand people better when we're able to see each other in person. Suddenly the "other" shifts from being a simple idea I wanted to hold onto to something much richer—a real person. Buddhist Author Stephen Bachelor says, "Just as you peer out beyond yourself to scrutinize others, so do they gaze from their interiority to wonder about you."[5] He imagines the shared message of our gazes as this: "Do not hurt me."[6]

Joanna Macy went on to tell Dahr Jamail the importance of inner seeing—taking stock, acknowledging the pain we experience from the violent world we live in. "Refusing to feel pain, and becoming incapable of feeling the pain, which is actually the root meaning of apathy, refusal to suffer, that makes us stupid, and half alive," she explained. "The most radical thing any of us can do at this time is to be fully present to what is happening in the world."[7]

We hope for a lasting peace, a stable peace, a hiding place of permanent peace. Yet we are in a world of flux. In any moment something terrible might happen and, thanks to the internet, we can stay up to date about it. With an endless stream of awful news, how can we react? We're witnessing life eating life.

The work of Joseph Campbell and countless others makes it clear that the destructive aspects of the world, and the knowledge that each of us will die, has forever been a deep challenge to reconcile with a celebration of life. It's not getting easier. There's a web of relationships in a globalized world that make it difficult to live without being destructive. Even when sincerely striving to be peaceful, we may still be violent. When trying to help, we can cause harm. The laptop I use to write about peace runs on Congolese conflict minerals.[8] Even something as simple as a toothbrush has a vast meaning when we explore it:

> An electric toothbrush needs circuit boards dotted with materials of tantalum in a capacitor to store energy; neodymium, dysprosium, boron, and iron magnet to provide the power to spin brushes at 31,000 strokes per minute; batteries made from nickel and cadmium or lithium. The 35 metals needed come from 6 continents.[9]

Environmental destruction and forced labor uphold many of these supply chains.[10] We can reject violence, but our lives, from toothbrushes to treasured childhood toys, can be full of its products. Add to this that the average lifestyle in countries like Canada is profoundly unsustainable and causing havoc on a planetary scale while inequality continues to increase.[11] Some level of inequality might be a good thing, but an article in *The British Medical Journal* explains a bit of what major inequality can mean:

Inequality matters because, as a robust and growing body
of evidence shows, the populations of societies with bigger
income differences tend to have poorer physical and mental
health, more illicit drug use, and more obesity. More unequal
societies are marked by more violence, weaker community
life, and less trust. Inequality also damages children's wellbeing, reducing educational attainment and social mobility.[12]

Are our social and political structures themselves sometimes forms
of slow violence—"a violence of delayed destruction that is dispersed across time and space"?[13] Whatever we call it, we can get
a sense of why Jamail saw the culture around him—one avoiding
so many pressing issues—as suicidal. Part of our blindness to the
deeper structures of violence is our omission bias. If we push someone to their death, we consider ourselves guilty of murder, but if we
don't bother to catch a falling person, we're not so sure. We have a
sense that what we *do* matters more than what we don't do.[14]

So how can we engage in a violent world? As we've seen again
and again, honesty and openness help in building power-with and
finding our power-from-within. A Canadian Quaker book of wisdom
and advice says, "Let us be open to discern how the seeds of destruction of our planet are present in our ways of living. We are thankful
that so much joy and beauty has been offered to us."[15] We can try
to do the work of seeing ourselves and our own lives, observing for
signs of violence we may not want to witness, while remembering to
be thankful for all the good things we come across! We can celebrate
life without claiming that we're separate from its problems.

In a violent world, we humans are ever resilient builders of
community. We engage in design-led changes, thinking through
the lifecycles of products and building them in sustainable ways.[16]
We trade, share, and reuse to reduce our dependence on destructive
production and over-consumption.[17] We buy fair trade when the option is available and within our means. We make ethical investment
decisions.[18] We access better information than ever before, using it
to make informed purchases.[19] A few, like Quakers Tom Findley and

Keith Helmuth go so far as to grow their own food and live simply as an expression of spiritual connection with life.[20] Others chose to take personal risks like finding it morally right to withhold taxes that would go to pay for war.[21] Yet with all this, the calamities we face demand large-scale changes, and our best individual efforts can't extricate us.

We saw previously that we tend to think of ourselves as more fixed than we really are, until we get some simple training to make our views more realistic. We can learn to see violence too. Studies suggest that training makes people newly alert to it by highlighting "both the harm and the avoidability of many kinds of violence."[22] What was a narrow frame suddenly opens. However, seeing violence and choosing a response is still a process fraught with ambiguity.

Recall that to reduce our tendency to rationalize our decisions it helps to be clear about our values, to define the rules of the game. In doing this, though, power-over judgments have a tendency to creep up. I think it's great that so many of us are able to see the connections of various problems—to name them and to challenge each other about them. But we can readily speak from pain in ways that mostly just multiply pain. We get a bit too good at dissecting the world to find violence lurking, and we forget to build ourselves up by building up those around us.

We can always go further in calling more and more of life "violence," but at some point we lose all balance and our efforts are no longer fruitful. They turn into a quest for an impossible purity, a power-over attempt to make people and the world fit with our abstract ideas about how we imagine they *should* be.[23] In 1939 Friend Horace Alexander saw violence and worked for change. In doing so he explained that since war "involves the mobilization of all the human and material resources of the State, it is hardly possible for any citizen to keep clear of all entanglements. Each of us must draw the line somewhere, with charity towards those who for reasons that we may not appreciate draw it elsewhere."[24]

Whatever approaches we choose, we can take care not to try to escape from life. As Jamail and countless others have discovered, we can't be healed through lying to ourselves about what's happening. Hugh Campbell-Brown once put it succinctly during a Quaker Meeting: "Pain is like counterfeit money, it keeps getting passed on until someone accepts the loss." We benefit from having the right kinds of space for acceptance of the fullness of life, and for expression of the fears and challenges we go through in a violent world. (And there can be long-term health costs when we fail to do so.[25])

Here's an outlier who's a fascinating example—Friend Helen Steven. She saw violence and went to remarkable lengths to engage. She was arrested many times for peaceful involvement in social change campaigns, at one point risking losing her house over her arrests![26] She wrote that throughout these years, each time she admitted her fear and vulnerability, her isolation melted. Others felt empowered to really see her and help.[27] "By making ourselves totally open...by reaching down beyond our deepest selves to the very ground of our being, who knows what may happen? We are in effect offering a blank cheque of our lives. This may lead us in directions we had never dreamed of, to new challenges and new ways of living adventurously."[28]

On the other hand, we might reject that we have responsibility for violence. This could be based on all kinds of ideas. Here's an incomplete list:

- believing we humans are too small to know what's right and so shouldn't try to change things (uncertainty leading to faith in the status quo)
- faith that nature or the divine will help solve society's problems without us having to engage (faith-based determinism/fatalism)
- believing that trying to change things is impossible or too difficult and will ultimately fail, so isn't worth our efforts (fatalism/pessimism/defeatism)
- believing that everything is alright or is going to be alright (pure optimism/denial)
- believing that there are many problems but others should change them because it's not up to us or we don't have the knowledge/resources/expertise/energy (this is along the lines of what's called social loafing)

- fear that our enjoyment of life and our peace of mind may be lost if we try to change things (self-preservation/denial)
- wanting to live some way, but simply not doing it (inconsistency/denial).

Perhaps you resonated with some items on this list. That's OK! It's good to listen to ourselves. When our beliefs are right for us, they help us feel alive. If we discover ways that our beliefs are cutting us off from a celebration of our lives, they may need to be explored further with the exercises in this book. In this process we may discover that the challenges look monumental, so let's recall what we've already learned—acting on our peace concerns can actually be good for us on a personal level, both in the short and long term.

A study that followed 3,617 people from 1986 to 2006 as they aged found that "volunteer work was good for both mental and physical health. People of all ages who volunteered were happier and experienced better physical health and less depression." This wasn't just a statistical trend—becoming active with important social causes contributed to lowered depression in the same individual study participants. Another study showed reduced chronic pain. This appears to have been in part because of having a *sense of purpose*. Similar positive effects, at least in the short term, have been shown when donating to good causes. Brain scans suggest that giving feels rewarding.[29] Such findings make it "clear that helping others, even at low thresholds of several hours of volunteerism a week, creates mood elevation."[30] This is a reminder that we can benefit from becoming more deeply involved in life, not to brood or fixate on our roles in violent systems but to care for and connect with each other. We cannot escape the destructiveness of the world, but we need not be crushed by it. Even as the peace virus tests and pushes us toward our edges, it can empower us and help us heal.

## Tips from This Chapter

1. We're surrounded by violence, some of it more obvious and some more concealed. It runs through each of our lives. We tend to think of certain violence, like that resulting from our

actions, as morally worse than other violence, like that from our inactions. We may also forget to ask questions about the sources of the products we buy or the impacts of our investments. This shelters us from seeing the violence that may be embedded in day-to-day decisions.

2. There are many competing ideas and motivations that keep us from acting consistently with the ways we want to live. All of us need to decide where to draw the lines and to recognize the complexity involved in these choices. Acting in pro-social and helping ways is not only a challenge but also its own reward, boosting our health and well-being.

— 11 —

# What's Natural?

*Why are we violent but not illiterate?*
*Because we are taught to read.*

— High school student paper[1]

NOT ONLY CAN many of us be violent, we can go so far as to get a pleasurable *thrill* from it. We can crave more, the same as in other addictions.[2] Isn't this proof that violence is in our DNA?

It seems that nearly every conversation about peace comes around to big questions. Perhaps war is inevitable, given the scarcity of resources on this planet, or it's just part of human nature. If we believe humans are naturally violent, exploitative, and selfish, we can readily decide that yes indeed, "Greed is good."[3] One of the strongest inoculations against the peace virus is beliefs like these, so let's explore them a bit. A great deal has been written about violence among chimpanzees and bonobos and what this may or may not say about humans. I don't think we need to get into that. Instead, let's talk about human violence.

Firstly, it helps to differentiate interpersonal violence from war. Aggression and interpersonal violence certainly have a strong biological basis, but these phenomena *do not relate to war*.

The psychological and physiological mechanisms that cause one individual to strike another have nothing in common with the chains of command in an invading army.... Even in its most brutal and chaotic aspect, war is an organised and institutional form of violence. Warfare is essentially a

123

problem-solving device that leaders have turned to during
key periods in history...[4]

We talk about wars as if they suddenly erupt—like toddlers feeling
hungry and crying. War is *nothing* like that. Soldiers are very deliberately trained. Battles are carefully strategized, based on many
people's decisions and analyses. Wars are conducted within hierarchical structures of command, so individuals must be cool under
pressure, disciplined, and predictable—the *opposite* of acting in a
fit of rage. A modern war is nothing like a barroom brawl, and the
causes of the two are not closely related. The existence of a tendency
to resolve interpersonal problems through aggression (and sometimes violence) doesn't mean that the complex and systematic actions resulting in wars are "natural."

There's also a difference between "natural" and necessary. The
naturalistic fallacy holds that because something is "natural" it's
moral, and the is-ought fallacy says that because something *is* a particular way it *ought* to be that way. We may apply these fallacies in
some cases, but we don't do it consistently. We're not born knowing
how to read and write, but few of us think that that makes illiter-
acy morally superior. The ability to read is not natural, in that for
most of human history it didn't exist. Yet it turns out that most folks
can learn to read if the right systems for transmitting this skill are
present.

In the chapter Conflict we saw how alluring it is to look for one
simple "primary cause." Some authors argue that the human love
of violence explains all sorts of diverse aspects of our evolution and
behavior.[5] I'd agree with critics who've pointed out that there's no
obvious reason to pick violence as the primary cause. We could just
as readily create a story about why any other common behavior—
say, dancing—explains human behavior.[6]

It's been argued that the archaeological record shows the oldest
war being fought just 10,000 years ago. This view is based on multiple examinations of evidence from around the world. If true, this
would be striking because it would mean large-scale interpersonal
violence was absent for the first 99% of human history.[7] There's

speculation that the invention of farming, and the greater resulting population density and hierarchies, were important in increasing interpersonal violence and then organized warfare.[8]

Psychologist Steven Pinker is among the many who contend the opposite—that our past has always been filled with gore. Pinker explores the evidence at length and argues that people today are actually more peaceful than ever. He feels that claims to the contrary are based on romanticized and wishful thinking.[9] His work has been the subject of major debate. Anthropologist Brian Ferguson suggests that Pinker ignores the many archaeological sites that don't provide evidence of violence, and misrepresents some sites as showing warfare when they don't.[10] Another anthropologist, Douglas Fry, suggests that Pinker's claims about contemporary cultures are equally problematic. Fry says the assertion that violence and warfare are widespread among Indigenous peoples is based on looking at only a select few societies that fit that narrative.[11] Fry has written about examples of 70 different Indigenous peoples who have no practice of warfare.[12] Among some of these peoples, homicide still exists, but in a few cases there's simply no evidence of any killing at all.[13] Then there are older explorations of this question, such as one study of 625 different Indigenous peoples, where the authors claimed that only about a third engaged in anything that might fit a definition of "war."[14]

Once again, ambiguity helps us feel that our beliefs are right (no matter what they are), and a lot of this debate seems to come down to what we consider "war" and what we think is meaningful evidence of it. A few archaeological sites show clear violence; many are ambiguous. In terms of modern cultures, they're not static. Indigenous peoples have always adapted, and in recent centuries they've had to be incredibly resilient in the face of colonialism and countless outside pressures. The practices of Indigenous peoples today can't tell us how their ancestors lived thousands of years ago in very different situations! So, contrary to Pinker's claim that studying violence among contemporary Indigenous peoples tells us about violence their ancestors committed in the distant past,[15] what a cross-cultural analysis today can tell us is what's possible today. What we see is that almost all cultures have some violence, but they've also developed specific processes for transforming conflicts.[16] Physical aggression, both between individuals and between groups, is not actually a common conflict strategy.[17]

In the territories that today are called Canada and the United States, highly effective peace systems were developed, like the Haudenosaunee Great Peace, a sacred agreement between the Mohawk, Onondaga, Oneida, Cayuga, Seneca, and later the Tuscarora. These peoples had been enemies and violently attacked each other until they negotiated the Great Peace, which continues to thrive today.[18] It's exemplary but not alone. Other peace systems include those among the Chewong and other Semang peoples in Malaysia.[19] In Brazil, the Xingu maintain peace through embedding peaceful values deeply into their worldview. For example, "they view aggression as a pathetic mark of failed leadership and self-control" and war as immoral.[20]

The Batek of Malaysia and the Moriori of the Chatham Islands never participated in warfare and have complex systems of maintaining harmony and positive peace without major coercion or violence. This does mean sometimes fleeing as a whole community from people who refuse to change their aggressive and violent ways. The peace virus is also transmitted through modeling it to children.

> The Batek taught their children to act nonviolently, though the youngsters sometimes did fight with one another. Adults believed they would grow out of this behavior, which they felt was normal. Parents would separate fighting children, then laugh to try and minimize the importance of the issues they were fighting about. Adults normally did not use physical discipline. By the time children were four years old, they had learned that, in their society, people just do not fight.[21]

This sounds like power-with, using humor and guiding the children through modeling positive ways to deal with frustrations. It's not possible to know if violent impulses are simply being repressed in Batek children, but it seems like they may be finding constructive expression instead. If children as young as four can learn to stop fighting because they don't see violence modeled for them, that would suggest that although the *capacity* to behave violently might be natural, that doesn't make violence (much less organized warfare) a *necessary* or *unavoidable* part of the human experience.

Contrast this with the views of author Gerard Jones, who argues that, in this big scary world, children all feel powerless and afraid and so benefit from the stories of violent heroes. The violence helps kids connect with natural instincts for aggression, a desire for power-over. Jones is concerned about a push to keep young kids from such stories: "I see kids being deprived of an important component of emotional balance by not having their aggressive fantasies acknowledged." For Jones, kids don't learn to be violent from the media but from parents, so kids won't learn violence if the parent isn't violent. Jones argues that violent imaginary play teaches kids the important lesson that, "good is accomplished by the courage to engage with violence."[22]

Looking from a cross-cultural perspective it seems less like Jones is expressing what kids *need* than *one way* kids can be raised. The line of thinking misses a few points. For one thing, the power-over narrative of the comics and video games Jones references (that superior physical force triumphs, and that "good" must fight "evil") is one we've already seen the drawbacks of. It promotes simplistic thinking that can cause conflicts to become entrenched. Another issue is that children are actually incredibly creative. When not fed specific narratives by adults, kids have the capacity to invent their own games and stories and can readily do so without being told about violent superheroes.

The research evidence also doesn't support Jones' views. According to six top US medical and health associations, "Well over 1,000 studies…point overwhelmingly to a causal connection between media violence and aggressive behavior."[23] That doesn't mean that every child listening to violent music will become violent. But violent media does help establish what we think is normal, how aggressive we feel, and for some of us it contributes to our violent actions. This is true not only for children. Adults engaging with violent media can readily be desensitized to violence and become more aggressive.[24]

To sum up, there's a common assumption that aggression is always there within us, and if we're not engaging it we're caught in the inner violence of denying our true urges. The evidence we've seen suggests just the opposite—we can train our neuroplastic brains through engaging with aggressive and violent worldviews and cultural materials to feel aggressive and violent. But the fact that we have this ability doesn't mean we're expressing our "true nature" that was just repressed otherwise. One reason we might struggle to make this distinction is that the patterns of violence and power-over have roots so deep they may seem innate, independent from culture. The UN reports that 60% of the world's children experience regular physical violence from caregivers.[25] We might not remember our earliest years, but it's possible that the faith, acquired in those fragile moments, that lashing out with physical force is powerful, natural, and makes sense when we're upset lasts us a lifetime.[26]

We've seen it with masculinity, implicit bias, and now with violence—we can readily be wired for a range of behaviors without them being the only possibility. It seems that violence and war are very possible in the right conditions and that narratives about the righteousness of violence arise from specific cultures and then get projected out onto the world and called "natural."

Our beliefs about what's "natural" to expect can readily become self-fulfilling prophecies too. Studies have shown that telling teachers which students are gifted and likely to excel leads those students to perform better than their peers—and this happens when the "gifted" students are actually just chosen at random. The teachers' expectations shape their interactions with students and influence the students' future results.[27] Might this happen in the domain of violence too? In the chapter Who Benefits? we'll see an example that suggests the answer could be yes.

To return to the question we started this chapter with, the brain regions involved in our craving violence are key in much complex behavior. They help keep us focused and positive, for instance.[28] So we can learn to enjoy violence, as we can learn to enjoy gambling, without proving that we're all natural-born poker players or that poker defines us as a species.

The news makes it easy to discover just how horrible humans can be. There's no disputing that we have a "gift" for cruelty, contempt, and domination. Violence comes fairly easily to some of us and certainly has evolved biological underpinnings. However, we're safe to say that our destructiveness is not *the way it is*, so much as *a way* we can adopt, with other possibilities available.

## Tips from This Chapter

1. The mechanisms behind organized systems of violence, such as wars, are not closely related to the biology or psychology of interpersonal violence. Wars and barroom brawls are completely different.

2. Humans have a capacity for violence, but this capacity is brought out, or not, to varying degrees in different cultures, just like other capacities (e.g., to learn to read and write). The existence of cultures with little interpersonal violence suggests that violence is not an unavoidable part of being human.

3. Just because behaviors are commonly possible doesn't mean they're moral or inevitable. The naturalistic fallacy says something is good because it's natural, but few of us consistently believe this.

4. Not learning to be violent doesn't necessarily mean that violent urges are still present but being repressed in damaging ways. The evidence is clear that, in fact, violent cultural influences *cause* us to be more aggressive and accepting of violence.

5. Experimental evidence shows the existence of self-fulfilling prophecies, and our belief that large-scale violence is natural and inevitable may be one. (During a war it's all too easy to call it proof that we live in a violent world and need military might to maintain our safety.[29])

# Safety

*It is much safer to be feared than loved...*

— Niccolò Machiavelli[1]

MACHIAVELLI had no qualms about safety—for him, domination was the way to go. One gets ahead by instilling fear and obedience in others. Lying and manipulating are fair game. We've seen many examples of why Machiavelli's ideas were limited and unrealistic, but we may still wonder: aren't there people like him who are so dangerous they make power-with impossible? If we become too peaceful, aren't we going to get taken advantage of? If a few Machiavellis get too much power, won't everyone be in trouble?

Let's make this discussion clearer by naming a specific person, one of the most disturbing in history—infamous serial killer Ted Bundy. Bundy was an expert liar, seen as charismatic, and had apparently no limits to his brutality. His array of unspeakably terrible crimes, like ruthless sexual violence and keeping strangers' severed heads, are among the most heinous ever committed. A member of Bundy's legal team said, "Ted was the very definition of heartless evil."[2] Bundy was given the death penalty in Florida in January 1989. The *LA Times* reported that he spent the night before his execution weeping and expressing remorse, but many were unconvinced that this was more than just an act.[3]

Certainly we need protection from individuals like Ted Bundy! It likely requires some power-over, some way to physically stop them from doing whatever they want. But this is an area where our biases can run wild. As we stated previously, we suffer from an attention bias (we notice something vivid like a bomb going off far more than the innumerable times and places where a bomb doesn't go off) and the availability heuristic (we remember these vivid occurrences and rely on them to make decisions later). Research from the UK and Luxembourg suggests that when the topic is scary, we pass along stories in particularly biased ways that keep making them scarier and scarier. Psychologist Thomas Hills explains, "The more people share information, the more negative it becomes, the further it gets from the facts, and the more resistant it becomes to correction."[4] (Recall when we saw how a false story about razorblades in Halloween candy created massive distress and even generated new laws.) We seem to have a biological tendency toward negativity because our brains process and recall negative events *differently* from positive ones. So it can literally be easier for us to hang on to the negative and to recall it as if it were incredibly frequent and significant.[5] (In a future chapter on self-care we'll look at a way to overcome the negativity bias.)

Only very local media will cover nonviolent break-and-entry crimes, but most will cover a bomb going off anywhere in our country. Although we all likely know this, reporting of violent crime still skews our views about the world. How significant is our misunderstanding of the real threats we face? In the US people overestimate the risk of their personally falling victim to extremist violence by a whopping 1.7 *million times!*[6] This fear is present in spite of the nearly $6 *trillion dollars* spent on the "war on terror."[7] No matter how much power-over we have, it never seems like enough to make us feel safe. In reality, very few people are psychopaths,[8] and of these, even fewer become violent. Our sedentary lifestyles are *far* more likely to kill us, but Ted Bundy gets our attention.

Recent data suggests that in Canada 85% of crimes involve no physical threat or violence of any kind.[9] When violent crimes do happen, they tend to be committed by *people we know*, not the strangers we fear. And whether by a stranger or friend, a great deal of violence is committed when people *without* major mental health problems just "snap." While violently snapping, many of us feel that our outburst is wrong. We may find it deeply out of character. We often feel remorse right afterward. So if we want to protect ourselves from violence, we need to examine what's going on when people snap.

Neuroscientist Douglas Fields has studied the phenomenon, and in his view, "We all wish to believe—need to believe—that we are in control of our behaviors and actions, but the fact is that in certain instances we are not."[10] There are at least two different ways each of us can predict (maybe accurately, maybe not) and process threats—one path seems to be conscious, working slower, and the other unconscious and much faster.[11] When the latter is triggered, in a split-second, with little or no conscious awareness, we may launch into violence we never would have expected from ourselves.

Various influences can make us more prone to such snapping—being hot, hungry, impatient, in a noisy or high-stress situation, or being mentally tired or sleep deprived. One factor you might not think of is that whether in the lab or other environments, the simple fact of seeing a picture of a handgun, rifle, or knife can push us into an aggressive mode we aren't really aware of.[12] (This suggests that the media, when showing pictures of weapons, could actually be making us more aggressive and less creative in our thinking about important security issues.)

Since we may snap before even becoming conscious of feeling angry or threatened, it would be wrong to think that anger was the *cause* of the snapping.[13] But neuroscience does seem to show that the categories we use to make sense of our worlds are key to our experiences of emotions like anger, as well as to our perceptions of situations as threats.[14] So training ourselves to evaluate and categorize what's happening in less hostile and aggressive ways can help us have greater control, perhaps preventing future snapping. As we touched on in the chapter Communication, if we get cut off in traffic we might have any number of responses, like a sudden rage, and immediately sense that we need revenge. Instead though, we could re-categorize the events by telling ourselves a different story.

Maybe this is an inexperienced driver and they cut us off acciden-
tally. Even if it was somehow deliberate, maybe getting revenge isn't
that worthwhile. Re-categorizing seems to help prevent snapping
because we train ourselves *over time* to interpret and categorize situations more generously (again—assume good intent!) so that when
a situation arises that might have provoked us, we experience it
more positively *automatically*.[15] Singing to ourselves during stressful situations is another way we can regulate the sudden impulses
we're generating.[16] It's worth pointing out too that the capacity we
have to start choking someone in a split-second also allows us to
perform incredible acts of heroism. We can "snap" altruistically into
actions that put our lives at risk, saving others without giving it a
second thought.[17]

Policy decisions to maximize safety are complicated, but if we're
not careful we can easily provoke the conditions that *create* the bulk
of violent crimes, putting us in greater danger. In 1981, Canadian
Quakers came together to discuss their concern that prisons are
expensive and fail to increase safety. Almost everyone who goes
to prison will be released to be our neighbors again someday, but
many inmates don't learn to be better future neighbors. They have
the opposite experience—learning to become more violent, bitter,
and quicker to snap. This isn't surprising. We've seen that there's
no evidence to suggest that putting people in painful and isolating
conditions will train them to develop skills like self-regulation. So
Friends called for new approaches that address human needs. In
doing so they stated, "We recognize a need for restraint of those few
who are exhibiting dangerous behaviour."[18] (Yes, there is definitely
a need for protection from Ted Bundy!)

Norway has had success in reducing rates of reoffending through
a heavy focus on building inmates' skills, giving them the greatest
chance of reintegrating successfully into the community. Interestingly, guards at a maximum security institution are *unarmed*.[19] The
Norwegian model is undoubtedly imperfect, but if we're concerned
about our safety, looking to the most successful examples we can
find seems like a good starting place.

Another intriguing example comes from Glasgow, Scotland. When it was rated the "murder capital" of Europe, Glasgow decided its policing wasn't working. Instead of investing in even more of the same, the city compiled evidence on the factors *causing* the violence (poverty, alcoholism, masculinity…) and began to respond to them like it would to treat a public health epidemic. The data showed that violence was spreading between people just like an infection. The city started a coordinated campaign to address the conditions that were easiest to change, and the murder rate dropped by 60%.[20]

Multiple US cities have had some success with hiring people from dangerous neighborhoods, who have relationships and credibility there, to work as violence interrupters. They spend their days in violent areas, for instance, staying with people after a shooting and helping them to cool down instead of seeking revenge.[21]

Let's look at one particularly important factor in building safety. You might not be surprised to learn that Ted Bundy didn't have a happy childhood.[22] An analysis of serial killers suggests this is nearly universal, in particular the experience of isolation and loneliness as children.[23] We're learning more and more about what are called adverse childhood experiences (ACEs)—like neglect and physical, emotional, and sexual abuse. Their effects on our lives are far-reaching. Researchers have studied a large group of people since the '90s and found that the more ACEs experienced, the worse we tend to do (but certainly not always). Our cumulative ACEs score has a strong relationship to social, behavioral, and health problems throughout life.[24] Someone with an ACEs score above four is seven times as likely to become an alcoholic as someone with an ACEs score of zero. A person with an ACEs score above six is 30 times more likely to attempt suicide.[25] Nadine Burke Harris, a pediatrician who's studied ACEs, says, "Children are especially sensitive to high doses of adversity because their brains and bodies are just developing." This has been studied in more than 20 countries with similar findings. The fact that people who've experienced more ACEs tend to engage in more dangerous behaviors like heavy drinking appears to only explain about half of the increased risk of health problems.

Another major contributor is one we keep seeing—chronic stress—made all the more damaging because it started in childhood.[26]

In his work with people with serious drug addictions, physician Gabor Maté discovered that everyone he treated had a history of abuse in childhood. Maté explains a wealth of research about how isolation, trauma, and neglect harm the developing brain, including various parts of the prefrontal cortex that help us regulate our impulses and weigh future outcomes of our actions. In essence, the result can be adults lacking not a free will, but a "free won't."[27] They can have particular difficulty interrupting the snapping that we saw is so common in violent crime.

What we've just seen is a feedback loop. ACEs lead us to be particularly impacted by stress but also to live in high-stress circumstances—with addictions, inadequate housing, and countless other factors further wearing away our impulse control. These conditions tax our brains[28] and feed into a complex downward spiral. As it worsens, we're more and more likely to violently snap. Given this picture, it becomes clear why prison is so often a failure—we didn't become violent from carefully deciding to be, and fear of punishment wasn't likely to help us learn the impulse control we need.

The dynamics of this feedback loop can be changed, though. The environments we grow up in might make a major difference between a person with the genetic traits of Ted Bundy becoming violent or expressing the peace virus instead. We've seen many examples of how the situations around us shape us in dramatic ways. So if we want to be safe, we'd be wise to work for the conditions that give children the possibility of growing up with their needs met.

The sad truth is that some of us will likely always be violent and dangerous, but what's become increasingly clear as evidence mounts is that security works best when it's *shared*. The idea of individuals (or indeed, individual countries) building security for themselves in isolation doesn't make much sense. It's the isolated power-over mentality again. In reality, we aren't alone, so our interests are best served when we foster healthy dynamics and protect the natural resources we all depend on.[29] The point isn't to absolve individuals of any misuse of their personal power or responsibilities (Bundy wasn't merely a passive victim of his life circumstances), just to recognize what will give us the best chance of security. One of the problems with focusing on the worst case scenarios like Bundy is it can be deeply disempowering, feeding our fears of what we can't control instead of encouraging us to look at what we *can*.

## Tips from this Chapter

1. Attention bias and the availability heuristic mean that we notice things that stand out in our environment, and we remember them more readily. This can warp our views about the world, leading us to make poor personal decisions or support poor policies.

2. Most crimes are not violent, and most violent crimes are not committed by strangers but people we know. Violent crime tends not to be committed by psychopaths but by average people who simply snap. When we snap and become violent we may regret our actions almost immediately, but we may lack the "free won't" to consciously interrupt our impulsive violence.

3. Many factors like being hot, hungry, or sleep deprived can make us more likely to snap, and conditions around us (such as seeing a picture of a weapon) can prime us to be more aggressive even when we're not aware of it.

4. Evidence shows that re-evaluating situations can help prevent violent snapping. Waiting until the moment when we're already snapping is too late, though—we must build this skill through repetitive practice so we automatically interpret situations in ways that are least likely to cause us to snap.

5. Singing to ourselves when we're snapping may help calm us down.

6. When thinking about our safety, we can look to build shared security, in particular protecting children from neglect and abuse. We'll never be completely safe, but we can choose to support policies based on what has the greatest likelihood of preventing the bulk of violence.

## Activity: Accepting *Everyone*

Facilitators ask the group to divide into concentric circles and speak to the following questions:

1. Is it possible to vigorously oppose actions and policies without opposing people?
2. How does the idea of not rejecting anyone feel in your body? What are your immediate physical reactions to it? How do these relate to your thoughts on the topic?
3. If we never discounted one brutal dictator, one Muhammad Suharto, one Efraín Ríos Montt, if we worked to stop them without hating them—what would that look like?

## Example: The Nashville Sit-ins

In Nashville, Tennessee, in the '60s black people aren't allowed inside many of the city's businesses. Students get together and come up with a strategy—a series of sit-ins to silently challenge segregation, using lunch counters as a symbol and focal point.

The students carefully plan the campaign. They have to be ready to suffer greatly and draw on their power-from-within. They spend long nights role-playing, being pushed and verbally abused, making sure that when the real thing happens they won't snap. They decide to dress well and be well-mannered so as not to give any excuse for mistreatment. The entire campaign is orchestrated to create a feeling of moral outrage. Every decision is made to maximize the discomfort of the segregation system, making continual denial impossible, bringing segregation's irregularity and repulsiveness into painful view. The students disrupt negative peace, making people see violence.

When arrested, the students refuse to pay their bail—increasing the tension and media coverage. They choose respectful and clear language to frame their campaign when speaking with the media. They're strategic in escalation. Once the campaign gains significant attention, but not before, they call for a boycott of all businesses in downtown Nashville. Boycotts are obviously directive and coercive, a type of power-over. Used with care in the context of a broader campaign, though, they can be effective in transforming the power imbalances in certain conflicts. Importantly, during the boycott the students continue to articulate their needs and to listen, *maintaining relationships* with the people they're trying to influence. This requires discipline and not losing focus on the long-term goal of the campaign.

While the students' lawyer sleeps, his house is blown up. This violent power-over backfires, galvanizing the students further and handing them a moment of public sympathy to seek a meeting with the mayor of Nashville. There's so much attention now that he can't refuse. They ask the mayor a simple question: does he think segregation is ethical? This forces him to go on record saying no. (Recall how we saw that when we publicly explain a belief and then see how we're acting inconsistently with it, we're more likely to change our act.)

Throughout the campaign, the students offer a strong example of the fortitude at the heart of a successful social change movement. The Nashville lunch counter sit-ins prove to be an important part of the wider US civil rights movement. Even after all of the students' successes, desegregation in Nashville still takes years,[30] and of course, to this day much remains to be done to address on-going violence and inequality.

History can make it seem like results were foregone conclusions, but for students in Nashville in the '60s the lunch counter sit-ins were anything but intuitive or popular, at least not at first. One of the student leaders, Diane Nash, thought the campaign was insane. She felt that only violent power-over would be taken seriously but recalls, "I kept going to the workshops because I couldn't find anyone else who was trying to do anything else."[31]

# When Hate Rises

*We all seem to have a craving for the situation
that allows no interpretation, no choice,
in which we can act with absolute commitment
not tempered by doubt.*

— Brian Murphy[1]

W E KNOW THAT life eats life and we're surrounded by violence. Some of it is even internalized—we've taken it *into* ourselves. In the first image we have the lunch counter sit-ins in Nashville. Activists are being assaulted by men who want to maintain segregation. In the second, we have one of many recent hate rallies where white supremacists wound up being attacked and beaten.

What do we see, looking at these images side by side? Both show us people, representing larger groups, who want to spread deeply controversial ideas. As we saw in the chapter Firm Belief, peace doesn't demand that we become boring relativists who think

Credit: Nashville Public Library

Credit: Reuters/Joshua Roberts

everything's equal, so we can say what's obvious—these ideas aren't morally similar in any way. The first image shows a spiritually grounded and love-based action that's trying to replace a segregation system founded on lies by showing the truth of our equality, the force of our connectedness. The second image is of a call for a new type of segregation, expressed with paranoia and hate. These positions are *profoundly* different.

Then there's this uncomfortable fact: there are similarities in these pictures as well as the major differences. In both cases, we have people acting in unpopular ways, rousing intense waves of negativity in those around them. In using violence, people in both pictures have good intentions; they believe they're doing what's necessary and right. If we saw brain scans of the people using violence in both pictures the activity might be similar, and they've both got elevated heart rates and adrenaline levels. Both are *expressing similar needs through similar responses*. The feeling of total disgust with the "other" gets expressed in the ways so many of us have learned. When we're most familiar with power-over, it makes sense that that's what we reach for. We begin by othering, using language that suggests that the students at the lunch counter or the white supremacists at the rally are *less than human*.[2] We mock with jeers and print materials in the '60s and with animated gifs today. To the extent that there's a plan, its logic is this: if "we" make life unsafe and uncomfortable for "others," we'll keep control over what's normal and acceptable.[3] We'll keep them from spreading their emotional contagion and getting more people on board.

Those are the similarities I can see between the parties on the attack, but there are many differences between the parties being beaten. One reflects again what we saw in the Communication chapter—a stimulus might be there, but it doesn't have the power to *make us* respond in any given way. The students in Nashville role-played being harassed specifically for this reason. They built their power to choose their course of action, rather than just reacting. We have a choice. To oversimplify: are we going for a response that will make us *feel dominant*, or one with the greatest chance of positively transforming the situation? Violence could be thrilling, but is it *strategic*?

A possible strategy is to oppose the spread of hate with whatever tactic makes life uncomfortable enough that hate groups hopefully just give up. Such battles to censor and shut each other down are ancient, as are the questions they raise about who gets to decide who to target. This has recently played out at universities in particular, where students engage in "no platform"—not allowing space for the expression of views they find repugnant.[4] Another tactic is finding and publishing the contact information of the "other," breaking their cloak of anonymity so they can be targeted and harassed.[5] Finally, there's physically attacking people. It's easy to imagine these techniques scaring and damaging some hate group members into silence. We can also find countless instances historically where being the target of aggressive power-over has actually galvanized and energized groups (recall that attempts to bomb the home of the lawyer for the student protesters in Nashville did just this), so, for some, that might happen instead. In any case, it's not easy to imagine this strategy winning over anyone who's already in a hate group, and it leaves the needs that drove them to join unaddressed.

A downside to the strategy is its use of the binary logic it opposes. It starts with acceptance of total division and total opposition. It sees that the "other" is using power-over, imagines that makes them strong, and decides to use *even more power-over with them*. This locks the conflict into a repetitive dynamic with no end in sight, perhaps accepting that this is less than ideal but feeling it's ultimately the only option.

To explore how to counter hate groups in other ways, we need to broaden the discussion. Importantly, there are many varieties of hate groups, focused on many target "others," and the ways we fall into these groups are complicated. So we need to be wary of one-size-fits-all approaches to counter-recruitment. They haven't worked well.[6] That said, we can explore some general trends.

Hate speech isn't harmless. Research from Poland suggests that with enough exposures it can desensitize us, increasing our aggression and prejudice toward "others."[7] (This fits with what we saw about the impacts of violent media.) As we know, beliefs—of whatever caliber—can spread, and as they become more familiar, more normal-seeming, they shape our views of the world and our framing of what's possible.

Today most hate speech likely spreads via the internet, so stopping it can be done with digital "no platform" implemented largely by artificial intelligence. Of course, this raises again the major problems around censorship, and if it's the social media companies who decide what to censor, it puts an incredible amount of power in their hands.[8] Still, successfully removing hateful content could be significant. Alexandre Bissonnette, who murdered six men while they worshiped in a mosque in Quebec City, spent a great deal of time seeking out opinions that would rile him up and appear to confirm his sense of being under attack. He was readily able to find them.[9] Would it have stopped his heinous crime if he hadn't had access to this content?

In the digital world various hate groups have had their materials removed by service providers. White supremacist website Daily Stormer has been taken down multiple times,[10] and in 2016 Twitter claimed to be suspending 40,000 pro-Daesh accounts *per month*![11] YouTube says it uses AI to remove content promoting violent extremism[12] and claims to redirect users toward "videos that confront and discredit extremist messaging and mythology."[13] But the results of these efforts are difficult to know.

On the one hand, perhaps some folks escaped recruitment because companies took down hateful content before would-be recruits found it. On the other hand, according to researchers who've studied hate groups' online activities, the groups can greatly *benefit* from being able to say they're victims, standing up for the truth while being persecuted by those who don't want the truth told. To would-be believers, the fact that sites get banned proves that the conspiracies they promote—for example, that a "white genocide" is underway—are true.[14] Violence does the same thing. In an attempt to intimidate him, white supremacist Brandon Spiller was badly beaten. Rather than making him give up on his cause, he told a jour-nalist that the beating proved whites are under siege and "definitely made me more likely to use my gun next time."[15]

Similarly, Daesh promotes a worldview that says Muslims can't be safe anywhere in the world except in the territory of its "caliph-ate."[16] The group has relied on violent attacks to provoke responses that help make this divisive story sound more believable. When they kill people in a bombing, that act is "highly dependent on reac-tion—on the ability to invoke fear, to stimulate outrage, to harden identities. To do this, it leans not only on shock and surprise, but on symbolism and stories. In other words, it is highly theatrical. Mark Juergensmeyer calls it 'performance violence.'"[17] Following a Daesh attack, Islamophobic government and media responses, which in-crease feelings of isolation among diverse Muslim communities, may be exactly what Daesh is looking for.

A 2017 study on reporting about violent hate crimes controlled for all reasonable factors like number of fatalities and found that a story got 449% more coverage from US newspapers if the perpetra-tor was a Muslim![18] Such skewed news can lead many of us to fear Islam (in a 2017 poll 46% of Canadians said Islam was damaging Canadian society; people were nowhere near as negative about any other religion[19]) or think that religious faith is the key cause of vio-lent extremism. But data in Canada from 1960 to 2015 found that only about 18% of violent extremism was perpetrated by someone claiming a religious motivation, and just 2% was perpetrated by a religiously affiliated group.[20] So while there's little doubt that in some cases participation in a religious community can fuel some of the deepest and longest-lasting divisions between "us" and "others," the importance of religious faith to violent extremism is often ex-aggerated.

The data show that another common claim doesn't hold up ei-ther—that those who join hate groups are "crazy." There's just no evidence to support this. Recruits do almost all have actual or per-ceived *grievances* though—something to feel enraged about and seek revenge for.[21] Many of the founding members of Daesh, for instance, experienced torture and dehumanization in US prisons in Iraq.[22] Interviews with fighters in armed groups in Syria confirm that traumas factor heavily in their decisions to take up arms.[23] But lots of people have or could invent reasons to seek revenge, and only a few join hate groups. Why is that? Again, the dark side of moral conviction seems to be at play. We're more likely to join hate groups if we see the world as a simple battleground where we have to fight against pure evil.[24]

Social psychologists who've studied data about hate groups in many countries say recruits are most often "males between 15 and 30 years of age—the same population most likely to commit violent crime in general, and the demographic group least likely to be deterred by the threat of physical force."[25] A key factor raised here and by other researchers, and very often ignored in the media, is that, while women can be instrumental in fueling hate,[26] the people committing acts of violent extremism are *overwhelmingly* men. Interviews with more than 100 recruits into various hate groups in Europe and North America uncovered over and over the same sense of frustration that the powers men felt entitled to weren't available to them. They were ashamed, and violence gave them a restored sense of pride and purpose.[27] This is consistent with what we've seen about violence and certain popular forms of masculinity, and about how, when things aren't going well for us, we scapegoat and oversimplify. Insulting and trying to intimidate hate group members begins to look, at best, woefully insufficient, when we consider that these strategies are being used against men who crave a sense of power and can't stand to be seen as weak.

Consider the case of Maxime Fiset—a socially isolated and angry man growing up in Quebec. Fiset met some white supremacists who treated him like he mattered, making him feel part of something bigger than himself. They shared hateful beliefs that helped his world make sense. They told him who his enemies were, who was stealing his power, and this resonated with his experience of painful isolation and struggling to get ahead. Soon Fiset bought books on making bombs.

Who did he plan to kill? "I don't know. Enemies of the nation. Everybody is an enemy of the nation when you're that alienated. News people. Muslims and minorities. Politicians. Every one of them could have been a target." Yet when Fiset tried to go ahead with his plan, the peace virus stirred instead. "You know why the army is training soldiers for years before they send them to battle? Because most people have this mental breaker that just snaps before you get to kill someone." Fiset wound up falling in love instead of blowing anyone up, and he left his hateful social circle.[28]

This is not uncommon. A major study following 1,000 men over time found that getting married and having children were strong predictors of not becoming involved in violent crime.[29] Unsurprisingly, it seems important to help young men overcome social isolation and find positive roles to play, and there are some examples of promising programs that claim to do this. (Again, these are complicated questions, and we might get into trouble if we try to generalize these findings too much.) In Saudi Arabia, art therapy has offered an entry point for thousands of men to change their lives and reject hateful ideologies. Art starts conversations. "To make a drawing that utilizes the principles of design: unity, harmony, balance, rhythm, contrast, dominance, and gradation...was not only calming—it opened them to an essential discussion about achieving balance and maintaining healthy rhythms in their lives, as well as on paper."[30]

In countering recruitment of youth in Morocco, the nonprofit Search for Common Ground found their work was most successful when it delivered emotional messages at a particular stage. The messages "highlight the value and potential of individuals, rather than framing targets of radicalization as marginalized or victims."[31] This agrees with techniques we've seen—making our thinking more complex by focusing on distinctions among individuals, remembering that we're not trapped in our current situation and can adapt and grow, and infecting people with positive emotions to motivate change.

One reason that such an infection is often possible is that *hatred is hard work*. We have to keep generating negative feelings, and

suffering their impacts (the toll of chronic stress), to keep the stirrings of the peace virus at bay. When Zak Ebrahim, who'd been
raised by a violent and hateful father, started meeting more people,
he found it tough to keep up the momentum of his hatred. Exposure
to "others" was softening his resolve and making him question his
firm beliefs. He confessed to his mother. "She looked at me with the
weary eyes of someone who had experienced enough dogmatism to
last a lifetime and said, 'I'm tired of hating people.'"[32]

How can we use all this to respond to a hate group's rally in our
town? Refusing to be drawn in can be powerful. As we've seen,
when hate groups plan marches or bombings they depend on the
responses they're expecting. Any response that doesn't fit with the
dynamic they're trying to create undermines their power. Recently
in Germany neo-Nazis were shocked to learn that, unbeknownst to
them, a group had organized to get sponsors for the annual Nazi
march. For every mile the hate group walked, local businesses were
chipping in ten Euros to a nonprofit focused on helping people escape white supremacy. A different creative tactic was employed in
North Carolina, where a "white power" march was met with a group
of happy clowns throwing white *powder* in the air as if they'd mis-
read the invite.[33] Picture this scene for a moment. With a bunch of
clowns jumping around, would you be able to maintain the intensity of your purpose and continue with a serious march about white
supremacy? You might start to pick up the positive emotional contagion instead. Even if you didn't, you'd likely feel distracted and
deflated. Would your event still be as exciting to on-lookers you're
trying to recruit? As activist Janey Stephenson observes, "Collective
joy can become powerfully subversive."[34]

Quaker clown Jack Ross encourages us to "assertively select the
setting and mode of nonviolent action so that those opposed will be
motivated to be their best selves." He explains how useful it is to be
clear what our objectives are and not to make anything we do about
a personal victory (to embarrass or frustrate a hateful person) but
the bigger picture (to positively transform the situation).[35] Recall
that we understand ourselves not through some consistent idea,

but through looking around and seeing what others are doing and who we are in relation to them. There's always this mutuality. Even a violent conflict is just a particular relationship. So we can help bring out the best selves of those we're in conflict with, and doing so is always strategic—creating the best chance of a peace infection. Dancing or offering a present like a balloon can sometimes be more powerful than throwing a punch.

Every group has "internal social structures, tensions and contradictions. Appeals to the personal sense of humor create individual and unique responses"[36] among group members. Remembering that groups aren't as solid as they appear, we can seek out the soft spots, the folks most vulnerable to the peace virus. Perhaps, like in Fiset's early days, there are members who aren't that committed and really just want to feel seen and valued, to not feel like failures as men. There's no perfect strategy for success here, and no one cause of recruitment to focus on, but responding to hate, while incredibly challenging, is possible.

## Tips from this Chapter

1. We can decide to use physical violence for many reasons. We don't need to think of them as morally equivalent, but it can actually be more difficult than it first appears to determine who deserves to be the target of violence, or even just of censorship.

2. When confronted with hate we need to decide whether we're responding to make ourselves feel better (more powerful or righteous) or to have the greatest chance of accomplishing a positive change. A helpful rule here is to act in ways likely to bring out the other person's best self.

3. Suppression of hate groups' materials is at best dealing shallowly with the conditions leading to recruitment. This could be helpful, but it may also contribute to the hate groups' narratives of persecution, fueling further recruitment.

4. Recruitment into hate groups is complicated, and there's no simple staged model that explains the process. This means that one-size-fits-all counter-recruitment hasn't worked well and

may make matters worse. What we *can* say is that hate group members tend to be young men. This demographic is unlikely to respond well to threats. Recruits are likely already seeking vengeance and longing for a feeling of powerful masculinity. In specific instances emotional appeals that highlight men's power to make choices as individuals have been proven effective, as have programs like art therapy. When men have families or find other purposes for their lives, they're far less likely to engage in violence.

5. Deflating hate rallies and events can often be done through breaking from expected responses. For instance, humor, when directed at situations in creative and non-threatening ways, can help diffuse hateful energy.

## Activity: Violence

Facilitators ask the group to divide into concentric circles and speak to the following questions:

1. When you support violence, what motivates you to do so?
2. Is there any part of you, perhaps one you don't like to acknowledge, that feels the urge to wield righteous violence?

## Example: Sammy Rangel

Sammy Rangel grows up in a home where he's raped by an uncle and beaten regularly by his mother. He's degraded in every possible way. By *age eight* he attempts suicide. At 11 he grabs a knife and imagines plunging it into his mother as she sleeps. Realizing he can't, he runs away instead and joins a gang. He recalls, "One of the older gang members asked me to slit a guy's throat, and when I said I couldn't, he showed me how to do it. Soon it didn't matter what I did." Rangel becomes extremely violent, dangerous, numb, and full of hate. At 17 he's sent to prison.

"I was excited about going to prison because I knew it was where I could gain power and authority… [Gang fighting in prison] gave my life a sense of meaning and legitimized everything I did…. I went into prison as a street punk and came out as a brutal leader with a killer mentality." He's out for less than a year before going back, this time for armed robbery. He winds up in solitary confinement after continual fighting.

> The first small change happened when this man called George came to the hole to talk to me one day. He confused me by calling me "nephew" and saying he wanted to see me in his office. I'd had no human contact for months and yet he got me brought from my cell to his office—which required four men putting me in shackles, handcuffs and chains—and then he told the guards to take off my chains. I couldn't believe it: it was like letting a werewolf loose on a herd of sheep. It shocked me that this guy, who was half my size, wasn't afraid of me. And then he asked me for my story—and I told him the whole thing. He didn't flinch or pity me—he just listened. Afterwards he said: "I want to help you get out of this place." I left knowing I'd been affected in some way. The meeting had left me feeling vulnerable.
>
> A year later I beat up four guards and I felt bad because I didn't want to do that anymore. I wrote to George and told him I'd "fucked up." I expected him to be upset with me, but he just said, "You don't owe me anything." Because he wasn't disappointed in me, it gave me hope to carry on.

Years after his first taste of power-with, Rangel's life has changed dramatically.[37] He explains that he holds out hope for others in similar situations. "I had a lot of mental health diagnoses that said I was incorrigible, I was anti-social...basically that I couldn't change, and yet here I am." Where he is is working with a nonprofit that helps people leave hate groups. He explains that what every former gang member he knows has in common is that experiencing compassion started to change them. His work with members of hate groups can involve individualized education, counseling, creating support networks, and placing people in job training. He says it's important that this model doesn't involve working with law enforcement. Instead of using tactics like threats or shame, all services are offered in a way that's confidential and non-judgmental. The focus is on helping people tap into their power-from-within. Rangel believes anyone can change—*no matter what they've done.*[38]

One turning point stands out for him—forgiving the person he hated the most. He's asked to sit facing an empty chair and imagine his mother in it. He has to express to her all of his feelings of torture and abuse at her hands. He does it with tears in his eyes, describing times she pulled patches of hair from his scalp or sent him to school in filthy clothes with open wounds on his body. Next he has to switch chairs. This he resists. *He wants to feel hatred toward his mother* for doing inexcusable things. But he agrees to try, and when he switches chairs, all he can say is, "I'm sorry."

Rangel goes back to his own seat and is asked to express all of his feelings in that moment. He speaks about being a victim, being abandoned, brutalized, unseen, and unloved. For Rangel the turning point comes suddenly, with the next question. "Sammy, have you ever hurt anyone the way your mother has hurt you?" "Since then," Rangel recounts in a choked voice, "my life has been one long apology."[39] Sammy Rangel, a violent and dangerous man, was infected with the peace virus. His work since is helping it spread.

# Violence in Social Change

*Pacifists do the state's work*
*by pacifying the opposition in advance.*

— Peter Gelderloos[1]

Imagine this: family members are wailing inconsolably. They're crying about what a loved one means to them. That person is dead or dying...and you pulled the trigger.

This scene is horrible beyond belief, and hopefully you and I never have to experience it. But many people do. When we make flippant comments about violence, are we really aware of what we mean? Unless we have a direct experience of killing someone and witnessing the anguish of their family and friends, we may struggle to comprehend just how monumental killing is. Dangerously, we might feel like we know all about it, simply because of sanitized popular depictions.

It's actually very difficult to predict what we would or wouldn't do in any new situation. What if you were taken hostage and had the opportunity to kill your captor to save yourself and other hostages, would you do it? Unless we've had that experience, we can't feel too confident one way or another. It's just an abstract question and *it's not too useful*. Let's leave the ethics of killing and examine instead the evidence about it.

In terms of changing social structures or overthrowing repressive governments, many think violence is the way to go. Activist

Peter Gelderloos, whose quote introduced this chapter, is among those who see nonviolence as often keeping people in a docile state of servitude, forcing them to accept their bad lots in life instead of fighting for change. He points to many examples where non-violence was woefully inadequate.[2] Others, like revolutionary author Frantz Fanon, have argued that violence is a pivotal way for the oppressed to get their dignity back.[3] The goal sounds laudable, but I think we've seen plenty of evidence about less-damaging ways to build dignity. Still, when we talk about large-scale social change, are the peace skills we're learning anything more than sometimes effective in the right conditions but often useless where violence would have worked?

Erica Chenoweth expresses a common refrain when she says that, after years researching for her PhD on political violence, she found the idea of using nonviolence to change oppressive regimes "well intentioned but dangerously naive."[4] You might feel the same way. You certainly know people who do.

Chenoweth debated the possible effectiveness of nonviolence with fellow political scientist Maria Stephan. Together they agreed to systematically look at the evidence—something they discovered had never been done. They combed through data on nonviolent and armed campaigns between 1900 and 2011 where at least 1,000 participants sought to overthrow a government or liberate a territory. What they discovered was jarring. Nonviolent campaigns were not as readily ignored or crushed as Chenoweth had assumed. They were *twice as likely to succeed!*

Amazingly, nonviolence succeeded even under brutal dictatorships. In fact, *no campaign failed* if it achieved the active and sustained participation of 3.5% of the population, and the *only* campaigns that got to that size were all nonviolent. Why would that be? If we think about it, it might actually start to make sense. Nonviolent campaigns *engage a wider range of people*, with all of their more diverse networks of contacts.[5] There was one more noteworthy finding—once they've succeeded in overthrowing a dictatorship, nonviolent movements are significantly "more likely to establish democratic regimes with a lower probability of a relapse into civil war."[6]

While this research may sound encouraging, nonviolent campaigns have been less successful since the '90s. Perhaps they're taken more seriously, and authoritarian regimes are developing more effective counter-measures. However, the effectiveness of violent campaigns has declined *even more rapidly* than nonviolent ones.[7]

Chenoweth and Stephan's research is not without its critics. One claim is that the distinction between nonviolent movements and violent ones is impossible to make. "There is no example of a nonviolent movement that did not occur in the same time and place as a violent movement. In other words, the success of the nonviolent movement is always related to the parallel existence of an 'unsuccessful' violent one."[8] Some also argue that the classification of nonviolence was too loose and inconsistent with popular ideas. For instance, Chenoweth and Stephan considered movements nonviolent even when they included throwing rocks, burning tires, and other destruction of property.[9]

Studies of social change movements that use a little bit of violence while being mostly nonviolent don't find that the violence helps, though. Violent factions don't protect nonviolent protesters, as is sometimes assumed—their presence actually just puts everyone in greater danger.[10] How can that be? Unsurprisingly, using violence increases indiscriminate police and military crackdowns.

We've looked before at what motivates us to take action: violence can definitely help some people to feel morally righteous and galvanized into an "us." It doesn't change the hearts of police or security forces and convince them to stop backing dictators though—something nonviolent movements often do.[11] Perhaps most importantly, movements using even a bit of violence make many in the general public *feel unsafe*. (Whether or not this feeling is justified, it's there.) Because of the bad publicity[12] and safety concerns they create, violent campaigns can shift public opinion from sympathy about the issues of injustice to a desire for "law and order." One study suggests this may affect not only our sympathies but even our voting patterns.[13] This seems consistent with the lab studies we saw in the chapter Us and Others that found that feeling safe, or feeling afraid, shifts our views on key social issues.

According to historian Laurie Marhoefer, deliberately holding rallies in hostile places where they knew they'd be physically attacked was a strategic choice that may have helped the Nazi party in Germany. Being beaten up in the streets not only got them lots of media attention, but all the street violence may have shifted the way many Germans *felt* about their country, fearing it was freefalling into disorder and needed the firm hand of the Nazis to restore it.[14] Whether or not she's right, it seems clear that nonviolence gives social change movements more legitimacy in the public's eyes,[15] and if done carefully, this brings many more people on board.

Our faith in violence makes us think governments won't take anything else seriously, but just the opposite may be true. "Governments invariably welcome violent protests. With soldiers, police and huge arsenals of weapons, they know how to deal with any form of violence. They also infiltrate protest groups with provocateurs to stir up violence."[16] Let's turn to a real-world example—one that shows the dynamics of violent activism at work. In October 1969, a group called The Weathermen planned a protest in Chicago, later dubbed *The Days of Rage*. They hoped the action would bring the violence of the Vietnam War to the streets of the US.

> They recruited extensively among white working-class youths to come to the city with helmets and such weapons as clubs, prepared to vandalize businesses and cars as well as assault police. They believed their action would help provoke an uprising against the capitalist state.
>
> During the "Days of Rage," the Weathermen did not attach themselves to a larger peaceful demonstration. They were on their own. So, the action provides a great case study about the feasibility of violent street tactics.

For starters, they discovered that it was hard to find recruits for their violent street army. Only about 300 people
showed up despite months of effort. And they found it
harder to enlist support for their actions even among those
who were friendly with them politically.

This is exactly what we discussed above. For many who wanted
to see an end to the Vietnam War, The Weathermen seemed ill-
informed about how change happens, and not worth backing. You
won't be surprised to learn that police had no trouble containing the
protest and bringing it to a quick end.[17] In the chapter Communication we looked at how difficult it is to imagine someone not knowing
the song we're tapping, because we're hearing it in our own heads.
Perhaps The Weathermen were experiencing this—the song of violence was playing so loudly for them that they just couldn't imagine
others having trouble picking it up and joining the uprising.

Far from a sign of power, political scientist Wendy Pearlman suggests that such violence often shows that a movement is fragmented
and desperate. When there's a clear vision and effective leadership,
there can be focus, cohesion, and nonviolence in the face of repression. It's when movements are struggling that violent factions seem
most likely to form.[18] If this is true of social movements, it's familiar
to many of us as individuals too. It's when we're exhausted and out
of ideas that we're most likely to lash out violently, not when we're
at our most alert and creative.

After watching a horror movie people who were asked what
they'd like to do with some upcoming free time had little to say. A
group that watched funny videos or got a bag of candy to put them
in a happier mood had many more ideas.[19] A wealth of evidence
along similar lines suggests that emotions like fear and rage may
rally our resources, mobilizing us to respond as quickly as possible
by narrowing us in on an immediate goal, while positive emotions
*broaden our perspective*, helping us adapt and think more imagina-
tively. This seems to be a very concrete reality. For instance, if given
a surprise gift, test subjects show increased eye movements during

future activities—*literally taking in more of the scene and generating a bigger perspective.*[20]

Narrow, violent rage is unsurprising given the awful conditions many people around the world are living in. While we can respect peoples' experiences and expressions of rage, the fact remains, violence is usually a counter-productive way forward. All too often violent rage winds up just being directed at nearby targets—like when rioting in low-income neighborhoods destroys local businesses. This won't promote change, but it's what was immediately available.

We might believe that, particularly when our anger feels justified, there's healing power in expressing it. There is evidence that putting our feelings into words helps us be more in control and less reactive.[21] (Recall what we saw in the chapter Communications about the multiple benefits of recognizing and labeling our feelings as precisely as possible.) What about punching a pillow or screaming into an empty room? These acts are based on an ancient idea—catharsis, the release of pent-up emotion so it doesn't linger within us. Today, in cities like Toronto, we have "rage rooms," where we pay to break things. Essayist Calum Marsh explains, "It's a sort of therapeutic exercise: destruction as a bid to relieve tension. And it works." Finding himself unable to get particularly worked up, Marsh had to learn to project his hatred onto dinner plates and then take a bat to them.[22]

Unfortunately, Marsh likely wasn't reducing his aggression. Studies that induce anger and then let people pummel a punching bag before engaging in other tests show that aggression simply *increases.*[23] Researchers propose that violent catharsis may fail in part because it's all about calling to mind and *ruminating* on feelings of anger.[24] So rather than "getting the anger out," we're holding on to it, putting our energy and attention there. As we know, our brains, through repetition, *strengthen* connections—for instance between a certain inner state (anger) and set of behaviors (aggressive responses). So over time, punching pillows might teach us to lash out when angry, making us quicker to do it next time and less patient and able to experience anger without an outburst of violence. While violently "letting off steam" doesn't help us become more patient, it *can* help improve our moods. To that extent, Marsh's observation that the rage room "works" is accurate. We already know this. Destroying things can feel exhilarating for some of us. But the studies show that our beliefs play a big role here. If we *think* we're going to feel better after the rage room, we're more likely to.[25]

A related finding is that acting aggressively toward others tends to build its own momentum. In the lab, when people are allowed to give out electric shocks, they tend to increase the intensity and length of the shocks over time, even with no reward or encouragement to do so.[26] When violence becomes normal, we might get more and more violent. Other tests have been done on killing bugs. It seems "the act of killing may provide its own 'fuel' for subsequent killing as part of a perpetrator's psychological efforts to justify his or her own morbidly violent actions." What may be happening is that, like we saw with putting up a sign in our window in Chapter One, we look to our past and see that we did something—in this case killing bugs. Since we don't want to feel that that was the wrong thing to do, we might instead devalue bugs in our minds, thinking of them as wholly "other" and feeling that their lives are worthless. Then we kill more bugs.[27] So we see again how the patterns we get into can carry forward.

To close, let's look briefly at the strategies used by nonviolent peacebuilding and social change movements, to help demystify them. Watching the news from a safe distance, we may think about the poor people living under brutal dictatorships or in dire poverty. Yet it's also the case that "in all circumstances, people have some type of power."[28] Social change movements, whatever the context, tap into and support peoples' power and drive to create better situations. One helpful framework for analyzing approaches to civil resistance is what Friend Gianne Broughton dubbed *The Four Elements of Peacebuilding*.[29] Movements are usually at their best when they use *all four elements* as part of a coherent strategy:

- *rights-based*—appealing to standards that are independent of the conflict, for instance, insisting that laws be applied or that recognized rights be respected. In South Africa in the '80s, appealing to the unjust laws of apartheid wasn't useful, but appealing to international law to explain how apartheid was a violation of rights *was*.[30] This highlights the need for good research and strategizing about which rights to focus on and make a moral and legal case for.

- *interest-based*—typically various forms of dialogue, bringing parties to the conflict to understand their interests and perhaps negotiate how these may be served without violence. Agreements must be established with great care. If one side takes all, we won't have the conditions for peace. A famous example is The Treaty of Versailles, which helped formally end a war but created deeply harmful conditions that contributed to the rise to power of the Third Reich in Germany and, of course—further war.[31]

- *power-based*—the use of nonviolent force and coercion to oppose and to push for changes. It rests on the idea that authority is given by people to their leaders, and people can successfully withdraw their cooperation when they feel the need to.[32] Political scientist Gene Sharp famously developed a list of 198 types of nonviolent action, which are primarily power-based ways of deliberately escalating tensions to (hopefully) hasten change.[33] Which techniques work best in which situations is a subject of on-going study.[34] Author Stephanie Van Hook explains the general issue well: "It would be wrong to reach for an extreme method like fasting too early or carry on with introductory level methods like letter writing past the point where it can be effective."[35] At its best, power-based work gains sympathy rather than alienating, although Sharp notes that fully converting someone to a new point of view is the least likely outcome and isn't necessary for a campaign to succeed.[36] Like the choice of protesting at lunch counters in Nashville, power-based work is often symbolic, one reason it will do little without the other three elements.

- *compassion-based*—the work that gets the least attention, compassion demands bravery but is ultimately *essential* for peacebuilding. Resilient and courageous people like those we've met throughout this book are continuously expressing compassion, awakening us from hatred, changing hearts and loosening firm beliefs and entrenched divisions.

You may still be feeling skeptical about these techniques, or thinking that violence can be right and useful sometimes. We each have to make our own choices about that. We can do so by paying honest attention to our values, listening deeply to ourselves.

## Tips from This Chapter

1. Few of us actually know if we would or wouldn't use violence in a high-stress situation, and debating about these issues in the abstract isn't overly useful.

2. In the case of promoting social change, while violent uprisings work at times, they're less successful than nonviolent ones. This seems counter-intuitive to many of us, but no matter how brutal the dictatorship, people always have power that they can exercise through many different nonviolent techniques. The success of nonviolent movements seems to be primarily because in all contexts, they appeal to and engage greater numbers of people and their networks. Violence is also easier for governments to respond to. Public opinion is of vital significance for social change movements, and the use of violence tends to sway public feelings from sympathy toward calls for law and order.

3. Violence may often be a sign or symptom of problems within social movements rather than a carefully understood tool of strategic value.

4. We can recognize where our anger and drive for violence is coming from without thinking that lashing out will benefit us as social change movements or individuals. Putting our feelings into words can help us become less reactive, but violent or aggressive outbursts seem to actually increase aggression and impatience rather than helping us to "get it out." In the lab aggressive

behaviors just increase over time. On the other hand getting into a better mood has been shown to make us more creative as we literally take in more of the scene before us.

5. Social change is most effective when various approaches (based on rights, interests, compassion, and, where necessary, coercive nonviolent power) are integrated and balance each other. For example, jumping straight to a protest without first having a relationship with the other side that will allow for expressing rights and exploring interests is escalating the conflict prematurely and may make matters worse.

## Example: Elections in Idlib City

In Idlib City, as increasing repression from the Syrian military begins to impact day-to-day life, citizens get organized. They try to engage with government officials, and they volunteer on community building projects. Still, violent government repression worsens. In 2015 an armed group, Jeish al-Fateh, expels the Syrian government and forms its own council to manage the city, including administration of public services like healthcare and schools.

Jeish al-Fateh appoints its loyalists to management positions without paying attention to their qualifications. Repression and rights violations remain rampant. But civilians continue to resist, working to establish a local council to prevent armed groups from interfering in civil affairs.

They continue to organize, for instance, doing humanitarian projects and directing traffic and crowds. This helps build up a profile and get popular support. Hundreds of citizens begin attending weekly meetings and strategizing about how to take back their rights. Jeish al-Fateh works to undermine these activities, but public support only continues to grow.

Women are very active in this process, establishing multiple organizations to speak out, provide vocational training, and support each other through activities like bringing food to others who can't leave their homes. Women persistently push to counter the narrative that they shouldn't be involved in civic life.

After about eighteen months of continual campaigning for changes, Jeish al-Fateh gets tired, perhaps deciding their efforts are better used fighting the Syrian army. They give in and allow the election of a local city council.

People get organized, and teams of election monitors are trained to prevent corruption and election violence. Throughout this process, Idlib City is being attacked by Syrian government forces. Yet in these remarkably difficult conditions, social change work continues.[37]

## Activity: Four Elements

Facilitators ask the group,

- Where does power come from in Idlib City? What powers does each of the actors involved have?
- How did the civil society campaign involve the four elements (rights, interests, power, and compassion), and why might this have convinced Jeish al-Fateh to call an election for city council?
- Did the story make you think of struggles in your own life or ways you could approach your own problems?
- In reading about the four elements, was there one you felt most drawn to or familiar with?

## Activity: Follow the Leader

1. Facilitators ask everyone to split into pairs. Each pair chooses a leader. The leader moves their open hand around, and the follower must follow the palm of the hand with their face. Wherever the palm goes, they must go, always keeping close to the palm.
2. After a few minutes, facilitators ask the two parties to switch roles, with exactly the same instructions as before.
3. After a few more minutes, facilitators invite both parties to take both roles at once—each leading with their own palm while also following with their face. There may be questions, but facilitators don't offer any further guidance, saying, "Try it and see how you do."

4. When the third round has gone on for a few minutes, facilitators ask everyone to stop and gather in a circle to share any reflections about this exercise. Facilitators ask,

   a. How did that feel?

   b. Did you prefer one role over the other?

   c. If you got into an uncomfortable position as a follower, why did you do it? This was just an exercise and you could have stopped at any time.

   d. If you put the other person in an uncomfortable position, why?

   e. What happened when both partners tried to lead and follow at once?

   f. Did anything surprise you about this exercise?[38]

# Who Benefits?

*The destruction of a structure of exploitation
liberates the exploiter.*

— Johan Galtung[1]

A MONG THE CLASSIC ways to think critically is to ask who
benefits from a particular action—who gets rich or gains
power. A hidden alliance or conflict of interest might suddenly
become clear. One example is Andrew Feinstein's deeply chilling
research in *The Shadow World*, documenting how corruption is central to the arms trade and the brutal violence this trade fuels.[2] Common ideas, such as that war is explained by ethnic strife or is simply
chaos, let those who profit remain hidden.[3] When we consider who
benefits, we might see that winning and bringing the war to an end
isn't that desirable to everyone.[4]

What about when we're not earning incredible sums that make
our decisions self-serving? Amazingly enough, many of us are
quietly stuck in bad situations, *and we know it!* For instance, "Studies
of gang members, prison guards and prison inmates, as well as
school teachers show that the social norms about proper behavior
that are widely shared by all these communities are often regarded
by their very members as too strict or even plainly wrong, but no-
body dares to question the shared rules for fear of negative sanctions."[5] Our fear of being cast out from the safety of the group ("us"),
and our drive to see the world we live in as fundamentally fair seem
to make us justify the way things are, even when we can see obvious

problems. "Much evidence suggests that people are motivated to engage in 'system justification'—defined as the tendency to defend, bolster, and rationalize the societal status quo—even when social change would be preferable from the standpoint of self-interest."[6] In other words, we regularly stand up for systems that aren't good for us!

Once something *does* change and becomes the new normal, we have the capacity to quickly shift the ways we think about it. In 2015 Ontario banned smoking on bar and restaurant patios. Smokers were surveyed two days before the ban and two days after. In this brief time they had started rationalizing why the new law wasn't as big a deal as they'd thought before it passed. They even remembered smoking on patios less frequently than they had previously reported, apparently "adjusting their memory in such a way that the new law would feel less upsetting."[7] (Again, this is an average. If we were outraged by the ban we might not have been so quick to soften how we thought about it.)

We've looked in-depth at firm beliefs, but consider this: even when fervently arguing for a position, we ourselves are sometimes not so convinced![8] What could possibly be going on here? Perhaps in addition to being consistent with what we've done before (remember back to Chapter One and the evidence that we save mental energy by following what we've already done) we're asking ourselves, "How will my beliefs be seen by my group? Will I still be part of 'us'?" We might be ready to rationalize all sorts of beliefs so long as they keep us in good favor.

As solid and planned out as they can seem, there's significant randomness in the formation of our identities and the groups we belong to. Two male students were placed in a competition to measure their reaction times. Each was given alternating access to a "noise weapon" to blast their opponent—so when they had it their opponent didn't, and vice versa. They could choose the sound level to use. Unbeknownst to Student B, the researchers in some randomly selected trials led Student A to believe that B was *aggressive*, while in other random trials, they led Student A to believe B was *cooper-*

*ative.* To start the game, when Student A expected aggression, he used high intensity noise levels 61% of the time. When he expected that B was cooperative, he used high intensity 28% of the time. In response, students who were expected to be aggressive *became* aggressive. Student A was then taken out of the experiment entirely and replaced with a new student who hadn't been told anything about Student B. B *continued to behave* aggressively or cooperatively. Remember this was now based on a randomly created expectation held by someone who was no longer even there![9] The study didn't ask him, but perhaps Student B had come to identify himself as an aggressive or cooperative person. Maybe this would even change who he associated with later. We saw how when teachers believed randomly chosen children were "gifted" those children wound up doing better in school. This could have changed the students' identities and the groups they wound up in.

Even when we're alone we can act in ways that couldn't possibly benefit us. One set of studies found that people will risk exposure to negative situations like being electric shocked, blasted by painful noises, or seeing disturbing images *for no reward.* If we have a 100% chance of being blasted, we won't do this. But if the outcome is ambiguous, maybe we get blasted and maybe not, many of us choose to see what happens. After this choice, people report feeling worse.[10] So much for the theory that all our violence and support for violence comes from a rational analysis of how we can selfishly benefit! It seems more likely that sometimes we're just bored, curious, tired of making decisions, afraid of being mocked by others, responding to peoples' expectations (even if they were created randomly)…and we quietly go along with a status quo we don't believe will be good for us.

There could be another reason for this too. Many of us have ethical concerns, but when researchers ask why we didn't speak up about them, we may say that *no one would listen.* Evidence indicates we could be wrong about this. Studies from workplaces, for example, suggest that bosses and coworkers are actually surprisingly likely to consider what we have to say, and change their behaviors as a result. And when they do, they often feel *closer* to us rather than resenting us for having questioned them.[11]

Our choices improve when we're in more diverse groups. A review of "decades of research from organizational scientists, psychologists, sociologists, economists and demographers" found that diversity in groups increases creativity and leads to better decisions. There's no doubt that diversity can create friction, as different beliefs bump (sometimes painfully!) against each other, but diverse expertise and viewpoints also help groups reach more effective solutions to problems. Importantly, "Simply interacting with individuals who are different forces group members to prepare better, to anticipate alternative viewpoints and to expect that reaching consensus will take effort."[12] Recall what we saw in the Communications chapter— our understanding of other people's views improves when we have to explain what they think but only if we feel accountable to them to be accurate in the explanation. When we don't feel that everyone will just agree with us it's less comfortable, but it leads us to stop caricaturing alternate viewpoints and to consider them more honestly, developing more precision about our own ideas as well.

We might accept that group discussions help us search for better answers, but many groups, especially operating under stress and tight deadlines, don't work this way. We fall into groupthink—an illusion of unanimity where we feel a silent pressure not to speak our truth. Groupthink can be particularly strong when the team has a lot of confidence, a lot of faith in "us." This could lead to devastating consequences—like making war the "only option" when alternatives haven't been explored. How is such blind faith in our group possible?

Imagine this: you're in a community where you feel loved. You're told that anything that happens to you, something as minor as a cold, is visited upon you for a sacred purpose. Life is fair, and you always deserve what you get. You get to study and learn the ideas of the leaders of the community and to recite them to yourself often. That's the reading that's allowed. You can't engage with any outsiders, who seek only to corrupt you. Doubting what you're told is considered a selfish lack of faith and a heavy sin, and no one ever talks about doubts. You learn that your group is constantly persecuted and needs to behave secretly to ensure your safety. Then you're instructed to become a prostitute for the good of the community. You feel depressed and alone but unclear why. Finally, after years of pain and confusion, you receive information from the outside world that you simply can't ignore. It causes a *total* shift. It dawns on you that your firm beliefs are wrong; the leaders are wrong; and you've been abused this whole time.

This is more or less what happened to Mary Mahoney, and many like her, who've unwittingly joined cults. She says, "It took a long time to come out of the haze of those 30 years, but when I did, I was appalled by my former self."[13] Can you imagine how difficult it would be to accept that you'd been wrong for so many years and about so much, or to decide to make a change? Mahoney's story is an extreme example of what groups can inflict on their members, and the tremendous pressures members feel not to speak up, even in situations where they're being deeply harmed. Sadly, Mahoney's experience seems to be just an intense version of a common problem. A majority of us will agree with a group even when we know what the group is saying is obviously wrong, provided that the group's views appear to be unanimous. Adding even one nonconformist, though, *greatly* increases our willingness to speak the truth.[14] Studies and many real-world examples have shown that a few people acting to change what's "normal" can get others to follow.[15] Are there situations where you wouldn't have just obeyed authority figures if you'd felt supported by someone else who was taking a stand? Reflecting on Mahoney's horror story, what might be required of a healthy community?

In any group, some ideas are mainstream, and some are marginalized. This is always true because being a group means having a shared identity.[16] (An idea isn't mainstream because it benefits the majority of members, though, it's mainstream because, for whatever reasons, it's come to be seen as normal or right.) The mainstream identity may be understood implicitly and never talked about, but it's there. Among Quakers opposition to nuclear weapons is mainstream, and support for them is marginalized. This doesn't mean all Quakers disagree with nuclear deterrence, it just means they tend to keep quiet about it around other Quakers.

Communities have the tough task of balancing between maintaining traditions and identities, and also transforming and changing over time as is constantly required in an ever-changing world. John Paul Lederarch notes that a big part of the process of dealing constructively with conflict, and of maintaining the health of a group, is feeling empowered to discover and draw on our own knowledge. "The movement from implicit to explicit knowledge is discovery," he explains.[17] Sometimes when we've said something out loud, we even discover not only how much it's been bothering us but that folks we thought of as adversaries actually agree with the need for a change.

There are simple ways to encourage marginalized ideas to be discovered, to avoid groupthink. One is for leaders to listen before stating their own opinions. (If a leader starts a group discussion by raving about a particular solution, others might not risk voicing alternatives.) Another option is to name a respected group member "to articulate alternatives, possible pitfalls, and flaws in the group's plans."[18] Because this is the person's formal role, they can feel safer in doing it, and others are less likely to be upset by the issues raised.

There's another way that even the apparently powerful don't benefit when participating in exploitation and violence. Our actions can shatter our confidence in ourselves and others at a deep level. For example, soldiers on the battlefield might act in ways that are totally out of line with their ethics. This can leave a debilitating and invisible wound (sometimes called a "moral injury").[19] In such circumstances, even if we'd never admit it, we're not benefitting from having power over people. To heal ourselves we may even need the love and care of the very people we've just been battling.[20] Somehow the power we're steeped in can find its way to all of our relationships, even how we relate to ourselves. For this reason, wielding violence that might make it look like we're in a great position could actually be dangerous for us. Author Kazu Haga notes, "In my work in the prison system, I have found that...the more time you spend dehumanizing someone or hurting another human being, the more you internalize violence and the more it plays out in other areas of your life."[21]

At the beginning of the chapter Treating Emotions with Care, we saw how making an effective change requires making it as easy as possible. Many violent conflicts get to the point of a mutually hurting stalemate, a standoff where people are not benefitting but don't know how to extricate themselves.[22] When Martin Luther King, Jr. negotiated about Montgomery Alabama's segregation laws he discovered this dynamic:

> An attorney for the city bus company who had obstructed... demands for desegregation revealed the real source of his objection: "If we granted the Negroes these demands they would go about boasting of a victory that they had won over the white people; and this we will not stand for." Reflecting on this, King advised the participants in the movement not to gloat or boast, reminding them: "Through nonviolence we avoid the temptation of taking on the psychology of victors."[23]

Even when we're willing to change our position, we want to be seen in a good light for doing it! The fear of being embarrassed as a "loser" blocks many transformations that could benefit everyone. In South Africa there was major concern about the potential for violence during the transition from apartheid. As we know, this was a system that appeared beneficial to one group and was devastating to another. This system, once mainstream, was now being pushed to the margins. How would you feel as a white Afrikaner having suddenly lost so much power-over? Amazingly, the immediate years of transition out of apartheid went much more gracefully than expected. The Truth and Reconciliation Commission played an important role in allowing stories to be heard and pain to be processed. Another factor was that many people, including folks from around the world, spent time with Afrikaners, helping them let go of their power-over *with dignity*, without feeling ashamed. They were welcomed into the world community in the new power arrangement.[24]

From Mary Mahoney in a cult to apartheid in South Africa, when deprivation becomes a way of life, problems go unnoticed. We're not seeing violence. There are countless examples, such as the prevalence of unaddressed serious mental health issues.[25] We often mistake damaging situations for ones that are normal, not worth changing, or to our benefit. Maybe we're benefitting in some ways while conditions are still far from what they could be. Author Rebecca Solnit explains this well in the case of sexism, saying it "silences both men and women.... All of us live in a culture that is attempting to limit the range of our humanity, and so we're all in this liberation struggle."[26]

## Tips from This Chapter

1. Thinking about who benefits can offer us new insights into why a problem persists. At the same time, we regularly support and justify systems that don't benefit us, and we engage in behaviors that have no possibility of ever benefitting us. Part of this may be wanting to believe that our world is fair and so the status quo is good. Part of it is rationalizing whatever will keep us in the group.

2. In every group some ideas are mainstream and others are still present, but marginalized. Our group identities, the expectations we believe groups have about us, and what the group considers mainstream, all have some randomness behind them and may not be that beneficial to anyone. In any situation there are people who disagree with what's happening but go along with it anyway. Most of us will agree with decisions we know are wrong if everyone else seems to be agreeing. If even one other person doesn't conform though, we're much more likely to express our actual views.

3. We regularly underestimate our influence, thinking that others won't listen to us or will resent us for speaking up.

4. Groupthink can lead to terrible decisions. When we're in leadership positions, we can listen to others before offering our own opinions. In any group, we can assign people to propose alternatives and bring up pitfalls with group decisions. Diverse groups are more creative and effective, in part because of a broader range of perspectives and in part because we think more carefully about our own and others' ideas when we know we'll have to defend what we say to someone who thinks differently.

5. Change needs to be made as easy as possible. If individuals or groups are expected to give up some power-over, it will be easiest if they're treated well and encouraged for their positive change. If we hope to bring out the best in others and to build power-with, gloating isn't strategic.

6. Even if we feel we're benefitting, a situation may not be genuinely fulfilling and there could be win-win ways to transform it.

## Activity: Mainstream and Margins

1. Facilitators explain, "Groups sometimes present themselves as more homogeneous than they really are. Underneath, there are usually many differences, and groups can benefit from recognizing them. This exercise will help with that."

2. Facilitators ask everyone to line up at one side of the room and explain that the exercise will be done in silence. Facilitators state an identity, and everyone who feels it fits them is asked to move to the other side of the room, turn around, and head back to the group. Everyone must decide for themselves if the identity fits, so no one can ask for clarification. Facilitators can adapt the list for the group, always putting several less emotionally charged identities first.

3. Example identities: 1) woman, 2) man, 3) elder, 4) youth, 5) professional, 6) brought up in an urban area, 7) brought up in a rural area, 8) migrant, 9) fluent English speaker, 10) highly educated, 11) not highly educated, 12) active in a religion, 13) agnostic, 14) atheist, 15) brought up in a wealthy family, 16) brought up in a poor family, 17) lost one or more relatives in war, 18) been in a

physical fight as a teen or adult, 19) been a target of oppression, 20) benefitted from oppression, and 21) been personally accused of oppression.

4. Facilitators ask the group to share some feelings or experiences that came up. If someone mentions an experience that facilitators sense was common, they can ask, "How many others felt that?"

5. After some time, facilitators ask what the exercise showed about differences and end on a discussion of differences in groups.[27]

# Oppressors and Victims

*It is but too common for some to say*
*both are to blame…which is a base neutrality.*
*Others will cry, they are both alike;*
*thereby involving the injured with the guilty…*

— WILLIAM PENN[1]

W E'VE LOOKED at many types of violence, its usefulness in shaping individual behaviors and social changes, and responses to people who are becoming hateful and violent. We've seen how certain dynamics may not benefit even the apparently powerful. Now let's look further into a key story we've hinted at thus far—the story of "oppressors" and "victims."

In violent situations, euphemisms sanitize what's really happening. Talking about "casualties" and "collateral damage" helps us feel comfortable with choices we might not make about mutilating people's bodies.[2] Journalist Symon Hill says to honestly commemorate wars, "don't refer to people who have died unimaginably painful deaths as 'the fallen,' as if they had just tripped over."[3] The words we use have evaluations embedded in them, so they matter.

Regardless of our politics or views about violence, we've seen how a lot of us are trying to protect a firm belief that the world is fair. Language helps here too. We can use language to suggest, and find ways to imagine, that when bad things happen the person they're happening to *deserves* it.[4] This can include minimizing, ignoring, or misconstruing the consequences of what we do, not accepting responsibility, and dehumanizing and blaming those we harm.[5] These are all forms of the denial we keep running into.

Narratives nourish our thoughts, so new stories make change possible. Oppression is faced by billions of people. One problem with categorizing someone as an "oppressor," though, is that we're back to the binary—either you are one or you aren't, and it sounds like it's in your DNA. We know that, like Sammy Rangel, many victims go on to become abusers, and many abusers were themselves victims of abuse,[6] so depending where we start and stop the story, the categories actually flip. This discovery led Rangel to forgive his mother. What's the impact of these categories of victim and oppressor in other cases?

George Lakey explains the importance of feeling safe. "As a gay man, I remember the first time I saw on the door of a campus office a triangle, signifying that this would be a safe place for me. Surrounded by rampant homophobia, I relaxed as I turned the doorknob." Perhaps you can imagine Lakey's feeling of being able to let down his exhausting mental defenses for a while. Many of us know about the constant fear of recalling painful memories or emotions. A safe space can give us the time to recuperate. If we feel deeply unsafe because we might be set off—triggered—at any time, it could be really tough to learn or engage constructively with folks whose actions might hurt us.

Lakey recognizes another need that's equally important, though—to feel agency rather than victimhood.[7] There's lots of experimental evidence that agrees. Believing we have control is huge for our wellbeing. What's fascinating is that *this is true even in situations where we don't actually have much control.*[8] When we frame ourselves as victims, on the other hand, we may be saying that we don't have any power or any role to play.

Here are some hints about how, even at subtle levels we're not aware of, the categories we think with might influence our actions. It's been found that after asking people to solve word puzzles (so they aren't focusing on the words they're sorting), those who work on words related to aging leave the experiment walking slower and more hunched over. These folks report no awareness of this or of having read anything about aging.[9] Students who pass through a room with the scent of a cleaning product are quicker in word association tasks that use words about cleaning. They also keep their desks cleaner.[10] A great many studies have shown these effects. It's what's happening when images of weapons make us more aggressive—it's priming. Might priming ourselves to think we're fragile play a role in making this our experience?

Lakey looks at safe spaces and trigger warnings in well-meaning groups and asks,

> Are marginalized individuals in a group excused from standing up for themselves and fighting out differences with other group members...? Are higher-status people coming to believe that oppressed people are by definition weak or even fragile? It wouldn't be the first time that the attitudes of dogooders diminished others, participating in the disempowerment of those they intended to help.

As a teacher, Lakey never tried to guard his classroom. "Oppressive behaviors including racism showed up and useful conflicts erupted..." He feels this was not easy, but empowering to students nonetheless. They had the opportunity to openly work through conflicts. "One result was a degree of community that was unheard of in a course in a huge university."[11]

Why did this course build community? Why did people of color want to take it when they might experience racism from their peers instead of a safe space? Part of the reason may be that much of what was actually being processed was *emotion*. In this case students weren't facing physical violence. Instead, they had to work through strong feelings of marginalization and oppression. All of this will be faced outside the classroom, too, but without a professor like Lakey there to facilitate. The chance not to avoid but to face emotional threats head on and learn to address them, to gain a sense of agency and power-from-within, may have kept students coming back to Lakey's class.

Clearly a balance must be struck in considering our needs for safety and agency. That balance may be shifting to over-policing, in particular on some university campuses.

> One teacher I know was recently asked by a student not to use the word "violate" in class—as in "Does this conduct violate the law?"—because the word was triggering.... About a dozen new teachers of criminal law at multiple institutions have told me that they are not including rape law in their courses, arguing that it's not worth the risk of complaints of discomfort by students.[12]

Examples like these are numerous, often generating a climate of fear and watchfulness so as not to trigger or offend. The intention seems good, but the results are questionable. Having future lawyers ignorant of rape law so that students can avoid discomfort sounds like a poor solution, and there are major problems with censoring everyday words like "violate." (This harks back to the questions about freedom of expression that we saw when discussing no platform.)

Another huge issue is that such strategies can't be equitably implemented because any word, object, or scent could trigger a traumatic memory for someone, and so be unusable. What's more, this might not even help! It could be useful to us to do any number of healing practices, like working with a therapist, and in this healing, safe spaces can be beneficial. But continual avoidance, especially for less severe fears, is unlikely to benefit us.[13] If we're afraid, the right exposure can fairly quickly help what triggers us to seem more normal and less distressing.[14] (This may be similar to how exposure to "others" works to reduce our biases, making folks we're feeling threatened by feel more acceptable and predictable.)

Safe spaces and no platform can readily turn into power-over techniques to shut down beliefs we just don't think we'll agree with. Author Debra Soh says, "The most concerning thing I've found in discussions with those in favour of censoring 'dangerous' ideas is that they frequently don't know what they are arguing against—they've either refused to read the speaker's work or are opposed to it based on misinformation."[15] Remember the game where one person tries to tap a song and the other guesses it? This is like playing while the listener sits in a soundproof booth. Authors Greg Lukianoff and Jonathan Haidt note this as one of the disturbing results of what they call "vindictive protectiveness." They believe that, in the name of protecting people, we often assume the other party has bad intent—to maliciously harm innocent victims—and we respond with what we know: power-over. Even without physical aggression and when claiming to promote compassion, power-over can just make a conflict more entrenched. There's a real danger of setting up "an environment in which students rarely encounter diverse viewpoints."[16]

We've looked at rationalization of behaviors like cheating. Evidence suggests, "Cheating is especially easy to justify when you frame situations to cast yourself as a victim of some kind of unfairness."[17] Again, we can use the victim label to justify the behavior we feel will set the world right. One reason this can be so powerful is that it's usually difficult to address the legitimacy of our claims. Victimhood is often based on a feeling. So a sense of being offended or upset may be enough to shut down a class or get a hasty apology issued (as we touched on in the example Who Gets Recognized?). There can even be what author Anis Shivani calls "hierarchies of grievance and victimization," where we compete to be the biggest victim.[18] This is not to suggest in any way that there aren't genuine injustices all over the world; it's just to say that we'd do well to think about the roles the victim label plays.

Phakyab Rinpoche, a Tibetan Buddhist, was held in a Chinese prison, where he was tortured for three months. He later made it to New York as a refugee and was enrolled in a program for survivors of torture. His cross-cultural insights are fascinating, and his story is all the more so. Here's what he recounts from meeting with his psychologist:

Although I can see this young woman intends to be genuinely benevolent and open to my story, a misunderstanding quickly arises between us as soon as I mention my detention and tortures. I will soon realize that Westerners easily indulge in victimization. This explains their amazement, and their total lack of understanding, when I joke about the ill treatments I suffered in prison.

In her eventual report, the Bellevue psychologist will state: "Mr. Dorje's affect was stable, however, it seemed inappropriate at times. For example, he was smiling, animated, and even laughed as he described his torture in detail and his survival."

She would have better understood my feelings had I acted like a punching bag and expressed myself with the tearful language of complaint. Then she would have sympathized and undoubtedly shared my wailing, my indignation, my anger, and my hatred toward my torturers. During our interview, I got the impression that she was driving me into a corner and wanting me to accuse my tormentors. That was when I burst out laughing.

How can I take on a hatred I do not feel?

In fact, on that day, even if I was only a penniless refugee and a sick man with a gangrenous leg, I was not the victim. The victims were my jailers. I had left prison, but what about them? They were locked up in a vicious spiral...[19]

This story powerfully illustrates a point we've seen—just how remarkably open our minds are to different evaluations of our experiences. A horrible event doesn't have to generate only one possible response, like hatred or seeking revenge. Phakyab Rinpoche's experience is dramatic, but overcoming trauma quite naturally may be surprisingly common. Even when terminally ill or uttering our last words, most of us are far less frightened, and far happier, than you might expect,[20] and overall, we're resilient.

Since everyone's responses to trauma are different, there's no one way to meet everyone's needs.[21] Contrast Phakyab Rinpoche's experience with that of Dahr Jamail who, as discussed in the chapter Seeing Violence, was using self-righteous anger to hide from the debilitating symptoms of PTSD. If, like Jamail, we're "actively struggling with the most severe levels of grief and distress" then counseling might help.[22] But if we're not, forcing a process of "working through" grief might actually make us feel worse. (In one study 38% of those in treatment got worse than they were before they started![23]) We might think that people who respond to trauma like Phakyab Rinpoche did are just repressing their true feelings. But multiple studies have looked for and failed to find evidence of, for example, repression of grief following a loss and that grief coming out later in some way. (Repressed PTSD was found but seems to be very rare.)[24] Yet, *if we force ourselves to think we're in denial unless we feel angry or like "victims," we might unintentionally create or increase those feelings.* (This seems similar to when we decide we must have violent impulses we need to discover and not repress, and then we actually cause or strengthen them through breaking things in rage rooms.) So it's important that we not assume we're *supposed to* feel a certain way or that we'll be unable to handle discomfort but instead check in with ourselves and honor our real feelings and needs.

There are countless cases of severe harms in the world, and everyone will experience these differently. A dangerous tendency to blame people for experiencing harms (like being raped) must continually be named and rejected.[25] While doing so, we also need to listen to people and not assume they want or need to be categorized as victims or kept in safe spaces away from oppressors. This isn't about minimizing the experiences we have; it's about finding the most empowering ways to engage with life and spread peace.

## Tips from This Chapter

1. We often choose words that make us feel better about our decisions and distance us from the realities of the harm we cause.

We try to see the world as fair by dehumanizing and blaming people when bad things happen to them. We also use categories like victim and oppressor in ways that can influence how we problem-solve, engage with others, and feel about ourselves.

2. Being primed with images, words, and scents can influence our later actions even when we're aware that this is happening.

3. Safe spaces and trigger warnings are helpful in certain circumstances. They also raise major questions about censorship and are an incomplete strategy because anything could be a potential trigger, and the right kinds of exposure, rather than avoidance, can actually be beneficial. There's a whole spectrum of feelings of distress and discomfort, and many are healthy to be exposed to, to help them feel less upsetting so we can gain a sense of control and agency in our lives.

4. Sometimes we assume we're more fragile than we really are. Evidence suggests that, following many traumas, the majority of us are surprisingly resilient—we're not just repressing our true feelings.

5. Any time we feel like applying the label "victim" to ourselves or others, we may want to consider why we're doing it. Is it ultimately helpful, empowering, limiting, or even condescending? Claiming victimhood can at times be a power-over tactic—one folks use to justify behaviors from cheating on tests to joining violent hate groups—so we need to think carefully when seeing ourselves as victims.

## Example: Pronouns

A bright and serious university professor has had enough. He's being compelled to address people with pronouns that sound unnatural. He perceives the situation as stunningly far-reaching: "There's a war going on at the heart of our culture." He feels he's in an epic battle against oppression, and he's being "tarred and feathered" for taking a moral stand. He senses that Canada is on the brink of likely decline into a communist hell where governments will control thoughts through legislating the words we *must* speak. He's studied history and knows he has to fight back.[26]

I'll admit, I had mixed feelings about writing this example. I'd love it if we all focused more on creative conflict transformation and spent less time on the sensational and polarizing. However, a great many of the issues we've looked at are present here, so it's a case study that seems too relevant to pass up. University of Toronto professor Jordan Peterson is a prolific public speaker with views on many topics, and the point here isn't to debate his ideas but rather to look at the *process* of a conflict emerging and what might have gone differently. To do that, we'll just look at a key moment in 2016. The parties seem to be Peterson, his supporters, trans students and faculty, their supporters, and the university administration.

Remember the headline about charity staff making big salaries and how the article actually hinted, if we did the math ourselves, that it was less than 1% of charity staff? Media can skip important details and present conflicts in simple ways that help entrench them. (We'll return to this issue when we discuss peace education.) So there's a lot we don't know. What we do know is that, as with many conflicts, unhelpful *assumptions* are everywhere. At one point Peterson says he would happily call a trans woman "she,"[27] so the actual scale of the conflict is unclear. It's possible the parties aren't starting off quite as far apart as it seems.

Perhaps constructive and respectful communication between Peterson and trans students takes place and just isn't reported. Publicly what happens is rallies and debates. Peterson—to many a charismatic fatherly figure with intense confidence—rapidly spreads his distress and his ideas about its causes. He rises to frame, in large part thanks to social media. Groups like the queer caucus of the union representing teaching assistants push back hard. They call for no platform for Peterson because "human rights aren't up for debate."[28] Passionate people show up to rallies both to support Peterson and to oppose and shout questions at him. Sometimes the questions are well thought out, sometimes not. This all generates a deepening sense of threat and distance between the parties. Apparently, instead of using any transformative approaches, the university opts for power-over, sending Peterson legalistic letters. As we'd expect, he resists and judges the letters evidence that he's being persecuted. Tens of thousands sign petitions both in opposition and in support of his right not to use someone's requested pronouns.[29] News media boost the frenzy, and Peterson winds up making more than $80,000 *a month*—all donated by folks who want him to share his ideas.[30] Clearly there are massive incentives for him to keep generating controversy and keep the TV and social media attention flowing.

*Analysis*

Let's take a breath and start by assuming good intentions. If we engage, our goal isn't to get the parties to fully agree with each other, just to offer them reminders that can nudge the conflict away from becoming overly simplified and entrenched. We're trying to bring out the best selves of everyone involved. Let's recall how easy it is for any of us to fall into binary logic and othering, to make broad judgments about *people* instead of specific ideas or actions. Let's notice our own feelings and recall our own confirmation bias. It will help if we listen carefully, remain curious, and do our best to look for evidence that *contradicts* what we want to believe. OK—here we go!

The parties each feel they're doing the right thing; they just have very different ideas about what that means. Labeling them with the binary of right- and left-wing won't tell us much, so let's get more complex. Of ten groups of values identified by researchers,[31] Peterson likely cares most about tradition and achievement, while the students likely care about universalism and benevolence. It's worth asking questions to test if we're right about this and keeping what we learn in mind, using it to frame our conversations. Perhaps Peterson could hear the students better if they spoke about tradition, and they could hear him better if he spoke in terms of universalism.

It's helpful to be clear on the central issue—gender—by exploring the deeper worldviews at play. In Peterson's case we have some sense from statements like this: "Bill C-16 [which added gender identity and expression to many existing grounds protected from discrimination] contains an assault on biology and an implicit assault on the idea of objective reality."[32] He seems shaken by what he takes as a challenge to clear and objective fact—that there are two genders and they're defined by genitals. One's experience of gender (or indeed *neuro*biology) doesn't seem to matter.

However, gender is different from biological sex, and in many places *gender doesn't get defined by genitals*. For some of us that's a jarring thought, but researchers like Will Roscoe have documented how fluid ideas about gender are across cultures and even through time within Europe. Many different cues have been and still are used to identify gender, and various cultures have *more than two* genders.[33] This might all feel like the floor is being pulled out from under us. As we've seen, those feelings can arise when we experience a challenge to our concepts, to a worldview that seems so totally obvious it appears to *be* objective reality. We can readily mistake something *we're doing* (collectively as a culture applying concepts and subtly getting people to conform to them to varying degrees) for something eternal in the biology of all humans or the laws of the universe. The issues surrounding gender are complicated, and the jargon sometimes used by academics doesn't help simplify them! It can be frustrating and confusing to feel like we're being told what we're sure we know is not only false but is also *oppressive*. That doesn't mean, though, that objective reality is under attack.

Perhaps Peterson is applying the is-ought fallacy here as well (just because something's common or mainstream doesn't mean it's automatically good or the way things "ought" to be). We could ask questions to explore this, but it might not achieve much, because Peterson has stated that he's highly familiar with gender studies literature.[34] Similarly we can ask questions to explore the worldviews and biases of the trans students, which haven't gotten media attention.

A huge feature of this conflict is mirror-image perceptions. Both sides label each other oppressive and ideologically motivated.

Both accuse the other of causing harm and unduly limiting their freedoms. Both call the other aggressive and difficult to talk to. Both think they know more about reality, while the other is uninformed. Both see the other's approach as dangerous, while they're standing up for honesty and truth. Both feel they're acting in protective and moral ways. Both feel that the other is complaining inappropriately, being too sensitive, and exaggerating the harms done to them. Because mirror-image perceptions are so common, making a claim like "I'm fighting against tyranny" is never likely to be useful. The other party can respond with the mirror—"No, *I'm* fighting against tyranny." It's also almost universal that when asked, we'll point to some action of the other side and say, "You see? They started it!"

Again, this isn't to say that both sides' positions are actually equal. Peterson's fears are largely about a terrible imagined future. Trans folks are *right now* shockingly likely to experience assault, rejection by family, discrimination in looking for jobs and housing, and these and other factors seem to contribute to very high suicide rates.[35] Many appear to feel that the new law is a hard-won victory offering some desperately needed protections.

Yet, as we saw in the chapter Communications, being told that our feelings are out of step and *should* change doesn't help. Peterson rightly states that none of us can enforce compassion on anyone else. If he doesn't feel compassion for trans students, he can't be coerced into it. If trans students don't feel compassion for Peterson, they can't be made to. As we'd predict, directive power-over has only increased division here.

Instead, what about encouraging the parties to articulate each other's situations accurately and to think about mirror-image perceptions? Could this be useful in generating more complex and generous interpretations? With trans students it might also help to discuss how applying judgments to Peterson and his supporters (e.g., "oppressor") could just be repeating the kind of fixed and binary logic they're working to change!

Violent language and the logic of power-over is easy to spot from Peterson too: "I'm fighting this as a battle of ideas." In making the "battle" as big as possible, he critiques vast domains—entire university departments, the "radical left," and the basics of Canadian law. The conflict heads into very absolute and certain statements. "I think huge swaths of the university are irrevocably corrupted: sociology, gone; anthropology, gone."[36] There *are* issues in academia. In one recent example three authors wrote various hoax papers full of absurd claims and analyses not warranted by their data. Seven of the papers were accepted for publication in peer-reviewed journals.[37] Similar hoaxes and absurd-seeming papers have been published in many other fields.[38] But statements like "sociology, gone; anthropology, gone," while sounding catchy, aren't useful. Without details, we can't understand, or seek to transform, problems.

The University of Toronto has large sociology and anthropology departments, with many different professors teaching many different topics, but Peterson seems to be creating a simple "them." Recall that asking someone to explain the details of *how* their beliefs work is often a good way to get beyond extreme certainty. Which professors are teaching this corruption? Which courses by those professors? Which lecture topics in those courses? How are the points made within those lectures? It may become clear to Peterson that he doesn't know as much about the details as he thinks. We can be fairly confident about this. There's an *incredible* amount we need to know to navigate through life. Each of us has to learn a vast array of information, so we couldn't possibly have time to know much of what's happening just in the anthropology department, much less in the world![39] Again, the more we explore the details, looking for information that *disconfirms* what we want to believe, the less we tend to over-generalize and be hyper-confident.

Critics are also making broad and insulting statements about Peterson and the intelligence of his followers,[40] so the same process of asking *how* questions could be used with them. Even if a conversation about the mechanisms at play doesn't shift anyone's certainty, it can help us get into specifics, so we understand the viewpoints more clearly. Everyone here feels misunderstood, so this is important. We can hopefully move away from big categorical judgments and talk about feelings and needs (I didn't see these discussed in the many materials I reviewed). As we ask about needs, we'd likely have to remind people this isn't a judgment or demand ("I need him to stop committing hate crimes") but a need—safety perhaps.

Now that we've explored who the parties are, the worldviews involved, and a few obvious issues with how the conflict is being framed and playing out, let's zoom out just a bit and look at the immediate context. We've previously explored issues like economic uncertainty leading to difficulty finding jobs and a sense of purpose, and, for men in particular, a feeling that powers they used to hold and are entitled to are vanishing. These factors seem to be contributing to why Peterson's messages resonate.[41] We may be seeing what psychologist Jack Brehm dubbed "psychological reactance"— a strong tendency to push back whenever we sense our control being limited. We're extra likely to fight to regain exactly the powers we're used to and feel slipping away.[42]

Peterson himself isn't facing economic hardship, but he's quite concerned about the changing academic climate described in the last chapter, one where he feels dangerously narrow approaches to language and ideas are taking over. He may have very valid causes for concern; we'd have to find out. Perhaps he's faced censorship in the classroom and it's contributing to his fear of collective power being used over him. We could mention that refusing to use a pronoun might be heard by a trans student as saying, "Society has the power to name you what we see you as, and you can't do anything about it. Your experience doesn't matter." In a sense this could feel like the *power of a collective* (Peterson and others who want to tell people what their genders are)—just what Peterson is worried about. Might exploring this issue of power shift the conversation at all?

Peterson has expressed admiration for democracy, so this might be a point of agreement between him and trans students. It could be a common ground to pick up on. We'd ask what the characteristics of a healthy democracy are. What values underlie one? Once the students and Peterson are clear, removing the ambiguity, we'd ask if pronouns actually fit *with* these democratic values, rather than with communism. We might bring up the concept of *balance* as fundamental to democracy. (I didn't see balance mentioned in the materials I reviewed.) The importance of balance has come up at many points in this book, like the previous chapter's discussion of the need to balance safety with personal freedoms and a sense of control. Turning the conversation in this direction might break open the simple binary judgments (freedom versus tyranny), fuelling more complex thinking.

In democracies, issues are rarely so absolute, and freedoms are balanced at every turn. Even a topic as simple as pet ownership comes down to balancing divergent interests. I may want to own dozens of dogs and walk them off-leash in downtown Toronto, but you also have rights that that could infringe upon. Both of us might think our freedoms are unfairly restricted, and we could likely find examples that seem to prove it. Again, since they impact so many people, it's usually possible to find a story of someone harmed by just about *any* law. This doesn't necessarily mean those laws are *tyrannical* though.

It's easy to think that because the parties involved are all intelligent people they can't possibly be susceptible to the simple-seeming biases and techniques to counter them that we've just discussed. That's possible. But recall again the evidence we've seen—the most intelligent among us are often *best* at hiding our biases behind stories that rationalize and seem to support whatever it is we want to believe. We might assume our intellects will help us win the debate and vanquish the flawed ideas of the other side, but ironically, that itself is usually a flawed idea, and one that hasn't been vanquished or gone away! As with so many attempts at power-over, we can persist in aggressive debates even when they're failing and there are more useful alternatives.

Rather than fuel a polarizing conflict process, the university might have facilitated a private dialogue, doing some of what we've just imagined. What if they'd gotten even more creative and brought in a trustworthy third party who invited the sides together to do something fun—maybe taking them to watch a comedy or go to karaoke to sing a few songs? What if they'd used the findings we saw about contact and had the parties do a volunteer project together, with the condition that they couldn't debate about pronouns while working? We've seen the power of fun and uplifting moments to shift conflicts and broaden our thinking. Studies confirm it's when we feel good about ourselves and our integrity that we're likely to take opposing views seriously and to make concessions.[43]

We also keep running into the fact that what we're feeling in our bodies—warmth from holding that coffee cup—impacts the decisions we make. As much as our culture might tell us our minds and bodies are totally separate entities, that's simply wrong. Whatever abstract beliefs we hold, they're influenced at least somewhat by our emotions and our current sensations. So would sitting down to discuss the issues again have felt any different after singing or doing something else to engage the body and lighten the sense of imminent threat? This isn't a bloody war (even in the midst of bloody wars people sometimes find time to get into better moods, like the famous incident of German, French, and British soldiers putting down their guns and dancing together on Christmas Eve, 1914[44]), and the two sides are talking (albeit loudly) to each other, so fun and humor instead of debates might have helped set a new tone. A coming chapter on mediators will look further at what they can offer.

It's very possible that none of this would have changed the conflict and it was destined to become this bitter. Even if that's true, change can and will still happen as the situation continues to unfold. We can keep engaging in conflicts through caricaturing the other side and assuming the worst about them, or we can test more creative options, which may or may not work. It's always up to us.

## Tips from This Example

1. We need to beware of making our views bigger, more abstract, or more absolute. That tendency can be countered by looking for precise details and by recalling that our ideas aren't coming from nowhere; we *always* have very immediate feelings and needs.
2. Particularly when we sense that we're losing control, we're likely

to fight to maintain it. We can expect this response from people any time we're trying to promote a social change.

3. We tend to engage in mirror-image perception. This means any critical judgments we make of other people *could likely be leveled by them at us*. This can give us pause for thought. In what ways would this criticism be justified if they aimed it at us? We may be surprised to find that we've got more in common with the other party than we expected!

4. It's very easy to fall into the trap of "common sense" assumptions. They may not be common to everyone involved in the conflict! To identify points of difference in worldviews or framing of the issues, we need to ask questions and listen. Sometimes what seems like objective reality is a concept we've learned and are applying, not something universal.

5. The decisions we reach are impacted to some degree by the sensations we're feeling in our bodies. Could we surprise the other party by trying to engage with them as a person, learning where we share a common hobby? Could we, perhaps with the help of a trustworthy third party, do something fun together and then return to the issues of contention with a better mood and a broader perspective?

## Activity: What's Changed So Far?

In the beginning of the book you did the activity Group Ideas—What Peace Is Not, where you wrote down assumptions you thought should be tested further and questions you wanted answered. Let's revisit them.

1. Facilitators explain, "We've come a long way together as a group. Let's take a look back at the questions and assumptions we wrote down."

2. Facilitators invite the group members to read out what they wrote and ask the group, "Have your assumptions or questions changed in any way?" "Does anyone have a new question or assumption that wasn't there in the first exercise?" Update the sheet based on what questions or assumptions are present now.

# 4

# Inner Peace

*In this section we'll explore other
key beliefs that may not be benefitting us,
by turning a bit further inward.
Skills developed will help us clear the way
to care for ourselves
and to let our inner peace spread.*

# Connection

*To come to know and value our own lives
is the basis of knowing and valuing
the lives of others.*

— EMMA DOUCET[1]

W E'RE UNDOUBTEDLY among the most restless of all species. A recent study in the US found that if left in a room without tasks or stimulation for just 15 *minutes* most men, and some women, give themselves mildly painful electric shocks for no reason other than to have something to do.[2] Examples of unhappiness, dissatisfaction, or "never-enoughness" are easy to find, whether in ourselves or our role models. Marketing that makes us feel inadequate and like we need more is everywhere. *Believing* we don't have enough (apparently whether we're right or not) creates increased mental strain, leading us to make worse choices and be less successful in resisting temptations.[3]

Technology offers us wonderful opportunities, but its continual advances also generate new strains. Computers encourage us to shift from task to task, leaving us feeling as if we're getting a lot done as we receive small neurotransmitter boosts. What's happening, though, is that constantly having multiple things on the go is reducing our skills and raising our stress levels, and it's even possible that it's reducing our abilities to empathize with others.[4] In the first chapter we saw how most of us are actually less happy when online than when *commuting to work*! Yet time in front of screens and on social media continues to increase, as does evidence that it can make us feel *worse*. (Studies have found that "spending more time on social media led to unhappiness, while unhappiness did not lead to more social media use."[5])

Essayist David Gessner says we're becoming "fast twitch animals."[6] Most people in the world now live in cities,[7] where background noise makes us irritable and on edge. Bright lights throw off our biological rhythms and can lead us to make worse decisions.[8] Brain scans suggest that living in places with larger populations makes us more reactive to stress.[9] As we keep seeing, some stress is useful—it helps us get out of bed and meet important deadlines. But living in a soup of *chronic* stress eats away at our mental and physical health. Long-term stress rewires our brains to make violent snapping more probable. The sleep deprivation, alcohol, and certain psychoactive drugs many of us use to cope with stressful lives further interfere with our abilities to consciously regulate our impulses.[10] Studies have also found that temperature increases may increase rates of violence.[11] Bustling with people and full of concrete that absorbs and radiates heat, cities can easily push us to be short tempered. The constant weight of getting by, and a fragmentation in our inner lives, leave us vulnerable to all kinds of disturbing behaviors. Add to this the pressure of groups...

In a crowded street hundreds of people gather below an apartment and begin shouting "Jump! Jump!" laughing together while someone on a ledge above contemplates suicide.[12] Would any of these folks be here mocking a suicidal person if the others weren't? On Twitter thousands of users persistently shame and attack a woman they see as having Tweeted something racist and insensitive. She loses her job and develops serious mental and physical health issues.[13] In a dim room students show fewer qualms about cheating on tests, and when wearing sunglasses, even just to play a computer game, they're more aggressive.[14] These are some of the many findings about perceiving ourselves as anonymous. Feeling anonymous, *even when we're not*, can embolden us to care less about the outcomes of our actions. Anonymity contributes to rampant online hatred, abuse, and bullying, directed in particular at women, commonly with graphic threats of sexual violence.[15] The evidence suggests that in general, though, feeling anonymous in a crowd impacts the actions of women just as much as men.[16] Feeling seen and accountable can impact us too. Even *a picture* of eyes posted on a wall can make us more generous![17]

These are powerful trends that interconnect in the urban lives most of the world now lead. Of course, there are many incredible things about cities, and the picture is by no means all bad. As those of us living in alienating and high-stress environments seek happiness, there's also some dramatic and freeing information emerging that connects us back to ancient peace ideas.

Imagine you won the lottery and suddenly had millions of dollars. Or imagine that, on the same day, instead of winning the lottery you became paraplegic in a grisly accident. You might reasonably expect that winning the lottery would make you very happy, while losing the ability to walk would be devastating. But the data from those who've actually experienced one of these two life-changing events shows that a year later, both groups are about *equally happy*. Whether winning or losing an election, gaining or losing a romantic partner, passing or failing a test, we consistently overestimate both how intense the resulting feelings will be and how long they'll last.[18] Many of us regularly get our *sense of causality backwards*. External events and conditions impact us much less than we expect. As we've seen, we're not just reacting to the world, we're actively constructing our experiences. This is great news for the peace virus! It's a timeless realization that means the conditions for peace to thrive and replicate aren't built only once we're high status or live in a pristine place. We don't need to be as concerned about what happens to us as we do about our ways of *being*. We can reframe our "never-enoughness" and build our inner peace viral count in surprisingly simple ways.

What ways? Well, "imagine a therapy that had no known side effects, was readily available, and could improve your cognitive functioning at zero cost."[19] Sound too good to be true? After three days of backpacking in a national park, people performed 50% better on problem-solving tasks. Research shows that living close to green space is associated with lower levels of mental distress as well as 15 different serious ailments—from depression to heart disease. Even just having a *view* of greenery means we'll recover faster when in hospital, and be less likely to engage in violence![20] More than 100 studies have demonstrated such positive effects of nature. Just seeing nature, *even in paintings and videos*, seems to help us generate positive emotions and calm ourselves.[21]

These effects all appear to relate in part to relaxation. Nature decreases brain activity associated with worrying and increases activity associated with empathy and altruism.[22] This is consistent with an experience many of us have had—being gentler with ourselves after going for a stroll in the park. Yet a lot of us continually underestimate the happiness benefit of being physically active and in nature. For instance, in the US adults spend less than 5% of their days outdoors.[23] A study in Taiwan involving over 400,000 people found that doing just *15 minutes* of physical activity a day increases life expectancy by *three years* compared to being inactive.[24] Of course, poverty plays a big role in our lifestyle—if we're working multiple jobs and living far from a park, we can be extra stressed and it can be tough to get outside. But activities like brisk walking for 15 minutes might be attainable for most of us, and to get some of the benefits of nature even *one minute* can make a difference.

When asked to remember a time when we felt awe, or to look up at a grove of beautiful trees for just one minute, instead of standing in the exact same place but looking at a building, we make more ethical and more generous decisions. What's happening seems to be that we're remembering the truth—life is much bigger than just us. We're recalling our connectedness. The positive effects of awe are found even after we watch a frightening video like a volcano erupting. It too reminds us how small our self-centered worries really are.[25] This is ancient wisdom being verified by modern science. We can spend a minute now and then and reclaim a sense of wonder and mystery.

For centuries many Quakers have seen simplicity as a way to feel deeply alive. According to Friend Mark Burch, who's written extensively on the topic,[26] living simply is not about running away from the world, rejecting luxuries, self-loathing, denial, or opposition to the beauty or richness of our surroundings. Quite the opposite: it's about removing cumber. "Cumber" originally meant wood placed in the way of an oncoming army to impede its progress. This is a vivid metaphor for an obstacle to the flow of life. In a sense, many possessions, and even general busyness, can readily become cumber. If we don't make space, we're blocking the movement of our time and awareness, clogging up our chances for meaningful connection with ourselves and our world. Cumber can make us less alert to peacebuilding opportunities, and it contributes to the feelings of desperation that can underlie some violence. Growing simple is not about feeling bad for having too much or learning to hate possessions. It's about learning to cherish what we have, looking for a balance where we can use and enjoy it. This requires us to say no to the cumbersome.[27]

Consistent with Burch's characterization of simplicity as enjoying and being present to life rather than denying life, according to a thorough review of studies about happiness (which didn't look at causation), those who take time to experience pleasures every day tend to be happier than those with negative attitudes about pleasure, or who try to limit pleasures in their lives for moral or philosophical reasons.[28] It's possible these folks are connecting with life rather than building walls of cumbersome shame and power-over themselves.

Whether we know it or not, and as much as we might try to isolate ourselves, we're deeply connected with each other already. Here's an incredible illustration—one of my favorite studies from this whole book. Framingham, Massachusetts is a town of about 67,000.[29] Since 1948, researchers have been going there to collect information from thousands of people. In 2008 a team decided to dig into these heaps of data to see what they could find about the health, emotional well-being, and social networks of 4,739 residents of Framingham. Exploring who each person was connected to every few years over a 30-year period led the researchers to a remarkable discovery. This complex web of relationships showed that if a friend becomes happier, it significantly increases the probability that *we*, who may think of ourselves as totally distinct individuals, will *also* become happier. If a *friend of a friend* becomes happier, someone we might never have met, *our* happiness increases. Even *a friend of a friend of a friend* significantly affects *our* happiness! Think about that for a moment. Picture your closest friend, picture who their friends are, and then try to imagine the friends of those friends. The fact that those folks' happiness would impact yours is remarkable. Only by four degrees of separation do effects on our happiness stop showing up.

Examining this data over time allowed researchers to look at *why* happiness was changing. They suggest that "clusters of happiness result from the spread of happiness" rather than happy people seeking out and befriending other happy people.[30] This is a beautiful demonstration of our connectedness, and of the way that states of being can spread between us, like a virus. Of course, as we've seen, it's not only positive states we're vulnerable to. Aggression built while playing violent videogames spreads to others in our social networks, even people who don't play the games.[31] Some forms of depression, where negative thoughts play a significant role, hang around in university residences year after year "like a lingering flu."[32]

In addition to emotional states, our behaviors can spread, influencing people we've never even met. This has been demonstrated from games in the lab measuring cooperation to choices in the real world, like whether or not to become an organ donor.[33] The example of people losing their individuality in the mob and shouting "Jump!" is a chilling one showing just how much the situation around us can impact our choices. But we can use this knowledge to build peace as well. It's been proven that mobs don't just bring out the worst in their members. When we're feeling connected in a group that puts positive and constructive pressures on us, we act *more* ethically and altruistically than we do on our own.[34]

## Tips from This Chapter

1. We're often restless, and our dissatisfaction and insecurities are being stoked from many directions. Technologies can help us feel like we're being productive and getting a lot done without actually making us happier. Many of the conditions promoted by life in cities in particular have been linked to negative health impacts, poorer decision making, and an increased likelihood of violence.

2. When we feel anonymous, even when we're not, our behaviors change. In groups we can find ourselves doing horrible things we'd never do on our own. But groups can also make us more ethical.

3. Being active and spending time in nature makes us healthier, happier, better at problem solving, and less violent. Even a few minutes can make a significant difference, as can just having a view of nature or watching a nature documentary. A sense of awe at just how small we really are can be fostered very quickly and make us more ethical and generous.

4. Saying no to cumber can be a powerful way of picking how to use our limited attention and energy to be present to life and to what makes us happy.

5. Happiness has been shown to be contagious, spreading from person to person and having an influence on us across three degrees of separation. Other states and behaviors are also infectious and highly able to be passed on. Whatever we choose to do, the effects reach far beyond us to people we've never even met!

# Changing Ourselves

*The readiness to listen*
*brings the joy of healing.*

— URSULA FRANKLIN[1]

SOMETIMES WE DON'T listen to ourselves. Perhaps we decide to just "forgive and forget," but we're not actually ready. When she was 15, Margot Van Sluytman's father was shot and killed during a robbery. Her world was shattered. She was in so much grief that at one point she attempted to end her life. She survived these years of agony and found herself turning to poetry, trying to listen and care for herself again. Eventually she did what many of us might find unthinkable—Margot Van Sluytman, after so much pain, *met and forgave* her father's killer. The lead up to forgiving was a slow and agonizing process of transformation and, for Van Sluytman, *it had to be* before she could forgive. She advises, "To tell someone who is in pain to forgive is brutal. Forgiveness can't be prescriptive."[2] Many who've experienced such severe pain never get to the point that Van Sluytman did. For those who do, *when they're ready and not before*, forgiveness can indeed be healing. Studies suggest that forgiveness has positive health impacts and makes us feel like we have more control over our lives.[3] Getting to the point of genuine forgiveness can also make it easier for us to stop remembering the details of what happened.[4] This doesn't mean we ever fully forget, or think what happened has been set right, just that we might be able to stop reliving the painful details.

One study had some participants recall negative interactions and brood about them, while others tried to repress their negative feelings, and a third group practiced active compassion for the people who'd harmed them. The findings were clear—those who practiced compassion experienced more positive emotions and *greater feelings of control*.[5] Note that this compassion or kindness isn't about trying to ignore the harm someone caused. That was the emotional repression strategy in the study. It didn't work well. In general, trying to use power-over ourselves to suppress a feeling or idea fails and just makes the idea stronger.[6] Instead, compassion is about acknowledging the reality of the situation while still generating warm wishes for the person (not for their harmful *actions* but for them as a person).

What about forgiving ourselves? The fact is that much of our violence is actually directed *at ourselves*. One study found that 1 in 12 teenagers commit acts of deliberate self-harm like cutting or burning.[7] We can actually sense at a deep level that *hurting ourselves is moral*. Perhaps we think we deserve to suffer for the wrongs we've done, helping us maintain the belief we've talked about—that the world is fair. There's some evidence to support this. The longer people administer painful electric shocks to themselves, the less *guilty* they report feeling afterward, and brain scans have found that guilt and shame can generate activity related to feelings of *reward*.[8] I have a hunch that culture plays a big role here, in some cases training us to feel good about punishing ourselves, but I've been unable to find studies testing this question cross-culturally. As long as we try to build peace in the world around us while having a violent relationship in our inner worlds, I think we're in trouble. Yet in many countries there are *socially praised* ways that we battle ourselves.

"A 2013 survey of human resource directors in the United Kingdom found that nearly 30% reported that burnout was widespread within their organization." This is far deeper than just exhaustion from a busy day. When our bodies are telling us to stop and we keep pushing, even to do something positive like work for a good cause, it could be as violent as cutting our brains. We produce "distinctive changes in the anatomy and functioning," changes associated with more difficulty regulating our emotions, disruption of creativity, trouble problem-solving, impaired working memory, and difficulty paying attention (all hindering the peace skills we've been learning!). Burnout spreads through our lives and can make us cynical and resentful of things we used to enjoy. So again, power-over, pushing ourselves based on abstract ideas ("I *should* get more done") separated from our needs, can work in the short-term but with major long-term costs. There's a bit of good news, though. In particular if burnout has built over months and not decades, brain activity can return to normal after recovery in less stressful environments.[9] If we give ourselves the space to, our neuroplastic brains may be able to heal.

You've probably tried to quit a habit like over-working or overeating but fallen back into it. A lot of this book has been about change. We've considered this question at the social level, but how can we encourage *ourselves* to change? We often reward ourselves for successes and get angry and discouraged about failures. Maybe we find ways to do this that really work for us, maybe not. There are other options too. One way to build positive habits is by just getting started for a short time. Committing for 25 minutes could feel less daunting, but as we keep seeing, whether self-destructive or beneficial, once we're started in a given direction we might continue. Evidence suggests just getting started can really help.[10]

What if we want to make a change like quitting smoking? Firstly, we can acknowledge that, as we keep seeing, there are many causes driving our behaviors. Tobacco companies have systematically established conditions for our addiction by making cigarettes highly physically addictive, making them seem cool with advertising, hiding health risks with misinformation, and so on.[11] So if we struggle to quit, it isn't just a moral failing or proof that we aren't strong-willed enough! Recognizing that, there are still things we can do. We might identify why we want to quit, set specific and achievable goals to get us there, build up our confidence that we *can* make the change, and examine triggers to cut them from our lives. Perhaps we notice we always smoke around certain people and decide to stay away from them for a few months, looking for other social supports instead. Steps like these can all help.[12] We might also benefit from breaking our big goals (quitting forever) into smaller ones that feel more immediate and attainable (no cigarettes for the next week). When we hit this first milestone it gives us something to notice and celebrate. Evidence shows that setting attainable milestones and celebrating them can help keep us motivated. To find some milestones you may have already reached and ignored consider this question: "What's a hidden accomplishment that is worth surfacing and celebrating?"[13]

One technique that helps many people may surprise you, since most of us wouldn't think of it: *let* yourself smoke—*and really pay attention to it.* This takes you from *knowing* smoking is a bad habit with hugely negative consequences to *investigating* how it feels to smoke *in the moment* of smoking. It shifts from automatic pilot to a more conscious action. That doesn't sound too dramatic, but over time persistent investigation into what's really going on can lead us away from harmful behaviors. (It seems to work about twice as often as other respected methods for quitting smoking.[14]) Techniques like this aren't fancy; they're free; and they might help boost our inner peace. Again, hate narrows our focus, so with self-hate we might just block our awareness of our creative power.

Consider this classic experiment. A child sits in front of a table where an innocuous little marshmallow waits on a plate. An adult the child is familiar with and trusts says they can eat the marshmallow now or wait five minutes and get a second marshmallow as well. (This situation has been repeated with pretzels, mints, even colorful poker chips.[15]) The adult says they need to check on something but will be right back.

Some kids pick up the marshmallow in a tiny hand and gobble it down before the adult's even out the door. Others wait until the adult returns to hand them a second treat. Replications of this study have cast doubt on how important the child's ability to wait is as a predictor of future successes in life.[16] What's interesting and regularly gets ignored, though, is the *process* used by the kids who wait. *How* did they manage to hang on in an empty room with only a bright white marshmallow there to interact with? How did they set themselves a goal like getting a second yellow poker chip, and then follow through? The answer is illuminating. They didn't, as we might expect, have greater power-over themselves. They didn't sit in front of the marshmallow gritting their teeth and beating themselves up to resist temptation. They *changed the situation*. They got up from the table and invented a game, sang a song, or explored. Before they knew it, the adult returned with the second marshmallow.[17]

Studies of adults have found that the same trick can work quite well. For instance, distraction—shifting our own or someone else's attention—is an effective way to reduce aggression, and we've already seen many examples of changing the mental situation, picturing and imagining it from new angles that help us make more beneficial choices.[18] The marshmallow study and the finding about smoking attentively are both reminders that using power-over ourselves isn't our only option. There are often ways to change the situation. "Research shows that people with good self-control actually spend less time resisting desires than other people, because they avoid problem situations and cultivate good habits." We can often create situations that help us avoid the hard work of resisting temptations in the first place.[19] In changing habits, evidence also suggests we'd be best to make one change at a time.[20] Trying to implement everything you learn in this book all at once may not work out. Recall again—*process matters*, and sometimes changes will be slow but are still happening.

You're having a rough day. You notice you've made a few mistakes, forgotten an appointment, and now you're feeling tense. How do you talk to yourself? What are your go-to thoughts? You may have been taught to feel confident about yourself and cultivate your self-esteem. One challenge with this, though, is that self-esteem tends to be based on comparisons. To understand and value ourselves, we make comparisons to others—their possessions, behaviors, beliefs… When we think we're better than average, we have high self-esteem.

Psychologist Kristin Neff explains, "The desire to feel special is understandable. The problem is that by definition it's impossible for *everyone* to be above average at the same time. Although there are some ways in which we excel, there is always someone smarter, prettier, more successful." Even as we push ourselves to build self-esteem, we feel a lot of self-loathing for not being as good as others (or as good as we *imagine* them to be).[21] One popular response is the self-help technique of "positive affirmations"—saying into the mirror, "You're handsome, successful, and everyone adores you!" If we already feel good about ourselves, evidence suggests affirmations give us a slight boost. But if we don't believe them, they just remind us of how *we're not living up* to the judgments we're repeating to ourselves. If we don't feel handsome, successful, or adored by everyone, telling ourselves so actually makes us immediately *more* self-critical and depressed.[22]

The solution to these challenges may be surprisingly simple: learning to care for ourselves *and recognize* our flaws. When Neff learned about the concept of non-judgmental self-compassion she was excited but skeptical. "I don't know…if I'm too self-compassionate, won't I just be lazy and selfish?" We've come across this idea many times now. Neff had faith in power-over, believing punishment was necessary to motivate herself.

Still, Neff decided to research the new approach—power-with herself—and see what she found. Soon she discovered that she could be both *more* honest with herself, not less, and *assume more ownership and responsibility* for her actions. She was no longer fearful of what might happen to her if she admitted what she actually did, since now she was able to show herself compassion. This parallels what we've seen in conflicts with *other people*. When we don't make judgmental evaluations, we can have more enriching conversations. Through years of research and practice Neff came to define self-compassion as being gentle and understanding with ourselves rather than harshly critical, feeling connected with others in a sense of shared humanity, and neither ignoring nor exaggerating our experiences, simply paying attention to them. But is this actually any different than self-esteem? It seems that it is. Evidence suggests that self-esteem can lead to narcissism, self-absorption, self-righteous anger, prejudice, and discrimination. But a decade of research at Neff's lab finds that self-compassion has all of the benefits of self-esteem, and none of these downsides.

Perhaps the biggest benefit of self-compassion is that good feelings "don't go away when we mess up or things go wrong." So how would this work? In one study participants were divided into people who scored highly on self-esteem but not self-compassion, and those who scored highly on a rating of self-compassion (which also tends to mean above average self-esteem). Participants each made a video to introduce and talk about themselves. Half were given positive feedback about their videos, and half were given neutral feedback. How would you react if someone gave lukewarm feedback about you talking about yourself? The folks with high self-esteem were angry. They tended to deny that the feedback was true. Those with high self-compassion were more likely to accept the feedback as honest, and *were less bothered by it, whether it was positive or neutral*.[23] This is an illustration of both the vulnerability of self-esteem and how it can block us from trying to understand and engage with others.

Let's go back to what we imagined before: you're having a rough day. You notice you've made a few mistakes, forgotten an appointment, and you're tense. Now what? Neff recommends first noticing that something's gone wrong and it hurts. She suggests doing this before jumping into problem-solving mode. When we notice that we're actually in pain we can observe whether or not harsh self-judgments are motivating us to do better. Many of us will find that they're not. Making mistakes and feeling bad about it are both common human experiences, so it helps to recognize as much. Our self-criticism can generate a false sense of isolation, making the pain worse.[24]

Remember the negativity bias? We saw how our brains process

positive and negative information differently, making it easier to re-call the bad stuff. Here's how to counteract it. Celebrating life is not about denying the bad parts but *remembering to experience and express the good*. One study that randomly assigned a group of people to write just three letters of gratitude to another person (and not even send the letters unless they wanted to) suggested that express-ing gratitude led to significant benefits that lasted for at least *three months*.[25] Gratitude appears to reduce our sensations of aches and pains, improve our feeling of connectedness to others, and make us more optimistic.[26] The act of expressing gratitude increases our healing and resilience following trauma.[27]

Good things are happening all the time, and *it doesn't actually matter how big they are*, experiencing gratitude for them increases our positive emotions. Looking down I notice my shoes haven't come untied. That's good! Paying attention to that good feeling just for a moment, over time, feeds further positivity. So to counter-act the sense of meaninglessness and gloom, we can deliberately pause to notice positive moments, no matter how small. This is not about lying or being only positive. We've already seen how affirma-tion statements we don't believe can make us feel worse. Evidence shows that real positive emotions are *embodied*—they're associated with physiological changes that make us feel better in a way fake positivity doesn't.[28] (For that reason, what may be better than try-ing to fake positive feelings is faking the body language. Adopting more positive facial expressions and poses may lead to feeling more upbeat.[29])

This is so simple and yet so important it's worth repeating. Sci-ence is now showing that very briefly feeling grateful for small things throughout the day actually *changes the ways we think over time*.[30] At the beginning of the book we looked at the words of Con-golese peace worker Zawadi Nikuze, who advised to give what we have, even if it's only a smile. We looked at what impacts this might have on others. It seems we can now add that if we feel capable of giving a genuine smile and paying attention while doing it, it can really help us too!

It's important to note that savoring good moments and expressing gratitude isn't necessarily the same as feeling better off than others. That type of thinking ("I get to eat today while so many people go hungry") may be closer to the guilt we looked at at the beginning of the chapter—it might make you want to give yourself a painful electric shock instead of savoring the moment. It could also be power-over—telling yourself how you *should* feel happy and grateful all the time because of how lucky you are. Studies suggest telling ourselves we're better off than others might not produce the benefits generated when we feel gratitude.[31]

If we can't feel any gratitude or compassion right now—that's OK. Perhaps we need practice, or it's too soon after something bad happened and we need more time. Feelings and thought patterns like compassion for ourselves and others can be learned. In fact, even basic compassion training has been shown to change brain activity and to increase real-world concern for others, making us more giving.[32] In a moment we'll do an exercise proven to build compassion. Psychologists propose that this benefits us not so much because of the exercise itself as because of the positive actions we're influenced to take after the exercise. "Really it's just a shift in your own perspective that softens you and makes you more approachable. It helps you remember that not everything is about you..."[33] Changing the situation and the stories we tell is an infectious route to changing ourselves.

## Tips from This Chapter

1. Compassionate feelings involve care about the experiences and pain of others without condoning their harmful actions. This is not about trying to suppress non-compassionate ideas or feelings or forcing ourselves to forgive and forget.
2. When we're ready, authentically embodied positive states like compassion and forgiveness offer significant health benefits.
3. Self-loathing may be a learned pattern, and one we may engage in for various reasons, including that hurting ourselves makes us feel less guilty and more moral. Pushing ourselves to the point

of burnout creates long-lasting mental and physical problems. Reframing this behavior as a type of violence against ourselves may help us set healthier boundaries and priorities.

4. In promoting positive behavior change we can stop procrastinating by getting started on the change for short stretches. We can identify our motivations, set specific and achievable goals, build our confidence, examine triggers to cut them out of our lives, and look for social supports. We can break the change down into smaller attainable milestones and celebrate each time we reach one. We can also investigate our habits and how we actually feel *while doing them*. In creating good habits, we're best to pick one at a time and not try to change too much all at once.

5. People who meet personal goals are often skilled at not having to use exhaustive willpower. We can distract ourselves or others, changing our focus or the situation rather than gritting it out.

6. Self-affirmation statements and forced positivity don't seem to work well and can actually make us feel worse.

7. Rather than self-esteem (being better than others) we can build self-compassion—being gentle and understanding with ourselves instead of harshly critical, feeling connected with others in a sense of shared humanity, and neither ignoring nor exaggerating our experiences, simply paying attention to them.

8. Changing our posture, facial expressions, and body language has been shown to improve our energy levels and moods.

9. Gratitude has powerful positive effects that appear to come from paying attention to positives in our own lives, not comparing ourselves to others to feel better off than them. The simple act of consciously savoring positive experiences for a few moments has been shown to benefit us in multiple ways, countering our negativity bias with a more realistic understanding of how many good things are happening.

## Activity: Kindness Meditation

This is an individual activity but facilitators could read off the instructions to the group while members do the meditation.

Alternatively, each member could try it at home, and facilitators could ask for reactions to it as part of a group discussion.

Psychologist Barbara Fredrickson has studied the impacts of meditating on simple statements. This is an ancient method (in this case developed by Buddhists) used by countless people all over the world. It isn't offered to promote or appropriate from a particular faith tradition but because this widely available meditation has been tested both scientifically and through so many peoples' direct experience. What happened in the study?

Half of a group of 139 participants were randomly assigned to meditate or to be on a waiting list and learn the meditation only after the results from the first group were assessed. Most folks had zero experience with meditation and tried it for about an hour total over the course of a given week. The benefits for the meditation group were significant. Following seven weeks of brief training and practice, they'd developed increased social support, improved attention, and decreased symptoms of illness. Perhaps most interestingly, they actually felt an *increased sense of purpose and satisfaction in life*.[34] This is quite an impressive change after an hour a week!

Another interesting finding was an initial *decrease* in positive emotions among many of the meditators. Fredrickson and colleagues speculated that this may reflect the challenge of learning to meditate, that is, "doing something unfamiliar, difficult, and draining without immediate rewards." Those who stuck with the practice, however, started to experience significant improvements in positive emotions during week three.[35]

The point of this exercise is not to change anyone else or to expect that your wish will come true. The point is softening your own perspective—loosening your hold on your personal worries and self-centered stresses by exploring feelings of compassion for others. At first, this exercise is best done when you have 10 or 15 minutes where you won't be disturbed, so it's easiest to do in a quiet place. You may prefer to dim the lights.

1. Sit in a way that lets you feel comfortable, alert, and relaxed. Breathe easily. Dropping your shoulders and rolling them back

while sitting up straight can put you in a good position to let your lungs fill more comfortably. Let your eyes close or set them lightly on a single spot in front of you.

2. Pick someone you care about. Call to mind this person's positive qualities. Reflect on these qualities and notice your positive feelings about the person, as well as any sensations like warmth or relaxation, perhaps in your heart area.

3. Make the following statements out loud if you prefer or simply by thinking them. Do this slowly and with care, pausing after each statement. You can insert the person's name or picture the person as you say "you."
   a. May you feel safe.
   b. May you feel happy.
   c. May you feel healthy.
   d. May you live with ease.

4. If these statements don't feel quite right, you might want to adapt them, perhaps making them more specific. The most important point is to go slowly and focus on the positive emotions you're experiencing, not to mechanically repeat specific phrases without feeling them.

5. Leave some silence after repeating the statements.

6. Now move on to thinking of another person and go through the same process.

7. Many people find it helpful to include themselves in this practice ("May I feel safe...").

8. Once you're familiar with this practice, you might try pushing your boundaries by picking people you care less about. Eventually you could even think of people you actively dislike. Can you generate genuine good wishes for them?

9. If you notice any resistance come up, don't try to suppress it. Maybe this exercise feels silly, fake, naive, or even dangerous. Maybe you're agitated and don't want to continue. After trying the meditation for 10 minutes or so, you can explore what beliefs are creating your resistance and evaluate if those beliefs serve you.[36]

## Activity: Gratitude

This is an individual activity. Facilitators may decide to use it if your group is eating together.

Many of us find the practice of gratitude helpful. Perhaps you already pause before a meal to say thank you in some way. The next time you sit down for a meal, before you take your first bite, try pausing to recognize and thank all of the different people, animals, and natural processes involved. People grew the food, harvested it, packaged it, transported it, stocked it in stores, and sold it. The meal required energy from the sun, rain, atmosphere, and soil. This food exists in this exact way only because of the cultivation decisions of generations upon generations of farmers. The food needed to be labeled; the farms involved needed inspections. As we follow this line of thought we may realize that the conditions leading to our meal are countless, stretching across cultures, continents, and centuries. There's a great deal to be grateful for! The practice isn't to tell ourselves we *should* feel grateful if we don't. Instead, we simply imagine the people, animals, plants, and processes our meal depends on and see how we feel when expressing thanks. We might imagine that the people respond with "You're welcome," or smile at us, pleased that their work has been acknowledged and that they could help.

# 5

# Structural Peace

*We've already considered structural issues*
*many times, but now we'll turn more specifically*
*to some of the toughest large-scale problems.*
*How is the peace virus at work in deadly conflicts?*
*How might international crises be transformed?*

# Who's Dreaming?

*If we are looking once more*
*to [violent] force for our security,*
*the world has learned no lesson.*

— London Yearly Meeting of the Religious Society of Friends, 1919[1]

IT'S THE WEE HOURS of the morning of October 25, 1983, a Tuesday. On the tiny island of Grenada, most of the 96,000[2] residents are asleep. Suddenly, the US begins airdropping forces onto Point Salines International Airport. This is operation *Urgent Fury*.

The Grenadian army, numbering about 1,500 (plus some 700 Cubans, mostly construction workers trained to serve as soldiers in a pinch[3]), takes up defensive positions while shots ring out. An emergency statement from the United Nations "deeply deplores" the invasion as a "flagrant violation of international law,"[4] but the fighting continues. The official end date of the war is November 1, one week after its launch. US reports claim 70 dead and almost 1,000 wounded Grenadians and Cubans, and 19 dead and 116 wounded US soldiers. At least 24 Grenadian civilians are among the dead, many from the US bombing of a mental hospital.[5]

Why did I tell you this? Because this is the kind of clean military victory most of us think of when we think of war...and we're dead wrong. This was one of the *exceedingly rare* wars in the last half century that led to a decisive victory, and did so without devastating the countries involved. Given the militaries, it's hardly surprising. Overwhelmingly, modern wars fail to produce results in terms of one side

Credit: Public domain

Grenada, October 25, 1983

"winning." Instead, broadly speaking, they produce a great many losers, a few individuals and corporations that profit enormously, as we've touched on, and no real end. Typically, a negotiated political agreement finally ends the formal war but without adequately building conditions for peace. In recent years about 90% of wars in the world have been civil wars, often involving many armed groups.[6] More civil wars ended through negotiations between 1989 and 2004 than in the previous two centuries, but "one fifth to one third of all settled [violent] conflicts regress back into war within five years."[7]

A key to understanding the failure of wars is something we've already looked at—often power-over *seems to be working* because it produces an immediate change. If we want to think realistically though, it's important to recognize that once mass violence has started, *there is no great option.* Whatever response the international community makes, *there's no immediate fix* to problems that take so long to build. We'll look in the coming chapters at prevention and responses to atrocities—but it's important to start by admitting that once dynamics of mass violence are already playing out, our heartfelt desire to push for a quick resolution can be disastrous.

If our goal is that as few people should be harmed as possible *in the immediate term*, a bombing campaign to stop the advance of an army that's attacking civilians might seem promising. We'll kill and maim some civilians ourselves—but we may protect far more. However, if our focus is on the *longer term*, the bombing campaign isn't promising at all. It has further destabilizing and unpredictable effects, and it does *nothing* to build the conditions for positive peace—bombs simply don't have that ability, and it's not fair to expect it of them. So for all the rhetoric during war, as much as we say we'll blow our enemies off the face of the earth, what actually happens is that our enemies and their ideas continue to exist. We don't get rid of them. Even in wars, we're in relationship.

The continual failure of war to improve or settle anything significant isn't only the case in Afghanistan, Yemen, or Iraq, but even for the "war on terror" and the "war on drugs." Violent extremism has greatly *increased* as a result of the "war on terror," and violent drug cartels have become immensely more dangerous and powerful thanks to the "war on drugs."[8] What's going on? Rather than neatly crushing our enemies, extreme power-over seems to mostly help a climate of violence and corruption to spread. You can easily imagine many of the ways this happens, so I'll only mention one of the less obvious ones. The private security company TigerSwan built up its expertise when it was funded by the US government to operate in Afghanistan. Company documents show that TigerSwan then applied the strategies of the "war on terror" to combat overwhelmingly nonviolent protests against pipeline construction in North Dakota. Indigenous-led protesters, said TigerSwan, represented "an ideologically driven insurgency with a strong religious component," similar to "jihadist" fighters. The result was a heavy use of violent force by police receiving security briefings from TigerSwan.[9]

The militarization of policing has been dramatic in Canada as well, with a 2,100% *increase* in the deployment of SWAT teams (once considered a last-resort) between 1980 and 2017. Many deployments were for minor offenses like noise complaints and traffic violations![10] This is not happening by accident or in isolation. A militarized culture spreads as countries learn from each other about tactics tested in war. And the people most negatively impacted appear to largely be marginalized folks trying to exercise democratic rights.[11] Violent power and respect for each other don't easily coexist—as one rises, the other tends to diminish. As we use violence, we can corrode the social fabric, creating conditions for more violence.

Still, our faith in war can be so unflinching that we feel the way a Facebook user did in commenting on a video I shared about alternatives: "In other words spend and dream." With respect to spending, in 2017 the economic cost of violence was estimated at $1,988 *for every person on the planet*.[12] The UN and World Bank confirm that, in the most pessimistic scenario, the net savings of war prevention *for the international community, not even the countries involved directly in the war*, would be almost $700 million per year. And "the benefits of prevention increase over time, whereas the costs fall."[13] These numbers don't take into account war's contributions to pollution and climate change. As just one example, the US Department of Defense is "one of the world's worst polluters," creating thousands of contaminated sites and being "the single largest consumer of energy in the United States."[14] So whose dreams, or nightmares, are we living in? And more importantly, how can a new dream become more infectious?

We know enough to answer this question—how over-confidence, groupthink, othering, system justification, simple binary logic like the belief that some people are "pure evil," violent and euphemistic language, the media and games we're exposed to, beliefs like war is "natural," and certain experiences of masculinity all combine to create a narrow frame. They can make war seem inevitable.

We may also just *assume* that all other options have been exhausted, when this is far from true. One study asked a group of participants if they supported a war. A second group was asked the same question but was also told that there were no good alternatives. A third group was asked the question of whether or not they supported the war and was told that all alternatives had not yet been exhausted. Unsurprisingly, this third group was far less likely to support the war. What may surprise you is that the responses of the first two groups were identical—they both supported the war about equally.[15] Think about that for a moment. The finding suggests that unless people are told *explicitly* that alternatives to war exist, they simply assume that such alternatives *do not exist*, or that they've already been tried and failed (even when they haven't). The finding may well apply to policy makers as much as it does to the rest of us.

The good news is that frames are opening all the time! History can be instructive here. Slavery was an integral part of the British economy. It was considered an absurd dream to ever change this. The frame was clear—slavery was normal and the most one could do was debate the ways Britain engaged in it. Slave traders produced pamphlets advancing a number of arguments:

- Slavery was important for the British economy and Britain's successes on the world stage.
- Britain had to be involved in the slave trade because other countries were, so if Britain didn't involve itself, it would lose a competitive advantage.
- British slave traders were more ethical and humane than their rivals the French and Dutch, so Britain's involvement was good.
- Britain was helping slaves by removing them from Africa to places where they were treated better and kept safer by their slave masters.[16]

Eerily similar arguments are still with us today, used to justify war and the sale of weapons for war.[17] It's variously been argued impossible to outlaw slavery, to ban chemical and biological weapons, or to stop the use of land mines and cluster munitions.[18] While none of these has fully disappeared, much progress has been made in moving them from widespread and mainstream to marginalized and formally scorned. So let's not assume that our current narrow frame is the only option.

## Tips from This Chapter

1. Wars are inherently destabilizing and don't create the conditions for positive peace. Our enemies don't just disappear, so in the end we need to find ways to transform our destructive relationships with them.

2. We may support wars due to short-term apparent successes like keeping some civilians safe. What's clear is this is a bad choice to have to make, and the long-term impacts of using violent power-over are unpredictable and regularly make the situation worse.

3. Prevention of wars saves lives and money (even for countries not directly involved in the wars) and prevents environmental destruction. Wars also shift cultures. Once we've developed expertise in attacking people, this mentality of extreme power-over and domination tends to spread.

4. Seeing wars as the only option is an example of a narrow frame. Have we thought of other alternatives or just assumed they must be impossible or have been tried when they haven't? History shows that many institutions that looked too powerful and well-established to ever change have indeed changed.

# Just War, Just Peace, and Responsibility

*Many institutions and ways of doing things*
*persist because of the wide-spread acceptance*
*of TINA [there is no alternative].*

— GEOFF HARRIS[1]

W̲E MAY FEEL a visceral reaction when the importance of war is questioned. It can sound unpatriotic, or like the sacrifices of folks who serve in the military are being undermined. This chapter isn't about questioning the bravery of soldiers. We'll simply be asking, Since we know war regularly fails to increase security or stability—are there realistic alternatives? Can we save lives, including soldiers' lives, by not risking them in the first place?

We already know a lot about firm beliefs and how they form and linger. But to understand why we react so strongly when questions are raised about war, and why at a cultural level thinking about peace can be so narrow, it's worth briefly looking at the historical roots of a particular set of beliefs. When we go deep enough, the righteous savior "good guys" in Hollywood stories connect to strong *faith-based* beliefs about power. In many countries, this has evolved from Christian "Just War" theory. Whether consciously or unconsciously, lots of us act as if there's a source of divine judgment, and it can be doled out as fiery wrath. A study from the US and the

Netherlands suggests that being primed to connect with this image of a violent God can make us more aggressive *even if we're atheists!*[2]

War may not serve our need for security, but perhaps it does make us feel that evil people are being punished and that the world is fair. This faith in retribution can impact us at a level we never really question. If we can kill, we can make choices about life—we can control it and know that we're good and on the side of justice because we wield such violent power. It can feel like being closer to the divine (regardless of how far this strays from or conflicts with some or all of our religions' teachings). This is a deep expression of alienated power-over. In war as elsewhere, we're often ready to apply these power-over standards inconsistently. When asked if he thought waterboarding was torture, one prominent US lawyer and politician admitted, "It depends who does it."[3] There's no "It depends who does it" clause in Just War theory, but I think that when we feel war can be holy, we're forever close to the dark side of moral conviction, where pushing justice further—even engaging in horrific crimes—becomes easy to rationalize because God is with "us."

These issues aren't unique to Christians. Many religions have ways of framing violence as righteous in certain conditions and evil in others. This even happens within traditions often thought of as pacifist. Quakers have been involved at high levels of war planning, have served in the military, and have supported wars.[4] Buddhists from Thailand and Myanmar to Japan have found ways of philosophically and spiritually sanctioning brutal violence.[5]

Still, the doctrine with the widest influence is Christian Just War theory, which developed over centuries and today may seem like "common sense."[6] The theory doesn't work. For example, it relies on "discrimination"—that only enemy combatants are eligible for violence, and civilians must be protected. This has not happened, is not happening, and is increasingly impossible, given the challenges of distinguishing between civilians and combatants.[7] Even when they could be adhered to, the laws of war are regularly violated, and Just War theory is ignored on the battlefield (or in the drone control room).[8]

For its part, the World Council of Churches, representing almost 500 million Christians, has rejected Christian Just War theory, stating, "War can no longer be considered an act of justice."[9] It's never enough to criticize though. What we need is to deeply examine the current reality and propose viable alternatives. Maybe we can agree that war isn't good, but how can we protect people facing atrocities?

There's a formula of actions taken in large-scale peacemaking, peacekeeping, and peacebuilding. There can be no doubt from looking at the results that it's often ineffective. One analyst puts it bluntly: "The Western checklist approach to peace interventions can build neither a sustainable peace nor a functioning democracy."[10]

Perhaps the biggest problem with the checklist has been its narrow frame—it has focused too much on government officials and often ignored the knowledge and skills present in communities.[11] Grassroots groups with highly relevant expertise and local networks may have no idea what peace work the UN is trying to do, because they've *never been consulted*.[12]

We've explored how complex the causes of violence and hatred are. Conditions of mass violence come from *and* cause many messy relationships *all at once*. A linear top-down peacemaking checklist just isn't equipped to deal with this. Think about the weather. Weather stations around the world generate more than 1 million points of data *every day*, and even with extensive mathematical models, supercomputers, and brilliant folks working on predicting it, weather reports can be *way off*.[13] That's because we don't have a linear way to "solve" or understand complex systems. They're unpredictable even with a lot of data, as we discussed when looking at the possible outcomes of #duranadam protests in Turkey. Factors contributing to wars are as numerous as those affecting the weather, so these complex systems demand responsiveness and adjustments based on what's happening.[14] Given this, and the insufficient coordination between actors like the UN and people at the grassroots, it's easy to understand how, even when the international community genuinely has the best of intentions, it can produce friction instead of synergy and sometimes make matters worse.

An example is sanctions. Experts say they're "sometimes imposed for lack of better alternatives and without much expectation of effectiveness."[15] Sanctions can easily devastate a country, weakening healthcare systems and contributing to mass starvation.[16] Powerful and well-connected individuals and companies have little trouble getting around sanctions with the help of foreign banks,[17] so average citizens are the ones most likely to suffer. On the other hand, "smart sanctions," limited to arms and *vigorously applied*, could be huge in reducing violence.[18] It seems most times, though, that weapons continue to flow freely to war zones. In one illustration of just how poor arms controls are, a US Department of Defense internal memo showed that $1 *billion dollars worth* of arms sent to the Iraqi army was not accounted for and had likely fallen into the hands of Daesh.[19] If we genuinely want to increase security, strictly controlling the flow of arms seems like an obvious starting place! Some governments and civil society groups have made headway in this direction, but far more needs to be done. Another option for sanctions is to target specific leaders, but major questions remain about if and when this is actually effective.

Even as it fails, the checklist has been slow to adapt. Jennifer Welsh, a former special advisor to the UN Secretary General, notes that since the first mediator was dispatched by the UN in 1948, both the practice of peacekeeping and the nature of violent conflict have shifted dramatically. Formerly peacekeepers were asked to keep well defined warring parties separated. Now they're trying to stabilize situations that are far more confusing, where there's less peace to keep, and where more civilians need direct protection.[20]

One of the biggest criticisms of such peacekeeping has been its attempted neutrality. The most heartbreaking and famous example is Rwanda. Senior US military leaders and academics met to review the evidence and agreed that an international force of just 5,000 troops deployed in the window of opportunity between April 7th and 21st 1994 could likely have "averted the slaughter of a half-million people."[21] But this was far from the only window of opportunity. Months before the violence started, world leaders were *repeatedly* warned about clear signs that genocide was coming, and none took meaningful action.[22]

In 2005 the UN adopted the Responsibility to Protect doctrine (RtoP) with the hope of never again failing to stop such atrocities. RtoP attempted to transform what's been called the "right to intervene" into the "responsibility to protect." Canada put it well: "What is necessary is for the international community to change its basic mindset from a 'culture of reaction' to that of a 'culture of prevention.'"[23]

RtoP insisted that in cases where a government is unable or unwilling to protect its citizens, the international community, under and with the authority of the UN, has a responsibility to intervene to keep people safe. This has been controversial primarily because some argue it allows powerful countries to be selective about when they choose to take action. The strongest critics say that protection is granted for political gain rather than based on the real needs of people facing atrocities.[24] Still, many were happy with the UN's adoption of the position that, to protect civilians, military interventions are sometimes a key last resort after RtoP's other pillars have been fully attempted and failed.

Most of the world thinks it's a good idea to kill some belligerent combatants in the hopes of keeping people safe. What do you do if you're unsure about this but dearly want to save lives and build the conditions for justice and peace? Canadian Quakers, among those who grappled with this tough topic, spent a full year in discussions. Their answer in the end ran counter to what most governments and human rights groups were saying, and history appears to have already validated it.

The essence of what Quakers said was this: support the work of prevention by putting far more time, thought, and resources there, and stop talking about military intervention in the last resort. Why? "Thinking of military intervention as a 'last resort' assumes that it is inevitable [and] hinders non-military action..."[25] Quakers were concerned that, while most of RtoP offered extremely important steps, the discussion of military intervention might prop up the narrow frame. Since deploying the military remains an option on the table, it keeps drawing our attention and resources. To be sure, the international community said it was ready to take timely military action *"should peaceful means be inadequate* and national authorities are manifestly failing to protect their populations…" But not enough emphasis was placed on defining these "peaceful means" and bringing them to scale.[26] Canada, for instance, said RtoP "does not necessarily mean that every [non-military] option must literally have been tried and failed," only that there are "reasonable grounds for believing lesser measures would not have succeeded."[27] But if we haven't invested in or thoroughly tested "lesser measures," how can we possibly know they wouldn't have worked?

In the years since the adoption of RtoP, much inspiring and important work has been done to build governments' capacities for prevention.[28] But RtoP has also been interpreted in exactly the devastating ways Friends feared. In February 2011, UN Security Council resolution 1970 imposed a series of international sanctions on Libya.[29] The UN said this was in response to atrocities committed by the forces of Muammar Gaddafi against civilians.[30] (It's unclear why similar atrocities elsewhere didn't lead to a similar response.) Less than a month later, resolution 1973 authorized member states to take "all necessary measures" to protect civilians, while explicitly prohibiting foreign forces from entering Libya. This led to NATO member airstrikes. (Their legality and faithfulness to the resolution have been questioned.[31]) Brazil, a member of the Security Council at the time, said resolution 1973 "may have the unintended effect of exacerbating tensions on the ground and causing more harm than good to the very same civilians we are committed to protecting."[32] It's unclear *how*, during the rapid escalation to a bombing campaign, the UN or individual governments pursued and exhausted peaceful means.[33]

Canada was heavily involved. Foreign Affairs Minister John Baird signed a bomb destined to be dropped on Libya with the words "Free Libya. Democracy." But freedom and democracy weren't the result of these bombs. Instead, instability increased, Libya's institutions fell apart, and the countries that carried out the bombings didn't help Libya rebuild.[34] Just what Brazil feared had happened, and *quickly*. Libya's collapse played a dangerous and destabilizing role throughout the continent[35] and continues to make our world less secure today.

So was the solution to just stay home and let human rights abuses in Libya go uncontested? Some have argued for this approach. They're often criticized for "knee jerk anti-interventionism"— automatically opposing military deployment without examining the situation.[36] In 2000, Friend Diana Francis wrote the pamphlet *Lessons From Kosovo/a: Alternatives To War*. Francis noted that at the time Quakers "felt sorely challenged when NATO went to war against Serbia over Kosovo/a. Confronted by images of families in their thousands driven from their homes," many were loath to support war, but felt "personal doubts as to what else could have been done."[37] Francis outlined alternatives at every step that might have helped prevent and deescalate, together with the failed decisions taken instead. Her analysis highlights a pattern that's disturbingly familiar in Libya and elsewhere:

> There were no easy solutions to events in what was once Yugoslavia. We cannot say, "If only this and this had been done, everything would have been all right." We can say that there were constructive things that could have been done, given the will and resources, and that mistakes were made at many stages, because of national interests in the West, the lack of any coherent approach, the lack of respect for local populations, and the lack of any serious analysis of what the "military solution" was likely to achieve.[38]

Recently the UN has tried to address many of these issues.[39] A greater emphasis is being placed on integrated and agile approaches, coordination of efforts, early warning systems, and taking a broader perspective on prevention, including for instance building up legitimate institutions and assisting more locally-led and participatory conflict transformation processes.[40] Yet many challenges remain with all of this, and just because better UN frameworks exist doesn't mean that governments are taking action and providing predictable and sustained funding for prevention.

One challenge may be a lack of clarity about whose job it is. Imagine if we wanted to go to war but no government body had the responsibility to make the call, and planning our engagement was divided across dozens of different departments. Our military would be inefficient and couldn't do much. Most countries have highly coordinated militaries, yet few have a similar body tasked with developing strategic and coordinated non-military actions to prevent mass atrocities. An international campaign is calling for governments to establish Ministries of Peace,[41] an intriguing idea for improving the capacity and will to engage in prevention.

For most of this book we've looked at what influences us as individuals, so it's important to highlight again that wars and mass atrocities are very different from interpersonal conflicts. Certain factors we might think of as important in predicting where atrocities will happen—ethnic tensions, frustrations leading to scapegoating—don't seem to matter much. Political scientist Scott Straus has summarized the evidence about predicting atrocities, as well as possible approaches to preventing and responding to them. Most responses don't require the military.[42] In the chapters to come, we'll look at a few of these.

## Tips from This chapter

1. Our faith in war is, at a deep level, influenced by religious faith. This persists even among secular people and nations. Christian Just War theory is the most influential theory claiming wars can be moral. There are many problems with Just War theory, and the World Council of Churches has formally rejected it.

2. Because wars are complex systems, a linear checklist of responses is often ineffective. Recently, greater efforts have been put into defining and developing strategies for prevention, but governments urgently need to take this more seriously, which

may be slow to happen as long as no government body sees it as its responsibility.

3. The best time to engage with a war is decades before it starts, but at each turn responses can make matters better or worse. Better responses require a coherent approach, respect for local knowledge and needs, and careful reflection on the likely impacts of all actions.

## Example: Healing and Rebuilding our Communities

In an extremely tense environment and reeling from genocides, Quakers in Burundi and Rwanda ask for outside help. Proposals begin to coalesce around the need for healing from trauma. One program starts bringing people together to discover their inner resources. This is based on the methods of Alternatives to Violence Project (AVP), an informal and often powerful process developed in the '70s by Quakers volunteering in prisons. Friend John Shuford offers a reason why AVP is often so well received: "Within it lie the seeds of peace—building community through connection."[43] In difficult environments like prisons, people often feel the need to be tough to survive, and they long for a chance to be vulnerable, as Sammy Rangel talked about. In Burundi and Rwanda, new workshops are developed, turning AVP into the work of Healing and Rebuilding Our Communities (HROC).

Imagine being invited to sit down in a circle knowing that across from you will be someone who killed your family member. Not all HROC workshops do this, but in some cases, that's what happens. Amazingly—with its conviction that something good can be found in everyone—HROC proves popular. People are hungry for it. Facilitators are trained in trust-building activities and responding to trauma, helping participants move through it without being retraumatized.

Why does HROC matter to people? Béatrice Mukayiranga shares her story. A Rwandan Tutsi, Mukayiranga recounts,

Life before the war was good; there was enough food; I had friends, my family, and good neighbors. My father was a

veterinarian, and my husband showed people how to cultivate. I had a rich family. I got married in 1984, and had my
first child a year later. My whole family lived near me.

Nine years later Mukayiranga was forced to flee for her life with her
husband and children, taking refuge in the Shangi Parish, a local
church. But they weren't safe. Some of those hiding in the church
were murdered. "We stayed with the bodies of dead people for over
one month in the church," she explains. "One of my children was
already dead. I don't know how my other three children survived.
I felt I had to run, but I knew I could only take one of my children
with me. I didn't know whom to choose to save. My heart told me
to take my son." She and her five-year-old son tried to escape, but
were captured. Mukayiranga was raped and much later discovered
she had contracted HIV.

> I am now taking drugs, I have more other sicknesses like
> asthma. Sometimes I am allergic to the drugs; my legs get
> swollen, and my belly gets swollen. I try my best to get food
> and clothing, but we eat only once a day. I try to grow some
> crops, because I know I will leave my children behind. When
> you are sick you should be taken care of by your family, but I
> have no family left. Before, my family was many. But my four
> children, my father, my mother, six brothers, and two sisters,
> uncles, aunts, and many others in my family died....
>
> I used to have a continuous headache, and deep sorrow.
> I was angry when I saw people who were happy, I wet the bed,
> I always felt grief. But then I was with the people who hurt
> my family in the workshop. I can't remember all of them but
> they were many at the workshop. They killed people, and
> many of them asked for forgiveness, and we forgave them
> and now they are our friends. I personally forgave those who
> killed my people.... My anger has calmed down. My trauma
> symptoms are not finished, but they are not as strong. I
> thought I would seek revenge if I ever got the chance, but my

sorrow has lessened. I can now sleep and the fears that they were coming to kill me are all finished… I have accepted myself and accepted living with the killers. Other survivors who have not attended the workshop condemn us. People cannot understand how you can live with someone who killed your people; they say we are fools; they ask what the killers have given us to be forgiven.

Samuel Komezusense is a Rwandan Hutu, who recalls his involvement in the genocide:

They told me that I had to help. And because it was my family telling me that, I joined them, and many people died when I was there. After, we stole the dead people's belongings, burned their houses and divided everything. Those who remained fled to the Shangi Parish. I went there one day when the Interahamwe [the violent hate group composed mostly of Hutu youth] attacked, and they said that those who were still alive must be killed. More than 1,000 people died, and I was watching so that no one would escape.

After participating in this massacre, Komezusense fled to DR Congo. He returned to Rwanda two years later, and was imprisoned for six years.

In prison life was difficult, because food was not enough; there were many diseases, not enough space to sleep. Life was hard there. Some died of those diseases, and even myself I fell sick many times. I had severe stomach aches and had toothaches. I have few teeth in my mouth and am still poor because of my long imprisonment.

When Komezusense was released he was still in danger. "My family hated me because I mentioned what they had done. They poisoned my child, and he died in 1999… Once I was released, I had to move around a lot to escape from being killed."

Three years later, he was invited to an HROC workshop.

I was so impressed by these workshops. In fact I made a decision to seek the people I sinned against and ask forgiveness and help the survivors because I had caused their pain.... [Before HROC] I could not sleep. I could not eat and feel happy because I was always upset. I always had stomach aches, headaches, and after... I realized that I was traumatized. I had heard about trauma before through the government workshops, but this was the first time I understood. I was free to ask anything I didn't understand, and the facilitators were compassionate. Since then, the trauma is reduced. I can't say that it is finished, but I am not lonely. I have some people I can go to and tell them my problems, and I don't have the same headaches because I no longer spend sleepless nights, and I don't fear those I offended because [HROC] united me with them.

Now, if someone has a problem I can help him. If someone is asking for forgiveness I try to help him.... Each day I apply what I learned. The workshop has awakened me to teach others. I love genocide survivors and want to help those traumatized as I can. I put myself in the place of the survivors and look inside at my participation in what happened, so now I can be close to them and see their problems as my own. I have peace within myself and talk and have no fear. Now, I am human.[44]

These stories from both sides of the same nightmare at the Shangi Parish show both how horrible people can be, and how resilient. At their best, HROC workshops can help to re-establish a sense of mutuality, even respect. By no means will this work for everyone, but the transformations experienced by Béatrice Mukayiranga and Samuel Komezusense are not uncommon either. Their stories also illustrate how many pressures come at us to keep destructive cycles of violence alive. We often need to find our power-from-within to rebel. Abdul Kamara from Sierra Leone expresses the dilemma well:

My mother was very very disappointed in me seeing me doing this reintegration. She said, "What are you doing? These are the people who tortured you. These are the people who raped your sister. These are the people who burnt your house. And you know them. What are you doing? You are a disgrace." I found myself not knowing what to do whether to continue with my conviction to build peace or to do what my mother said.[45]

HROC is used today in Burundi, DR Congo, Central African Republic, Kenya, Nigeria, South Sudan, and Uganda.[46] Methods like this need to be further tested to find out when they work and when they don't. If the evidence continues to show successes, they need to be scaled up to reach those who are ready and longing for chances to heal.

# Unarmed Civilian Protection

*In severe conflicts, often moderates...are voiceless.*
*They can be exiled, intimidated, or threatened.*
*Citizen-based processes open space for voices*
*of moderation that have been silenced.*

— CATE MALEK[1]

FOLLOWING ITS TRAGIC failure in Rwanda, the UN has significantly revised its peace operations, including "investing in improved information and analysis capacities" and "improving guidance and training" for peacekeepers.[2] There are on-going challenges, but UN peacekeeping has been studied, and findings include that it can successfully reduce fatalities in conflicts.[3] Many would argue that more such peacekeepers are needed.

Have you ever wondered if *unarmed* people could keep each other safe in the midst of a civil war though? Most of us haven't, because it seems like a silly idea. Guns beat no guns every time. Yet in 2016 the UN started to recognize the importance of unarmed civilian protection, "a methodology for the direct protection of civilians, for localized violence reduction and for supporting local peace infrastructures."[4] In all war zones civilians play key roles distinct from UN peacekeepers (who receive military training and typically carry weapons). Civilians *think differently*—using relationship-based strategies instead of military ones.[5] Today there are a few academic institutions offering training in the methods used by civilians to protect each other, and interest in this approach is growing.[6]

Isn't going into war zones unarmed extremely dangerous? The data isn't too robust right now, but it may surprise you. There are dozens of organizations in the field, but the ones with careful records were able to provide data about 3,065 unarmed civilian protectors. Of these, only six died (one in a car crash not connected to civilian protection). "Comparing these numbers to the fatality rates of armed peacekeeping missions conducted by the United Nations shows that armed peacekeepers are 12 times more likely to die on duty than unarmed civilian peacekeepers."[7] It seems like the willingness to be vulnerable may itself offer a form of protection. There could be other reasons for this finding, and more research is needed, but the general point is that unarmed protection is risky but not as risky as we might assume. (Once again, faith in power-over, our idea that only threats of violence can keep us safe, may being misleading.)

International protection starts when a community asks for outside help. Systems of security and protection already exist in that community, so peace workers from around the world support and strengthen these existing systems (which may be ignored completely by UN peacekeepers). Protecting people takes responsiveness—using the right tools in the right moments. Art Gish gives an example from Hebron in the occupied West Bank. "I went up to one of the [Israeli] soldiers who had his gun in a Palestinian's face and calmly told him that it was impolite to point a gun at someone like that. He seemed rather stunned, and walked away."[8] This worked simply because Gish was present, a foreigner (had a Palestinian done the same thing it might not have gone well), and nonthreatening. He employed, in a high stakes situation, tips we've seen, like assuming good intent and acting to bring out the best self of the other party. He brought the soldier back to himself, reminding him of alternate values—much like the reminders we've seen help us not to cheat on tests. Gish was also letting the soldier know that he was not anonymous—his actions were being witnessed.

Related to this, civilian protection, like other forms of peacekeeping, often includes monitoring conflicts and documenting human rights abuses or crimes committed by all parties. Sharing quality information can help to counter the vicious rumors and othering that spreads and escalates violence.

Internationals also focus on supporting and strengthening local abilities to build peace. This includes helping people to understand and process what it means that violent conflict could last a long time,[9] training communities in the skills of protection, and, in some cases, civil resistance.[10]

There are many organizations involved in unarmed civilian protection, each with unique histories and approaches. I'll touch on three to show some of the similarities and differences. Nonviolent Peaceforce started in 2003 and pays peace workers to deploy for two-year terms.[11] They get theory training and go through many role-plays. Training specific to each country is provided on arrival to the country, where internationals learn local history, culture, and conflict dynamics. About 50% of Nonviolent Peaceforce's workers are women. It's non-partisan, secular, and has no affiliation with any government. Nonviolent Peaceforce aims to build relationships with all parties and to create space for them to work out their own solutions.[12] Its team will not stand in the way of bullets, but in rare circumstances where relationships are strong enough, peace workers may physically stand between warring parties to prevent an attack from starting. As they accompany people who are at risk, Nonviolent Peaceforce workers make regular risk assessments, planning the safest timing and routes of movement, and deciding in advance on what actions to take in response to different threats.[13]

Christian Peacemaker Teams (CPT) began with spiritual reflection on the controversial idea that those committed to peace should be ready to die for it. CPT was established in 1984 by Mennonites, Brethren, and Quakers to bring the same discipline and commitment to the use of nonviolence that soldiers bring to war.[14] Unlike Nonviolent Peaceforce employees, CPTers aren't paid. Another key difference is that CPT doesn't try to be neutral. They see it as important to their work to "get in the way" of injustice through nonviolent interference. This means that CPTers may feel led to take more direct risks, like standing in the path of a tank or engaging in civil disobedience alongside locals.

As a faith-based organization, a key part of CPT's model is engaging churches and support groups internationally to advocate with their governments, challenging the roots of militarism.[15] When a CPTer returns home, they typically give presentations and remain active in raising awareness about human rights violations they witnessed.[16]

Similar to Nonviolent Peaceforce, CPT trains its peace workers to understand the processes at play in nonviolent conflict transformation. Role-plays help CPTers simulate extreme stress and danger and learn "to be as present as possible when guns are all around."[17] The training includes such details as the many different types of military equipment one might encounter and various protective responses depending on the situation.[18]

Why do people volunteer to risk their lives? Reasons given by CPTers include wanting new experiences, to pick up skills that will help in future careers, and to practice their religious faith. Here are some direct quotes:

- "I am a veteran, so I am not afraid of danger. I know the fruitless evil of war. I want to recapture the excitement of visiting a foreign land."
- "It is part of my family culture to take radical stands on peace issues. I feel inadequate when I am living sitting comfortably at home."
- "I felt spirit-led in this journey; there was an amazing smooth flow to it… It was intense and fatiguing for months, but also beautiful."
- "I want to learn better how to confront my fear of death by facing it."[19]

Peace Brigades International is another organization Quakers were involved with founding. Unlike Nonviolent Peaceforce, volunteers with Peace Brigades have played roles like unarmed bodyguard, intercepting hit squads and being ready to take a bullet to protect human rights lawyers.[20] Like CPT, Peace Brigades does communications and advocacy to encourage governments internationally to respond to human rights violations that peace workers document.[21] Today Karen Ridd is a valued part of the Quaker community in Winnipeg, Manitoba. Her incredible story from volunteering with Peace Brigades in El Salvador in 1989 illustrates both the perils and the creative ways that power-from-within can spur us to respond when lives are on the line:

> ...I was in a church refugee center, trying to protect the safety of Salvadoran refugees and church workers who were inside. The Salvadoran military invaded the center, scattered the refugees, detained the workers, and took me and four other PBI workers to the Treasury Police Jail. I was blindfolded, handcuffed, interrogated, kept standing without food and water, and threatened with rape and mutilation.
>
> This was a torture center; that much I knew. I had Salvadoran friends who had been tortured in this prison, and I could hear torture all around me. Under my blindfold I caught glimpses of people, broken, lying on the ground. But I also knew that I had lots of people watching what was happening to me. PBI had activated a "phone tree" through which people put pressure on the Salvadoran authorities and my own government in Canada using phone calls and faxes. I heard later that the President of El Salvador had called the jail twice himself that day. As the pressure mounted, the guards relented, and then said they would release me.
>
> I said "no."
>
> I had been imprisoned with Marcela Rodriguez Diaz, a Colombian colleague, and my North American life was being valued more than hers, so I refused to leave the jail without her. Instead I was re-imprisoned and stayed until we could both be released.
>
> The guards, their questions laced with sexual innuendo, challenged me: "Do you miss us?" they asked, "Do you want us?" "No...of course I don't want to be here," I replied, "but

you are soldiers, you know what solidarity is. You know that if a comrade is down or fallen in battle, you wouldn't leave them, and I can't leave my comrade, not now, not here. You understand."

I don't know what response I thought I would get. After all, I was speaking to a group of torturers.... if they agreed with me they would have to implicitly acknowledge our joint humanity. If they disagreed they would show—even to them-selves—that they were inhumane.

The guards went silent. Then after a long while one of them said, "Yes...we know why you are here." ...I had found a connection—a shared space of humanity—in which the threat of violence could be confronted without alienating those involved.[22]

This bold decision, with no guarantee it would work, put the guards in a position to be their best selves and to acknowledge their similarity with their captives. Ridd and Rodriguez Diaz were both released.

As with HROC, more work is needed to further define the optimal conditions and approaches to unarmed protection. When does it work and when does it not work? Can it help transform large-scale conflicts like civil wars? There have been some promising studies,[23] but unarmed civilian protection still hasn't been tried at the scale necessary to see what it can do. It seems to be part of what the world was searching for when countries said they wanted to use "peaceful means" before the "last resort" of military intervention. I hope to see these techniques rigorously tested and that their use will increase if they continue to prove effective.

## Tips from This Chapter

1. Without weapons, people are keeping each other safe and building conditions for peace at the grassroots. This work is heavily based on relationships and on strengthening existing security knowledge and skills. It's no more—and appears to be *less*—dangerous than armed peacekeeping. Various types of unarmed

protection have been developed but haven't been invested in enough at large scale to know what their full impacts can be.

## Example: Bear Clan Patrol

Winnipeg can be a dangerous place. In 2014 residents are deeply shaken by the discovery of the body of 15-year-old Tina Fontaine. This feels to many like "the last straw" in a system where different levels of government and police fail to promote Indigenous well-being and safety.

The Indigenous-led Bear Clan Patrol forms quickly, meeting once a week. Starting with 12 members, by 2017 it grows to more than 500, both women and men, taking direction from traditional teachings and practices.[24] Patrol members rally around their responsibility to provide security in a non-threatening and nonviolent way.[25] Their website explains, "It is an effort to restore to our community the capacity to address our own needs."[26]

Bear Clan Patrol volunteers maintain a visible presence on the streets, witnessing situations, working to de-escalate and transform conflicts, and most often just shaking hands and building relationships. The volunteers are trained to deal with a range of situations—everything from applying first aid to basic trauma counseling.

At first some community members are skeptical about Bear Clan Patrol, wanting to see whether or not it's serious and will show up when needed. Once the Patrol proves sincere, the community embraces it. Soon agencies and individuals are stepping forward to donate. Suddenly Bear Clan Patrol has medical equipment, medications to administer to people in the midst of drug overdoses, a van to extend the range of the patrols, and food to give out most nights. Bear Clan Patrol's model is now spreading to other cities and towns.[27]

## Activity: De-escalation on the Subway

1. Facilitators read off this explanation:

    It's easy to think that if we saw a hate crime unfolding we'd intervene. But in the moment, we might not feel like we know what to do. This activity is designed to give us a sense of how it *feels in our bodies* to intervene. We may need to repeat this practice many times. A body of evidence suggests that when we decide *beforehand* how we'll act in a challenging moment ("I won't just stand there and watch when I see someone shouting at a stranger; I'll intervene") we're much more likely to *actually* act when the situation arises.[28]

The bystander effect means when there are lots of people around, we might assume that someone else will step up, so we don't have to. We might also be unsure what to do, or afraid to make the situation worse.[29] As we've seen though, one person not conforming and instead taking action makes it much easier for others to join in. So be ready to go first! Try to make eye contact with the person being harassed and see if they look like they want assistance. If you're with others, let them know you're about to intervene. If you're alone, try making eye contact with other bystanders.[30] Make your presence known, and take cues from the people in the conflict, using your voice, choice of words, and body language to

- Distract—we've seen this tip already. Try to move attention around so the building animosity is dispersed. If the situation hasn't turned violent, asking a question to distract one of the people involved could be enough to de-escalate it.
- Direct—confront the situation directly but not so aggressively as to escalate it. This may involve a quiet but firm statement that reminds people they're being seen and brings out their best selves. (Remember Art Gish telling the Israeli soldier, "It's not polite to do that.") Note that it's usually a bad idea to touch someone who's angry, as even a light and friendly tap on the arm to get their attention may feel threatening.
- Delegate—ask for help from others present, drawing them in so they become more than bystanders.[31]

In pressure situations most of us tense up, breathing shallowly or even holding our breath. This puts our bodies on edge, so it's important to do what top athletes and public speakers do and consciously take deeper breathes that expand the belly, with longer exhales. This helps us stay present and more relaxed.[32]

2. Facilitators now ask for volunteers for a role-play: one person is a middle-aged man, one is a young woman, and three others are bystanders, one who will intervene and the others who may decide to or not, after watching the first one. Everyone else in the room is observing.

3. The scene is that the middle-aged man has decided the young woman is a lesbian and will start saying her lifestyle is disgusting. The woman is uncomfortable and looking around, but not responding directly.

4. Facilitators let the scene play out for two minutes and then pause it and ask each participant what they're feeling and why they did what they did.

5. Facilitators ask the rest of the group what they observed. Did the intervention work? Could anything have been done differently?

6. Facilitators can decide to try other variations of this scene—for instance if a young man is taunting a blind person who's shouting back, or if the abuse is racial and the parties have started pushing each other. (I'd recommend facilitators instructing no actual pushing, just miming it without making contact.)

# Mediation

*A tense and watchful atmosphere of
almost universal mistrust may easily develop.*

— ADAM CURLE[1]

WHO HASN'T gotten into an argument and turned to a trusted third party for help? When you were young maybe you went to a teacher or family member to tell your story and get a power-over decision about whose version of events was right and who needed to be punished. There are processes along similar lines for adults—arbitration for instance. Often used in small-scale disputes that would otherwise go to court, the parties talk to arbitrators (an individual or a panel) to have a settlement imposed. Arbitrators don't try to get the parties to understand the conflict differently or propose ways to positively transform their relationship—it's a simple directive approach.

A different one is mediation, which isn't about defining "what really happened" or assigning or implying blame.[2] Mediation tries to transform the conflict, which demands that both sides have some interest in transformation. (I'll just write as if the conflict has two parties, although we know it's often more complicated!) If one side is stubbornly convinced that they can continue and win outright, the time isn't right for mediation. However, in large-scale conflicts like wars, efforts are *always* underway to build relationships with both sides, to break down "us" and "others" thinking, and to remind leaders of their positive aspirations and values. Then when

the time for mediation arises, it can sometimes make a big difference. Mediators don't just focus on politicians either, they engage
in other "tracks," involving civil society, business leaders, and key
religious figures.[3]

Having served in the military as a major, Adam Curle, a Quaker
who achieved great successes as a mediator, was anything but naive
about violence. Yet he was also able to meet with leaders making
choices that killed hundreds of thousands, while showing them sincere *respect*. Think back to the studies of complex thinking where
psychologists bring people with strongly opposing ideas together
in the lab. It was feeling *both* challenged by the other person's ideas
*and* feeling genuine warmth for them as a person that predicted
conversations that the participants felt were worth having. In high-
pressure situations in the real world, mediators like Curle often do
just that. "In order to have an effective relationship with someone
in this mediatory context, I must have a positive feeling for them.
To the extent that I go to meet them with hidden reservations, con-
cealing my revulsion with smooth diplomatic words, the meeting
will be a failure..."[4] Curle contends that the parties in the conflict—
in his case presidents and military generals—operate in incredibly
high-pressure circumstances with many conflicting demands coming at them. In this hugely stressful position, they're generally just
making the decisions they know how to make, and the mediator
can't silently loath them for it.[5]

Representing a different view in a very different context, Teresa
Wakeen, who has successfully mediated thousands of interpersonal
disputes, says she often has negative feelings for one of the parties
and that neutrality is a myth. While mediators can't actually be
neutral, according to Wakeen, they can explain to both parties, and
honestly act on, their ethical duty not to impose their personal judgments on the process they're mediating.[6]

Due to their belief that each of us has something sacred inside
*regardless of what terrible things we might have done*, Quakers have
often been drawn to the role of mediator. When not representing
governments, they sometimes access places where officials are

blocked, maintaining low profiles so talks are easier to keep confidential. This lets the parties engage in mediation without the fear of public accusations of being traitors who talk to the enemy. Quakers and other faith-based mediators also have the advantage of being seen as motivated by a spiritual desire to help, where official mediators can seem to have secret agendas from the governments that sent them.[7] One downside to the involvement of informal mediators can be a lack of coordination, though, where different people all mediating in the same conflict wind up working at cross purposes.[8]

There are many types of dialogue, and mediation isn't the same as another famous one—negotiation, where parties put forward proposals. However, in war, parties don't often talk directly, so mediators can carry offers to negotiate back and forth. The important point is that the mediator is just the messenger, not making the proposals, which could make them seem biased and dangerously compromise relationships. Sometimes what gets called "mediation" *is* actually just power-over negotiation by government emissaries. ("Take this action which my government wants and you will be rewarded by a fat loan or a squadron of new fighter-bombers; don't take it and aid will be cut and the planes will be given to your rivals."[9]) At other times, mediation and other forms of dialogue initiated by third-party governments may be more focused on building relationships of trust and on addressing needs. The UN claims such mediation has helped ease tensions in countries from Guinea to Kyrgyzstan.[10]

Whatever the approach, mediation becomes much harder when killing starts, because images of the blood of "us" spilled by "others" have a powerful psychological impact.[11] Like with unarmed civilian protection, mediators' continued presence can help break through information bubbles and confirmation biases, reminding both parties of just how horrible what's happening really is. This isn't done by reproaching the parties for being involved in killing but by telling them the ugly facts they want to avoid. Mediators persistently raise the existence of alternative options. This usually fails to end wars, but often achieves smaller successes, like helping facilitate the exchange of prisoners.[12] Conditions in the conflict can change suddenly, and when they do, the peace virus spreads, in part thanks to the groundwork of better relationships built through mediation.

In spite of their important role, mediators are unpopular. One major pushback tends to come from younger fighters. Since they've just started, they're less war weary and want to prove themselves in battle so they can work their way up the ranks. Peace would threaten their chances for status and career advancement.[13] Mediation is also unpopular with people on both sides who say mediators don't care about justice, they're just working to restore order (negative peace).[14] Rage at the enemy may also turn into rage at the mediator, who's known to have formed a respectful relationship with the enemy. William Ury describes an instance of being berated as he facilitated talks between Russia and Chechnya. He calmly thanked the speaker for his comments, framed them as expressing a positive intent, and redirected the conversation back to the goal of the meeting. The tone in the room quickly became more productive.[15] Being a mediator can mean having to take insults in stride!

It's fairly obvious that a major block to this work is egos. We often assume that talking to our enemies makes us weak, or, as Sammy Rangel puts it, "Listening is often mistaken for conceding something…"[16] There's a common worry about being co-opted, that engaging with the other side means settling for their way (the accommodating conflict style) or legitimizing what they're doing. As we've touched on, it *is* possible for formal peace processes to give warring parties an appearance of seeking peace that actually helps them maintain injustices, but unpublicized talks can't provide this cover. And a bad *negotiator* may be taken advantage of or wind up giving up too much, but just listening to someone is very different from negotiating with them or legitimizing their actions. On this point Curle is firm: "I must have contact with the individuals who carry responsibility if we are to have any chance of affecting a total situation in which thousands or indeed millions of people on both sides, most of them having nothing whatsoever to do with the conflict, are suffering. To fail to do this because of scruples about the morality of those I have to talk with would be the most gross form of self-indulgence."[17] This question raises again the issue of strategic responses versus ones that make us feel powerful. It might be pleasing to ignore the architects of brutal wars but not ultimately useful in transforming those wars.

There's another firm belief that makes mediation a real challenge. During conflicts, we're bombarded by messages about how the other side is pure evil, crazy, and can't be negotiated with. Yet we've already looked at how recruits from Daesh to members of white supremacist hate groups aren't just "crazy," and talking to them is very possible.[18] However disturbed a group's ideologies, if they've managed to form a group it means they have the ability to create and function in complex social structures, so they're mentally capable of thought and discussion, and they have interests. All armed groups need weapons, equipment, financial services... As individuals there are times when continuing a conversation may not make sense, or may even be dangerous for us—say, if we're trying to escape an abusive relationship. But, as much as dialogue could be frustrating and fruitless, *governments* or *armed groups* in conflict *are always communicating anyway* and aren't made safer by cutting off dialogue. Experienced negotiator Joshua Weiss explains:

> During times of crisis and conflict, more communication is needed, not less.... When negotiation is absent it is important to remember that communication does not stop, but that messages are sent with actions open to multiple interpretations. During tense large-scale conflicts between nations, when mistrust is high, most actions taken are assumed to be belligerent.

We're back to the tapping game with one party trying to guess the other's song. The guesses are assuming bad intent and looking only for ways to confirm that assumption, and there's no talking afterward to explain what the song was! A real-world example Weiss offers is one where the stakes could not have been higher—the "Cuban Missile Crisis" of 1962.

Despite incessant prodding by his military advisors that there was no other course of action but a preemptive strike, President Kennedy...kept a back channel negotiation open with the Soviet Union. It was that negotiation that kept the situation from escalating out of control. Kennedy's overriding interest was to prevent nuclear war, have the missiles removed from Cuba, and save face for the US and he did that as well as meeting the needs of the Soviet Premier Khrushchev.[19]

We've focused on large-scale violence where mediation is a major challenge and successes like this one are sadly rare. So let's close on an encouraging note—we know how valuable peacebuilding at the grassroots is, and mediation at this level can be much easier. Experts report that in situations involving a small number of people, often "one or two mediation sessions can turn around long-standing conflicts."[20]

## Tips from This Chapter

1. Dialogue takes various forms, one of which is mediation. When used in wars, it regularly wins smaller victories and only rarely helps produce lasting peace. Still, mediation can keep opposing sides informed of what's really happening on the ground, and may help reduce the levels of brutality. It's not about assigning blame but rather is a slow process of relationship building, reminding each party of their values and trying to pry open their narrow frames and information bubbles so they see other possible ways forward.

2. Mediation relies heavily on trust in the mediator. It could even demand that mediators feel genuine warmth for the people they're working with, regardless of who they are. This is one of many factors that make mediators' jobs difficult and that can make mediators unpopular.

3. Not all situations are right for dialogue, but in large-scale conflict there's no good reason not to talk to the other side, whether through third parties or in other formats, off-the-record when

necessary. Whether or not we're talking directly, we're communicating through our actions, and these get interpreted in ways that escalate the conflict, where direct communication can clarify our positions and reduce the impacts of rumors. Talking to others is not the same as conceding to their demands.

## Example: Concerned Citizens for Peace

*Many of our greatest victories are what doesn't happen: what isn't built or destroyed, deregulated or legitimized, passed into law or tolerated in the culture.*

— REBECCA SOLNIT[21]

Our world is full of violence. Yet all around us inner and interpersonal conflicts are being transformed in positive ways. Potential violence is regularly avoided with skillful and timely action. Many wars do not happen. These stories don't get told. An event that kills several people will generate far more attention than peacebuilding work that saves the lives of tens of thousands. Here's a story from Kenya worth celebrating.

It's 2008 and in the wake of a deeply divisive election that many feel was rigged, violence is taking the country "to the brink of destruction."[22] More than 40 people are being killed a day. Ethnic conflicts—attacks and counter-attacks—are escalating. Sexual violence is being used as a weapon of intimidation. Property destruction is widespread. Half a million people are displaced from their homes.[23]

Five prominent and experienced peacebuilders decide to meet and develop a plan. Calling themselves Concerned Citizens for Peace (CCP), they examine the situation and agree that the stories people are hearing are encouraging violence. So they plan out a new strategy focused on changing the narratives and creating opportunities for dialogue. But how can this be done? As a small informal group, *CCP has no budget!*

The five start by committing themselves to a process. They'll host an open meeting each day in the same spot at the same time and use it to plan their next moves. They identify those most vulnerable to the peace virus—people who are already active with peace-oriented organizations. CCP invites them to the daily open meetings.

Soon, networks are being built between all sorts of existing groups (including Kenyan Quakers) who are each already concerned about the deteriorating situation. These groups have many resources, but they haven't been linking up with each other. The outbreak of violence in Kenya could have caused each to turn inward for security, but instead they meet together at the daily open meetings and a shared vision is born—the *Citizens' Agenda for Peace*. One of the participants, George Wachira, describes the meeting that generated this peace agenda: "The spirit in that room was so touching and moving. I have never been through such a wonderful deep spiritual experience."[24]

The groups use their contacts to approach the media and—*success!*—they get peace messages onto primetime TV and radio. They also get the media to agree not to air any more hateful content. They convince a major phone provider to text all subscribers "calling on them to be peaceful and to shun hatred and tribalism."[25]

Famous Kenyan musicians are recruited to spread peace messages.[26] City officials in Nairobi give their support for creating and training local "citizen's peace committees." CCP meets the heads of universities, schools, and student associations to engage them in stopping hateful messages and working actively for peace. Business leaders are approached and brought on side. Finally, as the violent climate starts to shift, CCP uses relationships with politicians to help secure a formal mediation process. CCP continues to engage throughout the mediation, representing civil society views.[27] In the end, the civil war that seemed imminent *does not happen*.

# Peace Education

*Traditionally, little encouragement has been given to
young people to take responsibility for resolving conflicts,
to look for "win-win" solutions.*

— SUE BOWERS and TOM LEIMDORFER[1]

WHY IS THIS book necessary? I'm glad you're reading it, but the skills we've been building—communication, conflict analysis and transformation, self-care—are widely useful and could be a *focus* of our education systems. Education is absolutely fundamental to who we are and how we think, so we could all benefit from a world with high-quality *peace* education! Whether formal or informal, peace education comes to life when it focuses on the countless areas directly relevant to our day-to-day lives—topics like being in conflict constructively.[2] Countless examples exist: peace clubs in schools; education to identify and counter gender-based violence and family violence; peer mediation; meditation programs (which have been studied and found to have some positive effects on regulating stress, processing difficult emotions, and improving academic performance[3]); livelihoods programs to offer skills and employment; sports, arts, and culture programs with a focus on human rights and healthy community building...

In these varied forms of education, *how* peace is taught might be as important as the content. One major challenge to formal peace education is that it happens in schools steeped in hierarchical power-over. Parker Palmer explains: "The real threat to community in the classroom is not power and status differences between teachers and students but the lack of interdependence that those differences encourage."[4] In effective programs, teachers would focus on building interdependence—trusting power-with relationships—with students, parents, and other faculty, instead of just getting through the curriculum. The pressures on teachers can be immense, but peace education ideally demands that instead of presenting themselves as experts with all the answers, teachers be a bit more open, vulnerable, and inquisitive, which invites students to do the same.[5] "The learner often doesn't want an answer."[6] Instead, in some subjects in particular, we can gain a lot by experimenting, playing, and unpacking ideas. I think peace education is particularly powerful when it's *experiential*. Hopefully you've had the chance to do some of the activities in this book and you agree!

Even when schools are on board and teachers have the skills, outside of school, family and cultural influences can undermine the learning at every turn. Yet in spite of these challenges countless kids do absorb the peace virus. How does this happen? What makes peace education programs effective? Although peace education curriculums are in use around the world, many haven't been systematically evaluated. Testing their effectiveness requires both testing that students learned the content and that it was useful to them, that they applied it to spread peace. Studies have shown that many peace education programs are statistically effective, but some aren't.[7] For instance, an evaluation of a peace education program involving 1,500 students in Colombia, Nepal, and DR Congo showed that they became more active citizens, held fewer discriminatory views, and reported less violence and a more peaceful immediate environment around them, which they were contributing to. When the programs were at their most infectious, students were motivating each other, parents were brought on side to support their children's involvement, and local peace leaders were serving as active role models.[8]

Too much emphasis may be placed on education initiatives in isolation though. Mercy Corps has done studies of youth recruitment into hate groups and political violence in Afghanistan, Colombia, and Somalia. Their research finds what we've seen before: "The principal drivers of political violence are rooted not in poverty, but in experiences of injustice: discrimination, corruption and abuse...Young people take up the gun not because they are poor but because they are angry." They found that education, without necessary systemic changes, can *increase* this problem. Youth given job training by well-meaning nonprofits, but then unable to find jobs, often become *more frustrated and alienated*. And programs that aim to engage youth in civic causes, when delivered without addressing issues like government corruption, "may simply stoke youth frustrations with exclusive, elder-dominated formal institutions. This may explain why we found civically engaged youth to be more supportive of armed opposition groups, not less."[9] Education to help youth think in more complex ways, recognize biases, and moderate their faith in violent power-over might be helpful, as might training to nonviolently and strategically tackle corruption and injustices head on.

So that's education for youth and young adults, but peace education need not stop there. We learn throughout our lives, and every profession could benefit from skilled nonviolent communicators, conflict transformers, and people well versed in the elements of peacebuilding. There's one particularly important profession that's come up many times in this book, so let's touch on it—journalism. Journalism of the highest caliber is readily available to those of us with uncensored access to the internet, and it's helping the peace virus spread. I've drawn on the hard work of many journalists in writing this book. Some risk their lives to make sure important stories get told. Still, "peace journalism" is far from mainstream, and a great deal of the news we're exposed to doesn't serve us well. An activist considering a strategy for getting media attention expresses much of the problem: "Your coverage will often be limited to a two-minute clip that emphasizes an action more than its purpose."[10] Economics and attention spans are major issues, but I think how journalists are educated matters too.

In considering why we don't have more "peace journalism," Peace and Conflict Studies professor Jake Lynch explains, "News generally prefers official sources to anyone from the "grassroots"; event to process; and a two-sided battle for supremacy as the basic conflict model."[11] Educating journalists to report this way protects them from seeming biased yet also establishes a narrow frame based on assumptions we may be skeptical of by now. It's easy to ignore topics like the *quality* of the peace actions being attempted during a war, focusing instead on *quantities* like the number of bombing missions run or the number of combatants and civilians killed, leaving the illusion of being scientific while offering no depth of explanation. Reporters tend to stick to grisly details and get quotes from governments and opposition leaders while avoiding *key* questions: Where is this conflict coming from? How can it be transformed? What peacebuilding efforts (like those we read about from Concerned Citizens for Peace in Kenya) are happening? Journalists don't need to have *answers* to these questions, they just need to seek out and ask a range of people with relevant perspectives.[12]

Perhaps the biggest problem is that most journalists are taught or implicitly accept a flawed vision of what conflicts are and how they can be transformed. False "common sense" about power-over is uncritically presented again and again. We've seen the importance of complex and nuanced thinking, and the media have a major opportunity to present stories that promote it. Stories about conflicts are often framed by picking up on and amplifying points of disagreement, but journalists could do more to highlight points of common ground and of persistent uncertainty, assisting the public to become more curious and less hyper-confident and entrenched.[13]

## Tips from This Chapter

1. Peace education is offered formally and informally to people of all ages all over the world. It faces significant challenges, including building power-with learners and counteracting other forms of unpeaceful education and socialization! Peace education in isolation from work to address social problems like

corruption can actually make us feel more isolated and angry. However various studies have shown that peace education can be very helpful when done with care; for instance, it could include bringing teachers and parents onside, supporting youth to work together and motivate each other, and actively engaging mentors.

2. The education of many professionals, including journalists, suffers from narrow framings and thinking driven by simplistic binary logic. Peace education can have a positive impact on people entering these professions, but there are many challenges in overcoming entrenched practices like quoting official sources and reporting on numbers of casualties instead of asking questions about why a war is happening and what the quality of the peace process is.

## Example: Power with the Smallest Children?

There are many great models of early childhood education. One that's particularly peace oriented is the Montessori method. Working in Italy as a doctor, Maria Montessori felt that kids had more potential than was commonly assumed. Witnessing the impacts of war and the rise of fascism, Montessori also came to feel that children could be key in spreading peace.[14] She asked the question, How can children be supported in their development so they reach their full potential? For years she investigated children's needs and capacities and developed a way for them to regulate themselves and their shared environment—from the age of three![15]

Montessori designed, tested, and continually revised an enriching space full of distinct materials. With guidance from adults, children learn to use the materials and choose the ones they're drawn to, working with them to develop their skills at their own pace. Montessori's system wasn't about telling kids what they should do but rather consistently modeling it for them.

Quite the opposite of drawing all the attention to the most powerful figure in the room—the teacher—Montessori wrote, "The greatest sign of success for a teacher...is to be able to say, 'The children are now working as if I did not exist.'"[16] Her method is consistent with various findings shared in this book, such as that our environments deeply impact the decisions we make and that the way others see and treat us can bring out our best selves.

As in the real world, a finite number of materials are available in the Montessori environment. This means conflicts over who gets to use what are inevitable. When children discover that someone's taking too much for themselves, or that others are asking for a material to be shared but they'd like to hang onto it, they have to figure out what to do. Montessori believed that when kids are trusted to solve their own problems they're capable of a great deal and that stepping in, or making children's paths free of conflict, mostly hinders their development. The method isn't just "anything goes" of course. The room is meticulously planned out and there are many expectations children must learn when working with each other and the materials. Key to this is that nothing is arbitrarily decided by the "adult in charge," and expectations remain constant and apply to everyone equally.

When conflicts arise, children might come to the teacher, looking for an authority. But the teacher won't be playing the role of arbitrator or getting anyone in trouble. Teachers guide children to find out what they want and to discuss it. If a child complains, "She's using all the water and I want some to clean the tables myself," the teacher may respond, "I can see that. What could you do about it?" Initially, the teacher may need to provide options. Eventually, the child will learn to come up with these on her own. Children may still want support in carrying out their ideas, which teachers happily give if asked. ("Can you come with me to talk to her?") This process could be very slow as children think through their options, so teachers give them lots of time.

Let's look at an example. Most Montessori classrooms purposefully won't have enough chairs for everyone, so if a child wants to work at a table and there are no free chairs, they're left with a decision: demand that someone give them a chair, push someone off of a chair, stand near someone using a chair and wait for them to finish, choose to work on something else, ask someone using a chair to let them know when they're done. (These options might remind you of the different conflict styles we looked at.) What's important is that the child goes through the process of deciding which action to take and then lives the natural consequences of that decision. That way, children learn both that they're independent and that they're part of a community where their actions have consequences not just for themselves but for others.

That lesson is also reinforced by the way the room is set up, with children from three to six years old all together. If you're not familiar with kids, that might not sound like a big difference, but a typical three-year-old and six-year-old are in very different places in their development. This age mix guarantees that there's a mix of needs and abilities in the room. It means that older kids learn to help younger ones, showing them how to care for the room and keep the materials in good order, and younger ones learn to seek assistance from peers and not just authority figures.

What about when a child is acting out? A teacher might spot a child pouring water on the ground and ask if they'd like help. The teacher guides the child toward constructive choices by presenting favorable options and allowing the child to choose between them: "Are you going to tidy the spill on the table or the floor first?" Using passive voice frames this not as a problem with someone to blame but as a situation to change. Asking the question with enthusiasm helps the child not to think of this as a chore or punishment but simply something to do, just like any other task. Many of us assume kids are just like mini-adults, so if we don't like cleaning they must dislike it too and need to be coerced into it. But children aren't just mini-adults, and whatever the task, if we ask in an excited way, very often they'll be happy and excited about doing it. In this case the framing gives the child the opportunity to learn about the consequences of spilling without feeling judged. The process is designed to promote a sense of responsibility, of having value, and of being trusted. We've seen how important it is to have a sense of purpose and control in our lives, and these can be fostered at a very young age!

What about one child picking on another? A girl is poking a boy's arm, and the boy clearly doesn't want it to be happening. The teacher might come over and ask the boy, "Do you like it when she pokes your arm like that?" to which he shakes his head. The teacher provides language for the boy, "You can tell her that you don't like that and to please stop." He might repeat, "I don't like that. Please stop." Then, turning to the girl, the teacher could ask, "I can hear him saying he doesn't like that. Can you hear him?" Most often, the undesired interaction stops there. If it persists, the teacher can use a tip we've seen and change the situation, asking for the girl's help in doing something else. If it becomes an ongoing issue with the same girl, the teacher may suggest that they sit together in a certain spot and observe the other children in the classroom for a while. This is never described as punishment, so it doesn't tend to generate resentment or pushback.

What may be harder for some of us to understand and accept is that the Montessori method also avoids rewards. We looked early on at some of their drawbacks, but it might still seem heartless to deny rewards to adorable little kids. Maria Montessori found that children happily pick up social values like helping each other but are *less* excited to do so if they're told they should or if they're rewarded. In a sense, every time you praise a child for something they did, *you're taking it away from them*—it's no longer their own accomplishment based on their own decision. So Montessori teachers are instructed to be kind but neutral with feedback. When a child hands a teacher a drawing they've made they might hear, "It looks like you put a lot of effort into this. I could see you were really concentrating when you made it. How do you feel about it?" The teacher is showing the child that their efforts are noticed and appreciated but asking the child to make their own evaluations, not to crave the evaluations of others. Teachers are encouraging intrinsic motivation, so kids decide to draw because they're excited to and not because they want approval.

The result is a high degree of self-sufficiency, problem solving, and cooperation, instead of the competitiveness and chaos you might expect from a room full of 30 *young children* with only two or three adults!

Of course, there are challenges with all this. As with peace journalism, the Montessori method demands that teachers unlearn "common sense" power-over thinking and techniques. Also the role of the teacher can be exhausting, so it's probable that at times all of them forget about the ideal ways to be in the classroom and use some shortcuts like getting kids into trouble or praising them for being cute.

Another challenge is that Maria Montessori didn't copyright her name, so any school can advertise as using her method—whether or not the teachers or school administrators are trained in it![17] That said, entering a strong Montessori classroom is an immediate experience of the possibilities of working together to address our needs without coercive power. "There is respect for the environment and for the individuals within it, which comes through experience of freedom within the community."[18] Because some of us are thinking, "That sounds nice, but how do the students do?" it's worth mentioning that modern research findings about child development seem to support Montessori's observations, and studies of the method suggest that this power-with approach to education is indeed effective.[19] For instance, a randomized study placing children in either Montessori or regular public schools found "significant advantages for the Montessori students" on academic measures, as well as cognitive and social skills.[20]

## Activity: Peacebuilding Dreams

Facilitators ask the group to divide into concentric circles and speak to the following questions:
1. If your peacebuilding dream came true, in 10 years what would your life look like and what would you be doing?
2. Who has helped you the most to gain the peace skills you have today?
3. What kind of legacy would you love to leave?

## Activity: What is Peace?

We've already revisited what you wrote at the beginning of this journey, offering a chance to add to it in the middle. Now we're reaching the end.

1. Facilitators explain that this is a final wrap-up discussion. Facilitators read, or ask group members to read, the assumptions and questions about peace written previously.

2. Facilitators ask, "How has this process changed the ways you think, or the questions you have about peace? Has anything gotten easier or more difficult?"

3. After some discussion, facilitators ask one last question, "What will you commit to doing now to keep spreading the peace virus?"

# What Peace *Is*

*At its core, shared security is grounded
in what Desmond Tutu calls Ubuntu, an inherent
human connectedness that leads us to say,
"I am because you are."*

— American Friends Service Committee[1]

THE OXFORD LEARNER'S DICTIONARY calls peace a "situation or a period of time in which there is no war or violence in a country or an area" or "the state of living in friendship with somebody without arguing."[2] *Merriam-Webster's* definition is slightly broader:

> a state of tranquility or quiet: such as a) freedom from civil disturbance, b) a state of security or order within a community provided for by law or custom; harmony in personal relations; a state or period of mutual concord between governments; a pact or agreement to end hostilities between those who have been at war or in a state of enmity.[3]

Perhaps the limitations of these definitions are now clear. Peace doesn't mean there will be no more arguments, and it's more dynamic than a state of tranquility or order. Going beyond the dictionary, we quickly get into rugged terrain. As we've seen, our minds tend to categorize, to think in terms of solid "things." We can readily picture a toy tank—a distinct little metal object, its dark green wheels rolling it along. Peace is not just the opposite toy—a regrettably less exciting plastic dove that we don't really want as a birthday present. Peace is a process with endless value, but not one that's easy to make into a single tight talking point.

For thousands of years cultures have devised ways to maintain harmony and social cohesion, often through various forms and amounts of power-with. Cultures each have their own skills and contexts, but there have always been people practicing what Johan Galtung invented a word for in the '70s—"peacebuilding."[4] Governments only began to get in on the act and formally think about a "culture of peace" at the International Congress on Peace in the Minds of Men in Côte d'Ivoire in 1989.[5] Since then, countless definitions have been proposed. We started off with the exercise of examining what peace isn't, to help define the negative space, hopefully bringing the positive into better focus through showing its edges. I'd like to suggest that both surfaces will remain hazy and in constant motion, but we've considered enough angles on peace questions now that we may be ready to offer a positive definition without getting too hung up on it, or threatened by how it challenges what we take as common sense.

Galtung offers a succinct definition: "Peace is what we have when creative conflict transformation takes place nonviolently."[6] But his definition of violence is vast, including any "avoidable insults to basic human needs."[7] In additional to what he calls "cultural violence" and overt physical violence, he names two types of structural violence: exploitation and repression. He contrasts these with two types of structural peace: economic justice (the opposite of exploitation) and political justice (the opposite of repression).[8]

For Adam Curle, "Peaceful relationships would be ones in which the various parties did each other more good than harm; whereas unpeaceful ones would be those doing more harm than good."[9] This seems to offer more gray areas and messiness, less of a simple binary.

In terms of peace*building*, British Quaker Simon Fischer was lead author of a book that defined it as "undertaking programmes designed to address the causes of conflict and the grievances of the past and to promote long-term sustainability and justice."[10] Today some academic institutions keep the definition of peacebuilding narrow, while others include its broader implications. For example Johns Hopkins calls it

> a process that facilitates the establishment of durable peace and tries to prevent the recurrence of violence by addressing root causes and effects of conflict through reconciliation, institution building and political as well as economic transformation. Peacebuilding initiatives are not limited to the post-conflict environment. Most of the tasks described above are effective tools to prevent conflicts.[11]

The University of San Diego adds, "Peacebuilding is founded on an ethic of interdependence, partnership, and limiting violence.... Peacebuilding creates spaces where people interact in new ways, expanding experience and honing new means of communication."[12] The Quaker United Nations Office offers, "Peacebuilding is both the development of human and institutional capacity for resolving conflicts without violence, and the transformation of the conditions that generate destructive conflict."[13] Definitions like these all get at the challenge that peacebuilding has a structural side (creating conditions to prevent harms) and a responsive side (like taking action to halt atrocities once they're underway). There's overlap, but the tools needed vary greatly depending on the specific situation.[14] In 2016 the UN went from a narrow understanding of peacebuilding to a broader focus on "sustaining peace," which it called both "a goal and a process to build a common vision of society." Among other things, sustaining peace recognizes the importance of prevention of violence through addressing its root causes and involving a wider range of people in peace processes.[15]

Think about your own definition at the start of this book, and the questions you had. Have your opinions changed? Does reading these various definitions make new sense now, or do you just have new questions?

One Quaker Meeting, while looking at the Responsibility to Protect, suddenly realized just how immense this discussion was:

> We would have to look at building a culture of peace, and relate that to our relationships with each other, abuse issues, war, etc. How could we do this and not get the whole subject so diffuse that we are overwhelmed into non-action? The bigger and wider you make the discussion, the less you can focus on the immediacy of an issue.[16]

I hope this book has helpfully danced between big and far-reaching discussions and immediately applicable ideas and techniques. I hope you've experienced thoughts and exercises for living out and spreading the peace virus, whatever that means for you.

## Tips from This Chapter

1. There are many definitions of peace and peacebuilding. One challenge is that peace is actually so vast it can be difficult to discuss or act on. Another challenge is ideas about peace as a static end goal or a quiet hiding place where people aren't in conflict. Our world isn't like that, so the peace virus has to be spread here and now, not by waiting for "a state of tranquility" or an end to arguments.

2. We may have started this process with many beliefs about peace. I've heard folks suggest it's boring, cowardly, passive, a fixed state, unnatural, impossible, arrogantly self-certain, elitist, and naively ill-informed. We've now examined the evidence and done exercises that help us experience the peace virus directly. It's up to us to decide what to believe about our potential for peace and what to do from here.

# What We Mean
# by a Culture of Peacebuilding

*The following is adapted from Canadian Friends Service Committee's definition, which I helped to write.[1] CFSC chose the uncommon term a "culture of peacebuilding" rather than the common "culture of peace" to highlight that, for us, peace needs to be continually built.*

We believe that peace is always possible. Neither peace nor violence is inevitable. Relationships and social and political structures can influence us toward peace or toward violence.

Whatever CFSC can do to encourage peace is part of peacebuilding. This is clearly a vast definition, rather than a narrow or technical one. Peacebuilding is work that Friends historically, and still today, feel led to. It's an expression of all of CFSC's values, rooted in the Quaker testimonies of peace, integrity, equality, simplicity, community, and respect for all creation.

CFSC thinks of three levels through which the culture of peacebuilding flows:

- inner peace—attitudes, beliefs, and habits conducive to peace
- interpersonal peace—peace in interactions with other people
- structural peace—political and social structures that support peace.

Each is simultaneously influenced by, and influencing, the others. Peace-oriented social and political structures will encourage more peaceful interactions between people. More interpersonal peace will help us achieve more inner peace. Structural peace will be promoted when we understand and value inner and interpersonal peace and use it to recognize, and seek to distance our societies from, violence.

Our definition of peacebuilding applies equally to any country, whatever its present relationship to violent conflict. Because the conditions around us play such a major role in the decisions we make, peaceful conditions must be continually built. This process is complex and unpredictable, so peace must be cultivated responsively and with care.

CFSC considers the following interconnected elements central to a culture of peacebuilding:

**Justice**—This includes well-balanced systems of laws and standards, conflicts being dealt with consistently, protection of dissent, and fostering respect for the full human rights, dignity, and participation of all. Social institutions can't be founded on principles of retribution, exploitation, domination, or unsustainable use of resources. Because we live in a global and interdependent community, justice includes right relationships with others (other individuals, communities, nations, and species). Problems can't just be exported elsewhere in the web of relationships.

**Opportunities**—We need culturally appropriate, safe, and ethical services and entry points into a life that holds meaning for us as individual and communities. This includes education and child services, health services, housing, livelihoods, proper sanitation, arts, nutritious food and safe water, chances for fun and games, a sustainable pace of life, places and time enough to connect with the natural world of which we are a part, and opportunities for spiritual expression. We need a sense of control in our lives, within fair boundaries.

**Active support for peaceful change**—Cultures are not static; new ideas and directions are always emerging. Tension is inherent in such change. All elements of society need loving and supportive care, and space must be made to listen and encourage positive changes on a continual basis, while also maintaining and invigorating important traditions.

**Skills**—to live peacefully takes skill. This include the abilities to
- notice and analyze:
  - recognize our power,
  - maintain complex thinking and avoid the urge to harmfully over-simplify our understandings,
  - perceive and address othering in its many forms (in language, cultural events, economics, news media, entertainment, curriculums, government policies…),
  - reflect on assumptions, biases, and prejudices (personal and others'),
  - recognize signs that violence is building internally or in others,

- spot injustices and violations of rights,
- model healthy relationships with ourselves (inner peace):
  - identify and recall our values,
  - deal with negative emotions and pain so as to remain emotionally present and aware,
  - forgive and let go when we're able, but not avoid or deny,
  - treat ourselves with care, knowing that harsh judgments and pushing ourselves too much can do significant harm,
  - handle discomfort, apparent chaos, and ambiguity without becoming overly distressed,
  - identify what makes us happy and focus our time and energy there,
- model healthy relationships with others (interpersonal peace):
  - communicate our feelings and needs and listen with curiosity, assuming good intent and being strategic in bringing out the best self of the other person,
  - admit mistakes, like when we cause harm or when our beliefs prove inaccurate,
  - respect sometimes slow change processes as we build relationships and power-with others,
- imagine and enact change (structural peace):
  - envision positive and creative alternatives to current narrow frames,
  - resist group pressures and justification of the status quo and work for win-win alternatives.

This list (and it's far from complete!) clearly shows that something will always be lacking, leading us away from peace. At CFSC we're practical in our approach. Conditions may never be perfect, but now is always a good time to take peacebuilding action.

We believe that from inner and interpersonal to structural peace, helping people gain some of the skills above will uphold our core goal: *to contribute to creating a culture of peacebuilding.* (I wrote this book in my work for CFSC with that goal in mind.)

# The Basics of Facilitation

The facilitator's role is to help the group discover and draw out its own peace wisdom and skills. We're far more likely to learn when we feel safe and comfortable expressing ourselves,[1] so facilitators seek to create an environment where people feel this comfort. Facilitators aren't experts or authority figures.

Don't be shy about asking the group for help. Find out when they'd like to meet, where, and for how long. Will decisions be made by consensus or another model? Will you do the activities in the order they appear in the book or jump around? Each time the group meets it's useful to have someone bring flipchart paper or sticky notes, tape, and a few different colors of pens or markers. Who will take this on? This experience can be co-created, and facilitators don't need to figure it all out.

### What do I do when I first get to the room?

Before your meeting starts, you may want to allow time for people to chat. Try to notice if someone's sitting alone or looking uncomfortable, and go up to them to shake hands and share a few words of welcome. Once folks have arrived and had the chance to say hi to each other, you could introduce yourself if folks don't know you yet and explain any logistics, like where washrooms are and to turn cell phones off unless there's a vital reason to have them on.

I facilitate in Canada, so I begin with a territorial acknowledgement to frame the event with recognition of the long tradition of connection between people and the land, and to acknowledge the Indigenous peoples whose territory the workshop is on. (If you don't know whose territory you're on, this can be an interesting topic for research!)

You might invite the group to settle themselves for a moment, asking participants to let go of distractions and worries they're carrying and to center inward, thinking about the common good. You might say something like, "Whatever you have to offer in the activities that follow, let's all work to let go of our individual worries for now and focus on what serves the common good, which is bigger than any one of us."[2]

Next you might remind people what's happening, saying something like, "We've agreed to meet here in a group for the next 90 minutes to do several exercises from *Are We Done Fighting?*, all from the section called Violence and Interpersonal Peace. These activities may be challenging, and I encourage you to check in with yourself. Try to push out of your comfort zone into your growth zone. But feel free to sit out if you find an exercise pushing you beyond growth and into panic." In the first session the group makes a learning contract, so for subsequent sessions it could be helpful reminding the group about it. (If your group is already abiding by the learning contract you may not feel the need to bring it up.)

### How do I introduce an activity?

Tell people in general what's about to happen (for instance, "We're going to do a concentric circles exercise, so please arrange the chairs in one small circle on the inside and one big circle on the outside and find a seat"). Then wait for people to arrange themselves. Now summarize the *details* of the activity. (Remind everyone what they are and aren't doing during concentric circles. Then read out the questions.) This process gives everyone a better chance of hearing and feeling comfortable with what's happening.

Some folks benefit from seeing the activity name, the key topic being addressed, and the time allotted, so you could write this on flip-chart paper. Tell everyone you'll give a time warning before wrapping up each activity. Then make sure to actually offer the warning!

This book proposes some activities, but you may decide to make changes. Perhaps instead of discussing a particular topic in concentric circles you feel that your group could benefit from doing it a different way:

- small groups working together to make funny skits, inviting them to enjoy the process and be silly (a great way to build community—it's helpful to remind everyone, though, that skits aren't about mocking particular people);
- a group of people with similar experiences sit in the center of a circle and tell their stories while others on the outside silently listen to gain a new perspective;
- simple role-plays, giving each character their key concern or motivation in the scene;
- people strolling around outside in pairs discussing a topic;
- a group cartoon to represent an issue...

This book doesn't include ice breakers because there are so many you can find by doing a search. If you're at all like me, as a kid you used to love games that you never think about today. It can be surprisingly powerful to have time to be playful again—drawing a picture of a monster you invented and explaining it to the group, throwing stuffed toys around as a signal of whose turn it is to speak. There are countless ways to get to know each other and build trust.

### How do I respond to people as a facilitator?

Too much direction could be stifling to learning, but too little can stress some folks out, meaning they won't participate fully. Your responses are meant to help people without rushing ahead to explain or neatly wrap up a learning moment.

It's helpful to be attentive and thank people any time they make a contribution. This validates their experiences. When you're facilitating a discussion where hands are going up, let people know you've seen them and they'll have a chance to speak. It's easier for folks to listen once their desire to speak has been acknowledged and they know they don't need to keep trying to get your attention.

Don't be afraid to express uncertainty and use active listening as the facilitator: "What I think I'm hearing is...is that right?", "How would that work?", "Can you expand on that a bit so I make sure I'm clear?" Take care not to signal disapproval either verbally or through your body language (turning away, frowning, raising your eyebrows).

Writing key points on flipchart paper can help folks who prefer visuals to stay focused and can help to build the collective memory. If you can, try to write short sentences, summarizing the idea and including just enough information that it would make general sense to someone who wasn't in the room.

### What if people are speaking too much or too little, or the group looks bored?

Groups of up to about nine can do discussions well. Any bigger than that and it's a good idea to divide up so that everyone has a better chance to stay focused and to speak.[3] If a few people are speaking a lot, you may be tempted to ask them not to answer for a while, but often it's better to focus on drawing out the non-participating members rather than dampening the enthusiasm of the chatty ones.

You can ask for further feedback: "Does anyone else have a story to share?" and hope to hear from folks who aren't speaking as much. But if you see specific people looking like they're uncomfortable or don't want to participate, assuming you just need to give them more time to come out of their shells might be a mistake. The longer the shy or hesitant folks go before hearing their own voices, the more work it'll be for them to engage later. So ask them a direct and open-ended question early on. Responding can help them notice and work through their own uncertainties. After they've shared once, they're more likely to do it again.

If you ask an open-ended question to the whole group, expect that you may need to leave silence while people ponder their responses. This can get uncomfortable! You feel the seconds ticking by agonizingly and may want to jump in and clarify the question or offer your own thoughts first because no one is speaking. Try to resist this. Silence is not necessarily a sign of boredom or that something is going wrong.

To have a sense of what's happening, try to read the group's energy levels. When they *are* starting to get tired or distracted, it may be time to ask people to stand up, pick a new chair, and sit there. Or you could try dividing into smaller groups to get more participation. Alternatively, you could offer a very short question, have everyone sit in a big circle, and do a go-around with no one responding to what others have said, just sharing their own reflections. Another thing you can try is moving or speaking more animatedly yourself, using bigger gestures to recapture the group's attention. Finally, you can ask people how they're feeling and decide to save an activity for next time if everyone's too tired.

### What if strong emotions come up?

This book covers painful material that many of us feel strongly about. Expect that people will come with different reactions, needs, goals (which may be assumed to be the group's goals!), and definitions of what the problems preventing the spread of peace are. These tensions might quickly come to light through activities like What Peace is *Not*.

If you feel like there's resistance to some of the ideas the group is discussing, one way to learn what people are feeling is to have them either write or share verbally the end to one or more of these sentences:

- Thinking about peace, I feel guilty when…[4]
- A situation that leads me away from peace is…
- I don't live up to my values when…
- What challenges me personally from this book is…
- One reason I support violence is…
- One thing I plan to do differently over the coming month because of what I'm learning is…

Ask people to finish the sentence with whatever is meaningful for them. If you choose to have people write their response to a sentence like what they plan to do differently in the coming month, it can be interesting for them to write the date down as well, and keep the sheet of paper to refer to.

Try to notice ways that the group may be processing strong emotions by marginalizing or shutting down certain members or topics of conversation or otherwise holding back. For instance, if someone breaks into tears, that might make other group members uncomfortable or unsure what to do. As the facilitator, just acknowledge the emotion. ("I can see this is painful for you to talk about, so thank you for expressing yourself.")

Any time you feel the conversation is too heated, you can call for silence to let the momentum pass and give people the space to think again about the common good. After a few moments of silence it may be a good time to invite group members to each write their responses to a question, allowing further inward focusing and personal reflection.

If aggressive conflicts arise, or if you have questions about what to do, remember to trust the group and check in with them. Say what you observed happening and how you feel, and ask how folks would like to proceed. Perhaps you'll need to change plans on the fly to have more time for debriefing an activity that generated strong responses.

Before everyone leaves the room, it's important that you close in a way that brings the group together again.[5] You could say, "I know that parts of the conversation today weren't easy, but I found them valuable because..." You could then have the group form a circle and hold hands in silence before everyone leaves, or sing an uplifting song together. (I don't like group singing personally, but many folks love it.) Remind participants as they're leaving that the exercises they've shared aren't just relevant in the group but to life tomorrow as well.

### What do we do after an activity?

At the end of each activity it's helpful to debrief. This can be done with a simple question like, "How was that for you?", "What did that feel like?", or "What do you plan to take away from that?" You could do a go-around of the whole group, invite popcorn style responses where anyone can speak in no particular order, or throw a ball of yarn around the circle so everyone sees their connections to each other after answering.

### What if the discussion gets chaotic?

If the discussion is going in two directions at once, you may need to acknowledge both topics and say that you'll focus on one for a moment, take a few people's thoughts about it, and then switch to talk about the other. If you don't do this, folks may feel confused or like they need to push to keep the conversation on their preferred topic. If there are more than two topics, you could summarize what you hear coming up and ask the group which topic they'd like to discuss first, while writing the others down for later.

If someone is being repetitive, help summarize the point they're making and ask if you've expressed it fairly. If someone seems to be off on a tangent, ask them to help the group understand how the point they're making connects with the topic being discussed.

Experienced facilitator Sam Kaner offers a very helpful way to think about group exploration of difficult questions like the ones raised in this book. When groups are looking to come to new understanding and to make decisions, Kaner explains that the process often looks chaotic. Most groups try to bring this to closure quickly and efficiently, perhaps proposing a vote on the potential solutions raised. Yet sometimes apparent chaos is a valuable first step in creativity. Divergent thinking within a group usually takes the form of many ideas flying around with a lot of bewilderment and uncertainty. They start getting more and more diverse and farther away from each other. This doesn't feel promising! But if the group resists the urge to quickly pick one of the proposed options and move on, at some stage divergent thinking begins to narrow again, converging around shared ways of understanding the problem at hand, and the potential ways forward. Often this process, which can seem annoyingly out of control, leads to a new path that no individual in the group would have thought of.

For this process to work, groups need to cultivate unfamiliar ideas and opinions by allowing time and space for them. It helps if facilitators make the group aware that a participatory decision-making process is happening, it could be slow and irritating, and it requires that divergent ideas not be scoffed at. Invite group members to take the risk of stating their ideas out loud before they're comfortably formed.[6] (For more about these kinds of processes read the chapter Communication.)

# Notes

All hyperlinks were working when I wrote this book in 2017 and 2018. If links are broken, I recommend using Internet Archive (archive.org) or a search engine to find the content.

A digital copy of these Endnotes, with clickable links, is available for download at AreWeDoneFighting.com/citations.

### About Quakers and the Author

1. Arthur Dorland, quoted in *The Canadian Friend* 107, no. 2 (2011): 43.
2. Robert Byrd, *Quaker Ways in Foreign Policy* (University of Toronto Press, 1987), 191.
3. Gunnar Jahn, "Award Ceremony Speech," 1947, *The Nobel Prize*, nobelprize.org/nobel_prizes/peace/laureates/1947/press.html
4. Susie Steiner, "Top Five Regrets of the Dying," *The Guardian*, February, 2012, theguardian.com/lifeandstyle/2012/feb/01/top-five-regrets-of-the-dying

### Introduction

1. Srđa Popović in the documentary film *Bringing Down a Dictator*, directed by Steve York, 2002.
2. Edd Gent, "Scientists Call Out Ethical Concerns for the Future of Neurotechnology," *SingularityHub*, November 21, 2017, singularityhub.com/2017/11/21/scientists-lay-out-urgent-ethical-concerns-for-the-future-of-neurotechnology
3. Dale Dewar and Bill Curry, "Making the Diagnosis; Changing the Prognosis," *Sunderland P. Gardner Lecture*, Canadian Yearly Meeting, 2014.
4. Joseph Scimecca, "Self-reflexivity and Freedom," in ed. John Burton, *Conflict: Human Needs Theory* (Palgrave McMillan, 1990), 206.
5. David Shields, *War Is Beautiful: The New York Times Pictorial Guide to the Glamour of Armed Conflict* (powerHouse Books, 2015).
6. Douglas Fields, *Why We Snap: Understanding the Rage Circuit in your Brain* (Penguin Random House, 2015), 290.
7. I got the idea of a positive epidemic from a conversation with Fred Bass, an epidemiologist who studied smokers and came up with the plan of transmitting positive behaviors using a model similar to that of diseases, for instance, infecting the most susceptible parties first.
8. Quaker Council for European Affairs, "Building Peace Together," 2018, qcea.org/wp-content/uploads/2018/03/Building-Peace-Together.pdf, 9.

## Using This Book

1. The People's Response Team, "Bystander Intervention 101," 2017, peoplesresponseteamchicago.org/uploads/8/7/9/8/87981704/bystander _intervention_final.pdf, 13.
2. George Lakey, "To Succeed, Movements Must Overcome the Tension Between Rationality and Emotion," *Waging Nonviolence*, July 29, 2015, wagingnonviolence.org/feature/to-succeed-movements-must-overcome -the-tension-between-rationality-and-emotion/
3. William Wilson, "Scientific Regress," *First Things*, May, 2016, firstthings.com/article/2016/05/scientific-regress
4. Johan Galtung, *Peace by Peaceful Means: Peace and Conflict, Development and Civilization* (SAGE Publications, 1996), 265.
5. Positive psychology in particular has focused on such ideas. See, for example, Martin Seligman et al., "Positive Psychology Progress: Empirical Validation of Interventions," *American Psychologist* 60, no. 5 (2005).

## Chapter 1: What Peace is Not

1. Quoted in Kathleen Lonsdale, *Removing the Causes of War* (Headley Brothers Ltd, 1953), 8.
2. Kyoungmin Cho, "Sleepy Punishers are Harsh Punishers," *Psychological Science* 28, no. 2 (2016).
3. "The Science of Justice: I think It's Time We Broke for Lunch…" *The Economist*, April 14, 2011, economist.com/node/18557594
4. John Tierney, "Do You Suffer from Decision Fatigue?" *The New York Times Magazine*, August 17, 2011, nytimes.com/2011/08/21/magazine/do-you -suffer-from-decision-fatigue.html
5. Barbara McNeil et al., "On the Elicitation of Preferences for Alternative Therapies," *The New England Journal of Medicine* 306 (1982).
6. Lawrence Williams and John Bargh, "Experiencing Physical Warmth Promotes Interpersonal Warmth," *Science* 322, no. 5901 (2008).
7. Jonathon Freedman and Scott Fraser, "Compliance Without Pressure: The Foot-in-the-door Technique," *Journal of Personality and Social Psychology* 4 (1966).
8. Jonah Lehrer, "Why Smart People are Stupid," *The New Yorker*, June 12, 2012, newyorker.com/tech/frontal-cortex/why-smart-people-are-stupid
9. Quoted in ed. Laura Shipler Chico, *This Light That Pushes Me: Stories of African Peacebuilders* (Quaker Books, 2014), 62.
10. Lev Muchnik et al., "Social Influence Bias: A Randomized Experiment," *Science* 341, no. 6146 (2013).
11. Dan Ariely, *Predictably Irrational: The Hidden Forces That Shape Our Decisions* (E-book, HarperCollins, 2009).
12. Mathew Killingsworth and Daniel Gilbert, "A Wandering Mind Is an Unhappy Mind," *Science* 330, no. 6006 (2010).
13. Dan Heath, *Switch in 16 Minutes*, heathbrothers.com/member-content /switch-16-minutes/
14. Romans 7:15, studylight.org/bible/cjb/romans/7-15.html
15. I think I first came across the concept of three "levels" of peace in European Intercultural Forum e. V. Germany, "Mainstreaming Peace

Education," July, 2014, unoy.org/wp-content/uploads/Mainstreaming
-Peace-Education.pdf and adapted it from there. I've since seen it articu-
lated in various similar ways in other places, for example, Antony Adolf,
"What Does Peace Literature Do? An Introduction to the Genre and Its
Criticism," *The Canadian Journal of Peace and Conflict Studies* 42, nos. 1–2
(2010): 10–11.

16. Johan Galtung, *Theories of Peace: A Synthetic Approach to Peace Thinking*
(International Peace Research Institute, 1967), 12.

17. These issues are alive in the Kenyan Quaker community. At an international gathering of Quakers in Kabarak, Kenya, in 2012 someone posted
a homophobic statement. It became the basis of much reflection and
group discussion. Many Friends expressed how dangerous and hurtful
the statement was. The participants I spoke with felt that some at the
gathering experienced a genuine change of heart over the course of these
discussions and began to reject their former homophobia.

18. Jacob Kushner, "Look Who's Fighting Homophobia in Kenya," *Takepart*,
October 23, 2015, takepart.com/feature/2015/10/23/gay-rights-kenya

19. Quoted in Sarah Wildman, "Faith-based Equality," *The Advocate*, September 13, 2005, 37.

## Chapter 2: Us and Others

1. Quoted in Colin Beavan, "I Need to Start With the Racist Attitudes in Me,"
*Yes! Magazine*, August 18, 2017, yesmagazine.org/peace-justice/i-need-to
-start-with-the-racist-attitudes-in-me-20170819

2. Robert Cialdini and Noah Goldstein, "The Science and Practice of
Persuasion," *Cornell Hotel and Restaurant Administration Quarterly* (April,
2002), 40.

3. CBC News, "Syrian Refugees Confused, Disappointed by Pepper Spray
Attack in Vancouver," January 9, 2016, cbc.ca/news/canada/british
-columbia/vancouver-police-chief-constable-speaks-on-hate-motivated
-pepper-spray-incident-1.3397228

4. Marjorie Rhodes and Lisa Chalik, "Social Categories as Markers of Intrinsic Interpersonal Obligations," *Psychological Science* 24, no. 6 (2003).

5. Tom Jacobs, "Hatred of Outsiders Kicks in Between Ages 6 and 8," *Pacific
Standard*, January 29, 2014, psmag.com/social-justice/hatred-outsiders
-kicks-age-six-eight-73516; Tara Mandalaywala, "The Nature and Consequences of Essentialist Beliefs About Race in Early Childhood," *Child
Development* (2018).

6. Jennifer Kubota et al., "The Neuroscience of Race," *Nature Neuroscience* 15
(2012).

7. Theodore Johnson, "Black-on-Black Racism," *The Atlantic*, December 26,
2014, theatlantic.com/politics/archive/2014/12/black-on-black-racism
-the-hazards-of-implicit-bias/384028/

8. Keith Payne et al., "How to Think about 'Implicit Bias,'" *Scientific American*, March 27, 2018, scientificamerican.com/article/how-to-think-about
-implicit-bias/

9. Robert Livingston and Brian Drwecki, "Why Are Some Individuals Not
Racially Biased?" *Psychological Science* 18, no. 9 (2007).

10. Robert Sapolsky, "Why Your Brain Hates Other People," *Nautilus*, June 22, 2017, nautil.us/issue/49/the-absurd/why-your-brain-hates-other-people

11. Douglas Fields, *Why We Snap: Understanding the Rage Circuit in Your Brain* (Penguin Random House, 2015), 266.

12. Elizabeth Page-Gould, "Warning: Racism Is Bad for Your Health," *Greater Good Magazine*, August 3, 2010, greatergood.berkeley.edu/article/item /why_racism_is_bad_for_your_health

13. Yoel Inbar et al., "Conservatives are More Easily Disgusted than Liberals," *Cognition and Emotion* 23 (2008).

14. Simone Schnall, "A Sense of Cleanliness," *Edge*, December 5, 2010, edge.org/conversation/simone_schnall-a-sense-of-cleanliness

15. Douglas Oxley et al., "Political Attitudes Vary with Physiological Traits," *Science* 321, no. 5896 (2008).

16. George Bonanno and John Jost, "Conservative Shift Among High-exposure Survivors of the September 11th Terrorist Attacks," *Basic and Applied Social Psychology* 28, no. 4 (2006).

17. John Bargh, "At Yale, We Conducted an Experiment to Turn Conservatives into Liberals. The Results Say a Lot about Our Political Divisions," *The Washington Post*, November 22, 2017, washingtonpost.com/news/inspired -life/wp/2017/11/22/at-yale-we-conducted-an-experiment-to-turn-conser vatives-into-liberals-the-results-say-a-lot-about-our-political-divisions/

18. René Girard, *The One by Whom Scandal Comes*, Malcolm DeBevoise trans. (Michigan State University Press, 2014).

19. Quoted in Tom Jacobs, "Why We Engage in Tribalism, Nationalism, and Scapegoating," *Pacific Standard*, March 5, 2018, psmag.com/social-justice /why-we-engage-in-tribalism-nationalism-and-scapegoating

20. Dan Lassiter et al., "Videotaped Interrogations and Confessions," *Journal of Applied Psychology* 87 (2002).

21. Shelley Taylor and Susan Fiske, "Salience, Attention, and Attribution," *Advances in Experimental Social Psychology* 11 (1978).

22. Dacher Keltner, "The Power Paradox," *Greater Good Magazine*, December 1, 2007, greatergood.berkeley.edu/article/item/power_paradox

23. Marilyn Brewer, "The Psychology of Prejudice," *Journal of Social Issues* 55, no. 3 (1999).

24. Ronald Johnson, "Perceived Physical Attractiveness of Supporters of Canada's Political Parties," *Canadian Journal of Behavioural Science* 13, no. 4 (1981).

25. Amy Cuddy et al., "Stereotype Content Model Across Cultures," *British Journal of Social Psychology* 48, no. 1 (2009).

26. Jay Van Bavel et al., "The Neural Substrates of In-Group Bias," *Psychological Science* 19, no. 11 (2008).

27. Mary Wheeler and Susan Fiske, "Controlling Racial Prejudice," *Association for Psychological Science* 16, no. 1 (2005).

28. Jeremy Adam and Rodolfo Mendoza, "How to Stop the Racist in You," *Greater Good Magazine*, July 27, 2016, greatergood.berkeley.edu/article /item/how_to_stop_the_racist_in_you

29. Cialdini and Goldstein, "The Science and Practice of Persuasion," 43.

30. "Snapshot of Racialized Poverty in Canada," Government of Canada, August 16, 2013, canada.ca/en/employment-social-development/programs/communities/reports/poverty-profile-snapshot.html

31. Robert Byrd, *Quaker Ways in Foreign Policy* (University of Toronto Press, 1987), 160.

32. Thomas Pettigrew and Linda Tropp, "A Meta-Analytic Test of Intergroup Contact Theory," *Journal of Personality and Social Psychology* 90, no. 5 (2006).

33. Stephen Murphy-Shigematsu, "How to Help Diverse Students Find Common Ground," *Greater Good Magazine*, November 14, 2016, greatergood.berkeley.edu/article/item/how_to_help_diverse_students_find_common_ground

34. Pettigrew and Tropp, "A Meta-Analytic Test of Intergroup Contact Theory," 767.

35. Daniel Goleman, *A Force For Good: The Dalai Lama's Vision for Our World* (Bantam Books, 2015), 160.

36. Mike Merryman-Lotze, "When Dialogue Stands in the Way of Peace," *Friends Journal*, March, 2018, 21.

37. Edward Schiappa et al., "The Parasocial Contact Hypothesis," *Communication Monographs* 72, no. 1 (2005).

38. Amanda Sharples and Elizabeth Page-Gould, "How to Avoid Picking Up Prejudice from the Media," *Greater Good Magazine*, September 7, 2016, greatergood.berkeley.edu/article/item/how_to_avoid_picking_up_prejudice_from_media

39. Quoted in El-Hibri Foundation et al., "Neuroscience and Peacebuilding: Reframing How We Think about Conflict and Prejudice," March 5, 2015, s3.amazonaws.com/ehf-public/ehf-documents/Neuroscience+Conference+Summary, 6.

40. Jill Suttie, "Can Mindfulness Help Reduce Racism?" *Greater Good Magazine*, December 9, 2014, greatergood.berkeley.edu/article/item/can_mindfulness_help_reduce_racism

41. Rick Hanson, "Rick Hanson on the Neuroscience of Happiness," *The Greater Good Podcast*, September, 2010, greatergood.berkeley.edu/podcasts/item/rick_hanson

## Chapter 3: Power-over

1. *The Psychology of Peace* (Praeger, 2011), 41.

2. Starhawk, *Truth or Dare: Encounters with Power, Authority, and Mystery* (Harper and Row, 1987), 9.

3. Parker Palmer, *The Courage to Teach: Exploring the Inner Landscape of a Teacher's Life* (E-Book, Jossey Bass, 2017).

4. See for example Robert Thurman, trans., *The Holy Teaching of Vimalakirti* (Pennsylvania State University Press, 1976), 73–77; Lao Tzu, *Tao Te Ching*, Gia-Fu Feng and Jane English trans. (Vintage Books, 1989), 3.

5. Amos Schurr and Ilana Ritvo, "Winning a Competition Predicts Dishonest Behavior," *Proceedings of the National Academy of Sciences of the United States of America* 113, no. 7 (2016).

6. "Morton Deutsch, Pioneer in Conflict Resolution, Cooperative Learn-ing and Social Justice, Passes Away at 97," Teachers College, Columbia University, May 15, 2017, tc.columbia.edu/articles/2017/march/tc-mourns -morton-deutsch/

7. MacNair, *The Psychology of Peace*, 177.

8. Marcel Cremene et al., "A Strategic Interaction Model of Punishment Favoring Contagion of Honest Behavior," *PLoS ONE* 9, no. 1 (2014).

9. Christina Bicchieria et al., "Deviant or Wrong? The Effects of Norm Information on the Efficacy of Punishment," University of Nottingham, November, 2017, nottingham.ac.uk/cedex/news/papers/2017-14.aspx

10. Alex Ballingall, "Judge Drops $65,000 in Fines Against Former Homeless Man," *The Toronto Star*, October 4, 2016, thestar.com/news/gta/2016/10 /04/judge-drops-65000-in-fines-against-former-homeless-man.html

11. Ray Cunnington, *Towards Less Adversarial Cultures* (CreateSpace, 2016), 46.

12. Quoted in David Barash, "The Deterrence Myth," *Aeon*, January 9, 2018, aeon.co/essays/nuclear-deterrence-is-more-ideology-than-theory

13. "Active Engagement, Modern Defence, Strategic Concept for the Defence and Security of The Members of the North Atlantic Treaty Organization," The North Atlantic Treaty Organization (NATO), November 19, 2010, nato.int/cps/en/natohq/official_texts_68580.htm

14. Barash, "The Deterrence Myth."

15. Dane Archer, *Violence and Crime in Cross-National Perspective* (Yale Univer-sity Press, 1984).

16. Tali Sharot, *The Influential Mind: What the Brain Reveals About Our Power to Change Others* (E-book, Henry Holt and Co., 2017).

17. "Is Corporal Punishment an Effective Means of Discipline?" The American Psychological Association, June 26, 2002, apa.org/news/press/releases /2002/06/spanking.aspx

18. Nancy Eisenberg and Amanda Morris, "The Origins and Social Signifi-cance of Empathy-Related Responding," *Social Justice Research* 14, no. 1 (2001).

19. Edward Morris and Perry Brea, "The Punishment Gap," *Social Problems* 63, no. 1 (2016).

20. "Frequently Asked Questions," The Global Initiative to End Corporal Pun-ishment of Children, endcorporalpunishment.org/resources/faqs/

21. Daniel Pink, *Drive: The Surprising Truth About What Motivates Us* (E-book, Riverhead Books, 2011).

22. Monica Worline and Jane Dutton, *Awakening Compassion at Work: The Quiet Power That Elevates People and Organizations* (Berrett-Koehler Pub-lishers, 2017).

23. Anna Nyberg, "Poor Leadership Poses a Health Risk at Work," Karolinska Institutet, November 2, 2009, ki.se/en/news/poor-leadership-poses-a -health-risk-at-work

24. Jane Dutton et al., "Compassion at Work," *Annual Review of Organizational Psychology and Organizational Behavior* 1, no. 1 (2014).

25. Chip and Dan Heath, *The Power of Moments: Why Certain Experiences Have Extraordinary Impact* (E-Book, Simon and Schuster, 2017).

26. Daniel Siegel, *The Developing Mind: How Relationships and the Brain Interact to Shape Who We Are* (Guilford, 1999), 282.

27. Lars Schwabe and Oliver Wolf, "Stress Prompts Habit Behavior in Humans," *Journal of Neuroscience* 29, no. 22 (2009).

28. Shawn Achor, *The Happiness Advantage: The Seven Principles of Positive Psychology That Fuel Success and Performance at Work* (Crown Business, 2010).

29. Sharot, *The Influential Mind*.

30. Veena Vasista, "Wise Fools for Love? Arts Activism and Social Transformation," *Open Democracy*, November 14, 2014, opendemocracy.net /transformation/veena-vasista/wise-fools-for-love-arts-activism-and -social-transformation

31. Michael Kimmel in eds. Ingeborg Breines et al., *Male Roles, Masculinities and Violence: A Culture of Peace Perspective* (UNESCO Publishing, 2000), 240.

## Chapter 4: Power-with and Power-from-within

1. *Coming Back to Life: The Updated Guide to the Work That Reconnects* (E-Book, New Society Publishers, 2014).

2. Quoted in Calvin Trottier-Chi, "McGill Conference Discusses Truth and Reconciliation," *McGill Tribune*, March 15, 2016, mcgilltribune.com/news /trcs-work-future-final-report-031416/

3. Maggie Campbell and Johanna Ray Vollhardt, "Fighting the Good Fight: The Relationship Between Belief in Evil and Support for Violent Politics,". *Personality and Social Psychology Bulletin* 40, no. 1 (2014).

4. Jan-Willem van Prooijen and Evelien van de Veer, "Perceiving Pure Evil," *Social Justice Research* 23, no. 4 (2010).

5. Peter Coleman, "The Five Percent: Finding Solutions to Seemingly Impossible Conflicts," *International Focus* November 10, 2011, youtube.com /watch?v=FpmSC7ajIeU

6. Lucian Gideon Conway et al., "Integrative Complexity and Political Decisions that Lead to War or Peace," in eds. Daniel Christie et al., *Peace, Conflict, and Violence: Peace Psychology for the 21st Century* (Prentice-Hall, 2001).

7. Chadly Stern and Tali Kleiman, "Know Thy Outgroup: Promoting Accurate Judgments of Political Attitude Differences Through a Conflict Mindset," *Social Psychological and Personality Science* 6, no. 8 (2015).

8. Eolene Boyd-MacMillan, "Increasing Cognitive Complexity and Collaboration Across Communities," *Journal of Strategic Security* 9, no. 4 (2016).

9. Eran Halperin et al., "Can Emotion Regulation Change Political Attitudes in Intractable Conflicts?" *Psychological Science* 24, no. 1 (2012).

10. Starhawk, *Truth or Dare: Encounters with Power, Authority, and Mystery* (Harper and Row, 1987), 10.

11. Joe Hadfield, "Prescription for Living Longer: Spend Less Time Alone," *Brigham Young University News*, March 10, 2015, news.byu.edu/news /prescription-living-longer-spend-less-time-alone

12. Dacher Keltner, *The Power Paradox: How We Gain and Lose Influence* (Penguin, 2016).

13. Dacher Keltner, "The Power Paradox," *Greater Good Magazine*, December 1, 2007, greatergood.berkeley.edu/article/item/power_paradox

14. Mark Greenberg quoted in Julie Scelfo, "Teaching Peace in Elementary School," *The New York Times*, November 14, 2015, nytimes.com/2015/11/15/sunday-review/teaching-peace-in-elementary-school.html

15. Andrew Harris and Karl Hanson, "Sex Offender Recidivism," Public Safety and Emergency Preparedness Canada, 2015, publicsafety.gc.ca/cnt/rsrcs/pblctns/sx-ffndr-rcdvsm/index-en.aspx#a04

16. Circles of Support and Accountability Canada, cosacanada.com

17. Jill Chouinard and Christine Riddick, "An Evaluation of the Circles of Support and Accountability Demonstration Project," *Church Council on Justice and Corrections*, 2015, ccjc.ca/wp-content/uploads/2015/02/COSA-EVALUATION-FINAL-EN.pdf

18. Brian Goldman, "Doctors Make Mistakes. Can We Talk About That?" *U of T Magazine*, Autumn 2017, magazine.utoronto.ca/autumn-2017/doctors-make-mistakes-can-we-talk-about-that-brian-goldman/

19. Carol Tavris and Elliot Aronson, *Mistakes Were Made (But Not by Me)* (Harcourt, 2007), 232–233.

20. Maia Szalavitz, "When the Cure is Not Worth the Cost," *The New York Times*, April 11, 2007, nytimes.com/2007/04/11/opinion/11szalavitz.html

21. Quoted in Richard Thompson, "A Question of Balance," *Quaker Voices* 8, no. 3 (May, 2017): 12.

22. Johan Huizinga, *Homo Ludens: A Study of the Play-Element in Culture* (Martino Fine Books, 2014).

23. Sarah Lazare, "'Standing Man' Silent Protest Sweeps Turkey," *Common Dreams*, June 18, 2013, commondreams.org/news/2013/06/18/standing-man-silent-protest-sweeps-turkey

24. "Dynamic Systems Theory," The International Center for Cooperation and Conflict Resolution at Columbia University, icccr.tc.columbia.edu/dynamical-systems-theory-dst-the-foundational-paradigm/

25. Charlotte Werndl, "What are the New Implications of Chaos for Unpredictability?" *The British Journal for the Philosophy of Science* 60, no. 1 (2009).

26. Parker Palmer, "People Can Change," *Center for Courage and Renewal*, September 3, 2014, couragerenewal.org/people-can-change-parker-palmer/

27. This activity is adapted from an exercise first developed by Augusto Boal. It's one of many activities used in Theatre of the Oppressed.

28. This list is adapted from the "Transforming Power Mandala" developed by the Alternatives to Violence Project. See avp.international/

29. Note: this question was designed to allow someone from a marginal group to speak to a mainstream group. It is offered here in a different context because I think it has value in building trust and identifying power-from-within, not to suggest that we all have equally difficult and painful identities. Training for Change, "Diversity Interviews," trainingforchange.org/tools/diversity-interviews

## Chapter 5: Process and Change

1. "Spiritual Responsibility in the Meeting for Business," *Hartford Monthly Meeting*, neym.org/sites/default/files/Loring-Spiritual%20Responsibility.pdf

2. For one brief example see Medhi Hasan, "Blowback: How Isis was Created

by the US Invasion of Iraq," *The Intercept*, January 29, 2018, theintercept .com/2018/01/29/isis-iraq-war-islamic-state-blowback/

3. Daniel Aires, "The Challenge of Peace," *CBC Ideas*, August 14, 2017, cbc.ca/player/play/872643651511/

4. Jordi Quoidbach et al., "The End of History Illusion," *Science* 339, no. 6115 (2013).

5. Brent Roberts et al., "A Systematic Review of Personality Trait Change through Intervention," *Psychological Bulletin* 143, no. 2 (2017).

6. Carol Tavris and Elliot Aronson, *Mistakes Were Made (But Not by Me)* (Harcourt, 2007), 234.

7. Zhai Yun Tan, "Jewish and Palestinian-Israeli Teens Learn to Collaborate," *Christian Science Monitor*, October 26, 2016, csmonitor.com/World /2016/1026/Jewish-and-Palestinian-Israeli-teens-learn-to-collaborate

8. David Yeager et al., "How to Improve Adolescent Stress Responses," *Psychological Science* 27, no. 8 (2016).

9. Ewan Birney, "DNA is Not our Destiny; It's Just a Very Useful Tool," *The Guardian*, April 5, 2018, theguardian.com/science/2018/apr/05/dna -sequencing-educational-attainment-height; David Dobbs, "The Social Life of Genes," *Pacific Standard*, September 3, 2013, psmag.com/social -justice/the-social-life-of-genes-64616

10. Norman Doidge, *The Brain That Changes Itself: Stories of Personal Triumph from the Frontiers of Brain Science* (Penguin Books, 2007).

11. Jane Orion Smith, personal communication, and Matthew Legge, "Reflections on Service: An Interview with Jane Orion Smith," *Quaker Concern*, Spring 2018, quakerconcern.ca/reflections-on-service-an-interview-with -jane-orion-smith/

12. Gianne Broughton, "Canadian Quakers and 'Just Peace'," January 31, 2012, quakerservice.ca/wp-content/uploads/2013/05/12.01.31.Just-Peace -Seminar-presentation.1.pdf, 6.

13. Matthew Lieberman et al., "Do Amnesiacs Exhibit Cognitive Dissonance Reduction?" *Psychological Science* 12, no. 2 (2001). A related finding is that when we spend more time and effort building something we like it more. Shankar Vedantam, "Why You Love That Ikea Table, Even If It's Crooked," *NPR*, February 6, 2013, npr.org/2013/02/06/171177695/why-you-love-that -ikea-table-even-if-its-crooked

14. Michael Bartlet in ed. John Lampen, *No Alternative? Nonviolent Responses to Repressive Regimes* (William Sessions Ltd, 2000), 100.

15. UN High Commissioner for Human Rights, "Conscientious Objection to Military Service," 2012, HR/PUB/12/1, ohchr.org/documents/publications /conscientiousobjection_en.pdf

16. UN High Commissioner for Refugees, "Guidelines on International Protection No. 10: Claims to Refugee Status Related to Military Service Within the Context of Article 1A (2) of the 1951 Convention and/or the 1967 Protocol Relating to the Status of Refugees," December 3, 2013, HCR/GIP/13/10/Corr, refworld.org/docid/529ee33b4.html

17. Rachel Brett, personal communication and *Snakes and Ladders: A Personal Exploration of Quaker Work on Human Rights at the United Nations* (Quaker Books, 2012).

## Chapter 6: Firm Belief

1. *The Influential Mind: What the Brain Reveals About Our Power to Change Others* (E-book, Henry Holt and Co., 2017).
2. Vera Hoorens, "Self-Enhancement and Superiority Biases in Social Comparison," *European Review of Social Psychology* 4, no. 1 (1993).
3. Ellen Langer, "The Illusion of Control," *Journal of Personal and Social Psychology* 32, no. 2 (1975).
4. Michael Muthukrishna et al., "Overconfidence is Universal? Depends What You Mean," Harvard University, henrich.fas.harvard.edu/files/henrich/files/overconfidenceuniversal.pdf?m=1460547633
5. Takahiko Masuda and Richard Nisbett, "Attending Holistically vs. Analytically," *Journal of Personality and Social Psychology* 81, no. 5 (2001); Cara Feinberg, "The Placebo Phenomenon," *Harvard Magazine*, January-February 2013, harvardmagazine.com/2013/01/the-placebo-phenomenon; Alia Crum et al. "Mind Over Milkshakes," *Health Psychology* 30, no. 4 (2011).
6. Michelle LeBaron, *Bridging Cultural Conflicts: A New Approach for a Changing World* (Jossey-Bass, 2003).
7. Aboriginal Peoples Television Network, "Canada Guilty of Cultural Genocide Against Indigenous Peoples: TRC," June 2, 2015, aptnnews.ca/2015/06/02/canada-guilty-cultural-genocide-indigenous-peoples-trc-2/
8. Quoted in Jesse Sutherland, *Worldview Skills* (Worldview Strategies, 2005), 42.
9. Elaine Fox, *Rainy Brain, Sunny Brain: The New Science of Optimism and Pessimism* (HarperCollins, 2012), 19–22.
10. Heather LaMarre et al., "The Irony of Satire: Political Ideology and the Motivation to See What You Want to See in The Colbert Report," *The International Journal of Press/Politics* 14, no. 2 (2009).
11. Mark Synder and William Swann, "Hypothesis Testing Processes in Social Interaction," *Journal of Personality and Social Psychology* 36, no. 11 (1978).
12. Engin Bozdag, "Bias in Algorithmic Filtering and Personalization," *Ethics and Information Technology* 15, no. 3 (2013).
13. Sara and Jack Gorman, *Denying to the Grave: Why We Ignore the Facts That Will Save Us* (E-book, Oxford University Press, 2016); Karen Hopkin, "Musical Chills Related to Brain Dopamine Release," *Scientific American*, January 9, 2011, scientificamerican.com/podcast/episode/musical-chills-related-to-brain-dop-11-01-09/
14. University of Southern California, "Hard-wired: The Brain's Circuitry for Political Belief," *Science Daily*, December 23, 2016, sciencedaily.com/releases/2016/12/161223115757.htm
15. Maira Richter et al., "Do Words Hurt? Brain Activation During the Processing of Pain-Related Words," *Pain* 148, no. 2 (2010): 199.
16. Richter et al., "Do Words Hurt?", 198.
17. Chen Zhansheng et al., "When Hurt Will Not Heal: Exploring the Capacity to Relive Social and Physical Pain," *Psychological Science* 19, no. 8, (2008).
18. Francesca Gino, "Why Curiosity Matters," *Harvard Business Review*, September-October, 2018, hbr.org/2018/09/curiosity

19. Natalie Wolchover, "Are Flat-Earthers Being Serious?" *Live Science*, March 30, 2017, livescience.com/24310-flat-earth-belief.html

20. J. Eric Oliver and Thomas Wood, "Conspiracy Theories and the Paranoid Style(s) of Mass Opinion," *American Journal of Political Science* 58, no. 4 (2014).

21. Naomi Oreskes and Erik Conway, *Merchants of Doubt: How a Handful of Scientists Obscured the Truth on Issues from Tobacco Smoke to Global Warming* (Bloomsbury Press, 2010).

22. Urie Bronfenbrenner, "The Mirror Image in Soviet-American Relations: A Social Psychologist's Report," *Journal of Social Issues* 17, no. 3 (1961).

23. *Daily Mail*, "Three-second Memory Myth," January 7, 2009, dailymail.co.uk/sciencetech/article-1106884/Three-second-memory-myth-Fish-remember-months.html; Anahad O'Connor, "The Claim: Never Swim After Eating," *The New York Times*, June 28, 2005, nytimes.com/2005/06/28/health/the-claim-never-swim-after-eating.html

24. Robb Price, "CGI and AI are Going to Turbocharge 'Fake News' and Make it Far Harder to Tell What's Real," *Business Insider*, July 28, 2017, businessinsider.com/cgi-ai-fake-news-videos-real-2017-7

25. Paul Lewis, "Fiction is Outperforming Reality," *The Guardian*, February 2, 2018, theguardian.com/technology/2018/feb/02/how-youtubes-algorithm-distorts-truth

26. Anti-Defamation League, "ADL Task Force Issues Report Detailing Widespread Anti-Semitic Harassment of Journalists on Twitter During 2016 Campaign," October 19, 2016, adl.org/news/press-releases/adl-task-force-issues-report-detailing-widespread-anti-semitic-harassment-of

27. Samantha Bradshaw and Philip Howard, "Troops, Trolls and Troublemakers," *University of Oxford*, December, 2017, blogs.oii.ox.ac.uk/politicalbots/wp-content/uploads/sites/89/2017/07/Troops-Trolls-and-Troublemakers.pdf

28. Michael Medved quoted in "Media Violence," *Dawson College*, inspire.dawsoncollege.qc.ca/extreme-violence/media-violence/

29. Chip and Dan Heath, *Made to Stick: Why Some Ideas Survive and Others Die* (Random House, 2007), 14.

30. Danielle Polage, "Making Up History: False Memories of Fake News Stories," *Europe's Journal of Psychology* 8, no. 2 (2012).

31. Elizabeth Loftus and Jacqueline Pickrell, "The Formation of False Memories," *Psychiatric Annals* 25, (1995); Fox, *Rainy Brain, Sunny Brain*, 24.

32. Carol Tavris and Elliot Aronson, *Mistakes Were Made (But Not by Me)* (Harcourt, 2007), 6.

33. Tavris and Aronson, *Mistakes Were Made*, 94–99.

34. Micah Edelson et al., "Following the Crowd: Brain Substrates of Long-term Memory Conformity," *Science* 333, no. 6038 (2011).

35. Henry Roediger III and Andrew DeSoto, "The Power of Collective Memory: What Do Large Groups of People Remember—and Forget?," *Scientific American*, June 28, 2016, scientificamerican.com/article/the-power-of-collective-memory/

36. Lisa Fazio et al., "Knowledge Does Not Protect Against Illusory Truth," *Journal of Experimental Psychology* 144, no. 5 (2015).

37. Claire Warner, "Why Do We Believe Fake News? Accepting Inaccurate Information Is Less Work Than Being Critical, According To Research," *Bustle*, November 23, 2016, bustle.com/articles/196724-why-do-we -believe-fake-news-accepting-inaccurate-information-is-less-work-than -being-critical-according

38. Tim Gray, "If You Want Change, Learn When to Argue and When to Stop," *Open Democracy*, April 29, 2016, opendemocracy.net/transformation /tim-gray/if-you-want-change-learn-when-to-argue-for-it-and-when-to -stop

39. The Canadian Press, "Thousands of Charity Workers Earn Big Salaries: Report," *CBC*, July 10, 2011, cbc.ca/news/canada/thousands-of-charity -workers-earn-big-salaries-report-1.1022805

40. Tom Jacobs, "The Trick to Debunking Fake News," *Pacific Standard*, September 13, 2017, psmag.com/news/the-trick-to-debunking-fake-news

41. Philip Fernbach et al., "Political Extremism Is Supported by an Illusion of Understanding," *Psychological Science* 24, no. 6 (2013).

42. Steven Sloman and Philip Fernbach, *The Knowledge Illusion: Why We Never Think Alone* (e-book Riverhead Books, 2017).

43. Arie Kruglanski et al., "The Psychology of Radicalization and Deradicalization," *Advances in Political Psychology* 35, Supplement 1 (2014).

44. Megan Phelps-Roper, "I Grew Up in the Westboro Baptist Church. Here's Why I Left," *TED*, February, 2017, ted.com/talks/megan_phelps_roper_i _grew_up_in_the_westboro_baptist_church_here_s_why_i_left#t-194516

45. Linda Skitka and Elizabeth Mullen, "The Dark Side of Moral Conviction," *Analyses of Social Issues and Public Policy* 2, no. 1 (2002).

46. Meytal Nasie et al., "Overcoming the Barrier of Narrative Adherence in Conflicts Through Awareness of the Psychological Bias of Naive Realism," *Personal and Social Psychology Bulletin* 40, no. 11 (2014).

47. Stanley Cohen, *States of Denial: Knowing about Atrocities and Suffering* (Polity, 2001), 4–5.

48. Rachel MacNair, *The Psychology of Peace* (Praeger, 2011), 177.

49. Ryan Brown et al., "Moral Credentialing and the Rationalization of Misconduct," *Ethics Behavior* 21, no. 1 (2011).

50. Dan Ariely in Devin Stewart, "Thought Leader Dan Ariely," *Carnegie Council for Ethics in International Affairs*, February 6, 2013, carnegiecouncil.org /studio/thought-leaders/leaders/ariely-dan

51. Dan Ariely in Steve Mirsky, "Creativity's Dark Side," *Scientific American*, December 25, 2012, scientificamerican.com/podcast/episode/creativitys -dark-side-dan-ariely-on-12-12-25/

52. Roy Baumeister, *Evil: Inside Human Violence and Cruelty* (Holt Paperbacks, 1999).

53. Adam Gazzaley et al., "Top-down Enhancement and Suppression of the Magnitude and Speed of Neural Activity," *Journal of Cognitive Neuroscience* 17, no. 3 (2005).

54. Robert Cialdini and Noah Goldstein, "The Science and Practice of Persuasion," *Cornell Hotel and Restaurant Administration Quarterly* (April, 2002), 45.

55. Lisa Shu et al., "Signing at the Beginning Makes Ethics Salient and

Decreases Dishonest Self-reports in Comparison to Signing at the End," *PNAS* 109, no. 38 (2012).

56. Brian Resnick, "All Muslims are Often Blamed for Single Acts of Terror. Psychology Explains How to Stop It," *Vox*, November 30, 2017, vox.com /science-and-health/2017/11/30/16645024/collective-blame-psychology -muslim

57. Emmanuel Trouche et al., "The Selective Laziness of Reasoning," *Cognitive Science* 40, no. 8 (2015).

58. Peter Woodrow, *Clearness: Processes for Supporting Individuals and Groups in Decision Making* (New Society Publishers, 1976), 4.

59. Woodrow, *Clearness*, 8.

60. Virginia Coover et al., *Resource Manual for a Living Revolution* (New Society Publishers, 1985), 123.

61. Chip and Dan Heath, *Decisive: How to Make Better Choices in Life and Work* (E-book, Crown Business, 2013).

## Chapter 7: Treating Emotions with Care

1. Quoted in *Faith and Practice* (Canadian Yearly Meeting of the Religious Society of Friends, 2011), 74.

2. Dan Heath, "Switch in 16 Minutes," heathbrothers.com/member-content /switch-16-minutes/

3. I got this concept of "resonance" with someone from Richard Boyatzis and Annie McKee, *Resonant Leadership: Renewing Yourself and Connecting with Others Through Mindfulness, Hope, and Compassion* (Harvard Business Review Press, 2005).

4. Marco Iacoboni, *Mirroring People: The New Science of How We Connect with Others* (Farrar, Straus and Giroux, 2009).

5. Mona Chalabi and Simon Rogers, "Syrian Refugees: How Many are There and Where are They?" *The Guardian*, March 6, 2013, theguardian.com /news/datablog/2013/mar/06/syrian-refugee-crisis-in-numbers

6. Karen Jenni and George Loewenstein, "Explaining the Identifiable Victim Effect," *Journal of Risk and Uncertainty* 14, no. 3 (1997).

7. Stephan Dickert et al., "Affective Motivations to Help Others," in eds. Christopher Olivola and Daniel Oppenheimer, *The Science of Giving: Exper- imental Approaches to the Study of Charity* (Taylor and Francis Group, 2011).

8. Paul Bloom, "The Dark Side of Empathy," *The Atlantic*, September 25, 2015, theatlantic.com/science/archive/2015/09/the-violence-of-empathy /407155/

9. Paul Collier, "Doing Well out of War," in *Greed and Grievance: Economic Agendas in Civil Wars*, eds. Mats Berdal and David Malone (Lynne Rienner, 2000), 110.

10. Indra de Soysa, "The Resource Curse," in eds. Berdal and Malone, *Greed and Grievance*, 116.

11. Stephanie Sarkis, "11 Signs of Gaslighting in a Relationship," *Psychology Today*, January 22, 2017, psychologytoday.com/blog/here-there-and -everywhere/201701/11-signs-gaslighting-in-relationship

12. Roger Boesche, "Kautilya's Arthaśāstra on War and Diplomacy in Ancient India," *The Journal of Military History* 67, no. 1 (2003): 34–35.

13. Ryan Clow, "Psychological Operations," *Canadian Military Journal* 9, no. 1 (2008).

14. Martin Moore quoted in Carole Cadwalladr, "Google, Democracy and the Truth about Internet Search," *The Guardian*, December 4, 2016, theguardian.com/technology/2016/dec/04/google-democracy-truth -internet-search-facebook

15. Sandra Matz et al., "Psychological Targeting as an Effective Approach to Digital Mass Persuasion," *PNAS* 114, no. 48 (2017).

16. Carole Cadwalladr, "The Great British Brexit Robbery," *The Guardian*, May 7, 2017, theguardian.com/technology/2017/may/07/the-great-british -brexit-robbery-hijacked-democracy; Hannes Grassegger and Mikael Krogerus, "The Data That Turned the World Upside Down," *Vice*, January 28, 2017, motherboard.vice.com/en_us/article/how-our-likes-helped -trump-win

17. Kelvin Redvers and Tunchai Redvers, "Indigenous Youth are Their Own Heroes—It's Time We Listened," *The Globe and Mail*, September 10, 2017, beta.theglobeandmail.com/opinion/indigenous-youth-are-their-own -heroes-its-time-we-listened/article36217830/

18. Elaine Fox, *Rainy Brain, Sunny Brain: The New Science of Optimism and Pessimism* (HarperCollins, 2012), 155.

19. Cordelia Fine, "Is There Neurosexism in Functional Neuroimaging Investigations of Sex Differences?" *Neuroethics* 6, no. 2 (2013).

20. For example, Angelica Staniloiu and Hans Markowitsch, "Gender Differences in Violence and Aggression," *Procedia—Social and Behavioral Sciences* 33 (2012).

21. Robert Connell in eds. Ingeborg Breines et al., *Male Roles, Masculinities and Violence* (UNESCO Publishing, 2000), 22.

22. Bernadette Park and Sarah Banchefsky, "Leveraging the Social Role of Dad to Change Gender Stereotypes of Men," *Personality and Social Psychology Bulletin* 44, no. 9 (2018).

23. Search for Common Ground, "Transforming Violent Extremism," 2017, sfcg.org/wp-content/uploads/2017/04/Transforming-Violent -Extremism-V2-August-2017.pdf, 12–13.

24. Connell in *Male Roles, Masculinities and Violence*, 22.

25. Anita Tayler and M.J. Hardman, "War, Language and Gender, What New Can be Said? Framing the Issues," *Women and Language* 27, no. 2 (2004).

26. Joel Wong et al., "Meta-Analyses of the Relationship Between Conformity to Masculine Norms and Mental Health-Related Outcomes," *Journal of Counseling Psychology* 64, no. 1 (2017).

27. Carnegie Commission on Preventing Deadly Conflict, *Preventing Deadly Conflict* (Carnegie Corporation of New York, 1997), xxxii.

28. Laurel Stone, "Quantitative Analysis of Women's Participation in Peace Processes" in Marie O'Reilly et al., "Reimagining Peacemaking: Women's Roles in Peace Processes," *International Peace Institute*, 2015, ipinst.org /wp-content/uploads/2015/06/IPI-E-pub-Reimagining-Peacemaking -rev.pdf

29. Victor Asal et al., "Gender Ideologies and Forms of Contentious Mobilization in the Middle East," *Journal of Peace Research* 50, no. 3 (2013).

30. Radhika Coomaraswamy, *Preventing Conflict, Transforming Justice, and Securing the Peace* (UN Women, 2015), 293.

31. Fredericton Sexual Assault Crisis Centre, "Man to Man: A Tool-kit for Delivering Workshops to Men and Boys about Reducing Sexual Assault," 2009, accessed via fsacc.ca/en/learn, 265.

32. Bruce Dienes, personal communication, 2017.

33. Adapted from Virginia Coover et al., *Resource Manual for a Living Revolution* (New Society Publishers, 1985), 251–253.

## Chapter 8: Communication

1. "Marshall Rosenberg's NVC Quotes," PuddleDancer Press, nonviolent-communication.com/freeresources/nvc_social_media_quotes.htm

2. Rachel Pinney, *Creative Listening* (Annick Press, 1976), 2.

3. Alison Prato, "Does Body Language Help a TED Talk Go Viral? 5 Nonverbal Patterns from Blockbuster Talks," *TED Blog*, May 12, 2015, blog.ted.com/body-language-survey-points-to-5-nonverbal-features-that-make-ted-talks-take-off/

4. Chip and Dan Heath, *Made to Stick: Why Some Ideas Survive and Others Die* (Random House, 2007), 19–20.

5. Uri Hasson, "I Can Make Your Brain Look Like Mine," *Harvard Business Review*, December 2010, hbr.org/2010/12/defend-your-research-i-can-make-your-brain-look-like-mine

6. Tom Jacobs, "Conservatives' Love of Nostalgia Can be Used to Promote Liberal Values," *Pacific Standard*, February 1, 2018, psmag.com/news/the-grand-old-party-longs-for-the-good-old-days

7. Alison Wood Brooks and Leslie John, "The Surprising Power of Questions," *Harvard Business Review*, May-June, 2018, hbr.org/2018/05/the-surprising-power-of-questions

8. Liane Davey, "The Mistake You Make in Every Argument," *Medium*, January 21, 2018, medium.com/@lianedavey/the-mistake-you-make-in-every-argument-975caf7b004e

9. Daniel Dennett, *Intuition Pumps and Other Tools for Thinking* (WW Norton, 2013).

10. Hannah Tuller et al., "Seeing the Other Side: Perspective Taking and the Moderation of Extremity," *Journal of Experimental Social Psychology* 59 (2015).

11. Rachel MacNair, *The Psychology of Peace* (Praeger, 2011), 90.

12. Michael Nagler and Karen Ridd, "Humor but Not Humiliation," *Open Democracy*, May 7, 2014, opendemocracy.net/transformation/michael-nagler-karen-ridd/humor-but-not-humiliation-finding-sweet-spot-in-nonviolent-

13. The information about nonviolent communication in this chapter is based on Marshall Rosenberg, *The Nonviolent Communication Training Course* (Audio book, Sounds True, 2006).

14. Robert Cialdini and Noah Goldstein, "The Science and Practice of Persuasion," *Cornell Hotel and Restaurant Administration Quarterly* (April, 2002), 47.
15. Lisa Feldman Barrett, *How Emotions Are Made: The Secret Life of the Brain* (E-book, Houghton Mifflin Harcourt, 2017).
16. Feldman Barrett, *How Emotions Are Made*.
17. David Bohm, *On Dialogue* (Routledge, 2013).
18. Parker Palmer, *The Courage to Teach: Exploring the Inner Landscape of a Teacher's Life* (E-Book, Jossey-Bass, 2017).

## Chapter 9: Conflict
1. Quoted in *Faith and Practice* (Canadian Yearly Meeting of the Religious Society of Friends, 2011), 87.
2. James Gillian, *Violence: Reflections on a National Epidemic* (Vintage, 1997), 110.
3. Peter Coleman, "The Five Percent: Finding Solutions to Seemingly Impossible Conflicts," *International Focus* November 10, 2011, youtube.com/watch?v=FpmSC7ajIeU
4. Jennifer Beer and Caroline Packard, *The Mediator's Handbook* (New Society Publishers, 2012), 144.
5. Adam Kahane, *Collaborating with the Enemy: How to Work with People You Don't Agree with or Like or Trust* (E-book, Berrett-Koehler Publishers, 2017).
6. Kenneth Thomas and Ralph Kilmann, "An Overview of the Thomas-Kilmann Conflict Mode Instrument (TKI)," Kilmann Diagnostics, kilmanndiagnostics.com/overview-thomas-kilmann-conflict-mode-instrument-tki
7. Walter Wink, *When the Powers Fall: Reconciliation in the Healing of Nations* (Fortress Press, 1998), 26.
8. Miriam Toews, "How Pacifism Can Lead to Violence and Conflict," *Literary Hub*, November 28, 2016, lithub.com/how-pacifism-can-lead-to-violence-and-conflict/
9. John Paul Lederarch, *Preparing for Peace: Conflict Transformation Across Cultures* (Syracuse University Press, 1996), 16.
10. Lederarch, *Preparing for Peace*, 81.
11. Jesse Sutherland, *Worldview Skills* (Worldview Strategies, 2005), 85.
12. Malvern Lunmsden in eds. Ingeborg Breines et al., *Male Roles, Masculinities and Violence* (UNESCO Publishing, 2000), 268.
13. Adapted from Dorothy Vaandering, "Ripped Apart or Stitched Together," *Quaker Concern*, Winter 2015, 4.
14. Eric Butler, workshop on restorative justice, April 29, 2018, Centre for Social Innovation, Toronto.

## Chapter 10: Seeing Violence
1. "Audio: Lecture 1.2.3—Confrontation of East and West in Religion," *Highbridge Audio*, 2002.
2. Dahr Jamail, "On Staying Sane in a Suicidal Culture," *Truthout*, June 3, 2014, truth-out.org/news/item/24083-on-staying-sane-in-a-suicidal-culture

3. Jennifer Brown and David Sheffield, "Social Support and Experimental Pain," *Psychosomatic Medicine* 65, no. 2 (2003).

4. Yazmany Arboleda, "Bringing Marina Flowers," *The Huffington Post*, May 28, 2010, huffingtonpost.com/yazmany-arboleda/bringing-marina -flowers_b_592597.html

5. Stephen Batchelor, *Living with the Devil: A Buddhist Meditation on Good and Evil* (Penguin, 2004), 128.

6. Batchelor, *Living with the Devil*, 132.

7. Jamail, "On Staying Sane in a Suicidal Culture."

8. Morgan Winsor, "Congo's Conflict Minerals," *International Business Times*, September 18, 2015, ibtimes.com/congos-conflict-minerals-us -companies-struggle-trace-tantalum-tungsten-tin-gold-their-2102323; Todd Frankel, "The Cobalt Pipeline," *The Washington Post*, September 30, 2016, washingtonpost.com/graphics/business/batteries/congo-cobalt -mining-for-lithium-ion-battery/

9. Robert Howell, "Book Review: The Elements of Power by David Abraham," *A Resilient World*, August 12, 2016, a-resilient-world.blogspot.com/2016 /08/book-review-elements-of-power.html

10. These are huge issues, but see, for example, Anti-Slavery, "What is Modern Slavery?" antislavery.org/slavery-today/modern-slavery/; or a specific case study from just one industry: Kate Hodal et al., "Revealed: Asian Slave Labour Producing Prawns for Supermarkets in US, UK," *The Guardian*, June 10, 2014, theguardian.com/global-development/2014/jun /10/supermarket-prawns-thailand-produced-slave-labour

11. Will Steffen et al., "The Anthropocene: Are Humans Now Overwhelming the Great Forces of Nature," *Royal Swedish Academy of 2007* 36, no. 8 (2007); The Organisation for Economic Co-operation and Development, "Inequality," oecd.org/social/inequality.htm; Jonathan Ostry et al., "Neoliberalism: Oversold?" *Finance and Development* 53, no. 2 (2016).

12. Kate Pickett and Richard Wilkinson, "Immorality of Inaction on Inequality," *British Medical Journal* 356 (2017).

13. Rob Nixon, *Slow Violence and the Environmentalism of the Poor* (Harvard University Press, 2011), 2.

14. Mark Spranca et al., "Omission and Commission in Judgment and Choice," *Journal of Experimental Social Psychology* 27, no. 1 (1991).

15. *Faith and Practice* (Canadian Yearly Meeting of the Religious Society of Friends, 2011), 139.

16. Leyla Acaroglu, "Paper Beats Plastic? How to Rethink Environmental Folklore," *TED*, February, 2013, ted.com/talks/leyla_acaroglu_paper_ beats_plastic_how_to_rethink_environmental_folklore#t-566616

17. *Yes! Magazine* and others have helped to document many of these stories. See, for example, "Solidarity: How to Build Joyful Economies," Issue 84, Winter 2018.

18. Marc de Sousa-Shields, *Invest Like You Give a Damn* (New Society Publishers, 2018).

19. For example, Ethical Consumer, ethicalconsumer.org; Buycott, buycott .com/; and The Good Shopping Guide, thegoodshoppingguide.com

20. Gwen Anderson, "I'm Tom Findley," February 13, 2017, youtube.com /watch?v=mxO2KWirP1M; Keith Helmuth, *Tracking Down Ecological Guidance: Presence, Beauty, Survival* (Chapel Street Editions, 2015).

21. In Canada this campaign is promoted by Conscience Canada, and Quakers are among those involved. See consciencecanada.ca

22. Charles Collyer et al., "Sensitivity to Violence Measured by Ratings of Severity Increases After Nonviolence Training," *Perceptual and Motor Skills* 110, no. 1 (2010).

23. Frances Lee, "'Excommunicate Me from the Church of Social Justice': An Activist's Plea for Change," *CBC*, September 17, 2017, cbc.ca/radio/the sundayedition/the-sunday-edition-september-17-2017-1.4291332/excom municate-me-from-the-church-of-social-justice-an-activist-s-plea-for -change-1.4291383

24. Horace Alexander, *The Growth of the Peace Testimony of the Society of Friends* (Friends Peace Committee, 1939), 34.

25. George Bonanno and Jerome Singer, "Repressive Personality Style," in ed. Jerome Singer, *Repression and Dissociation: Implications for Personality Theory, Psychopathology and Health* (University of Chicago Press, 1990).

26. Helen Steven, *No Extraordinary Power: Prayer, Stillness and Activism* (Quaker Books, 2005), 66.

27. Steven, *No Extraordinary Power*, 52.

28. Steven, *No Extraordinary Power*, 58.

29. Meredith Maran, "The Activism Cure," *Greater Good Magazine*, June 1, 2009, greatergood.berkeley.edu/article/item/the_activism_cure

30. Stephen Post quoted in Maran, "The Activism Cure."

**Chapter 11: What's Natural?**

1. The student's teacher, Colman McCarthy shares this quote in Bob Myers, "Why Do We Use Violence?" roadofpeace.com/why-do-we-use-violence .html

2. Jeanna Bryner, "Humans Crave Violence Just Like Sex," *LiveScience*, January 17, 2008, livescience.com/2231-humans-crave-violence-sex.html

3. Jeffery Kluger, "Science Proves It: Greed Is Good," *Time*, March 28, 2014, time.com/41680/greed-is-good-science-proves/

4. Robert Hinde in *Preparing for Peace by Asking the Experts to Analyse War* (Westmorland General Meeting, 2005), xiv.

5. Dale Peterson and Richard Wrangham, *Demonic Males: Apes and the Origins of Human Violence* (Mariner Books, 1997).

6. Robert Sussman and Joshua Marshack, "Are Humans Inherently Killers?" *Global Nonkilling Working Papers*, 2010.

7. William Ury, *Getting to Peace: Transforming Conflict at Home, at Work, and in the World* (Penguin Books, 1999), 33–35.

8. Ury, *Getting to Peace*, 64.

9. Steven Pinker, *The Better Angles of Our Nature: Why Violence Has Declined* (Penguin Books, 2011).

10. R. Brian Ferguson, "Pinker's List," in ed. Douglas Fry, *War, Peace, and Human Nature: The Convergence of Evolutionary and Cultural Views* (Oxford University Press, 2015).

11. Douglas Fry, "Lethal Aggression in Mobile Forager Bands and Implications for the Origins of War," *Science* 341, no. 6143 (2013).

12. Milan Rai, "Abolishing War Part 3," *Peace News*, January 30, 2011 peacenews.info/blog/6490/abolishing-war-part-3

13. Douglas Fry, "War is Not Part and Parcel of Human Nature," *Peace News*, August, 2014, peacenews.info/node/7740/war-not-part-and-parcel -human-nature

14. Johan Galtung and Tom Broch, "Belligerence Among the Primitives [sic]," *Journal of Peace Research* 3, no. 1 (1966).

15. Steven Pinker, "The Surprising Decline in Violence," *TED*, March, 2007, ted.com/talks/steven_pinker_on_the_myth_of_violence

16. Leslie Sponsel, "The Mutual Relevance of Anthropology and Peace Studies," in eds. Leslie E. Sponsel and Thomas Gregor, *The Anthropology of Peace and Nonviolence* (Lynne Rienner, 1994).

17. Fry, "War is Not Part and Parcel of Human Nature."

18. "Confederacy's Creation," *Haudenosaunee Confederacy*, haudenosaunee confederacy.com/confederacycreation.html

19. Signe Howell and Roy Willis eds., *Societies at Peace: Anthropological Perspectives* (Taylor & Francis Ltd, 1990).

20. Fry, "War is Not Part and Parcel of Human Nature."

21. Bruce Bonta, "Centre for Global Nonkilling," December 1, 2011, *University of Alabama at Birmingham*, cas.uab.edu/peacefulsocieties/2011/12/01 /center-for-global-nonkilling-2/

22. Gerard Jones quoted in "Violent Media is Good for Kids," *Mother Jones*, July 22, 2000, motherjones.com/politics/2000/07/violent-media-good -kids-1/

23. American Academy of Pediatrics et al., "Joint Statement on the Impact of Entertainment Violence on Children," *Congressional Public Health Summit*, 2000, public.psych.iastate.edu/caa/VGVpolicyDocs/00AAP%20-%20 Joint%20Statement.pdf

24. Nicholas Carnagey et al., "The Effect of Videogame Violence on Physiological Desensitization to Real-life Violence," *Journal of Experimental Social Psychology* 43, no. 4 (2007); Christopher Engelhardt et al., "This is Your Brain on Violent Video Games: Neural Desensitization to Violence Predicts Increased Aggression Following Violent Video Game Exposure," *Journal of Experimental Social Psychology* 47, no. 5 (2011).

25. UNICEF, "Ending Violence Against Children," September, 2014, unicef.org /publications/files/Ending_Violence_Against_Children_Six_strategies _for_action_EN_9_Oct_2014.pdf, 4.

26. Joan Durrant, "Positive Discipline in Everyday Parenting," *Save the Children Sweden*, 2016, resourcecentre.savethechildren.net/node/7509/pdf /pdep_2016_4th_edition.pdf

27. Robert Rosenthal and Lenore Jacobson, *Pygmalion in the Classroom* (Holt, Rinehart & Winston, 1968).

28. Elaine Fox, *Rainy Brain, Sunny Brain: The New Science of Optimism and Pessimism* (HarperCollins, 2012), 48.

29. Johan Galtung, *Peace by Peaceful Means: Peace and Conflict, Development and Civilization* (SAGE Publications, 1996), 228.

## Chapter 12: Safety

1. *The Prince* (1532, Devoted Publishing reprint 2016), 40.
2. Polly Nelson, *Defending the Devil: My Story as Ted Bundy's Last Lawyer* (William Morrow, 1994), 319.
3. Barry Bearak, "Bundy Electrocuted After Night of Weeping, Praying: 500 Cheer Death of Murderer," *Los Angeles Times*, January 24, 1989, articles. latimes.com/1989-01-24/news/mn-1075_1_ted-bundy
4. Thomas Hills in Tom Jacobs, "News on Scary Subjects Gets More Negative as It Spreads," *Pacific Standard*, June 8, 2018, psmag.com/news/news-on -scary-subjects-gets-more-negative-as-it-spreads
5. Paul Rozin and Edward Royzman, "Negativity Bias, Negativity Dominance, and Contagion," *Personality and Social Psychology Review* 5, no. 4 (2001).
6. Peter Certo, "Here's the Thing About Terrorism Obama Won't Tell You," *Foreign Policy in Focus*, January 13, 2016, fpif.org/heres-thing-terrorism -obama-wont-tell/
7. Leon Shane III, "Price Tag of the 'War on Terror' Will Top $6 Trillion Soon," *Military Times*, November 14, 2018, militarytimes.com/news /pentagon-congress/2018/11/14/price-tag-of-the-war-on-terror-will-top -6-trillion-soon/
8. Studies in Great Britain have found that about 0.6% of the population meet the criteria for psychopathy. Jeremy Coid et al., "Prevalence and Correlates of Psychopathic Traits in the Household Population of Great Britain," *International Journal of Law and Psychiatry* 32, no. 2 (2009).
9. Statistics Canada, Canadian Centre for Justice Statistics, "Uniform Crime Reporting Survey," July 20, 2016, statcan.gc.ca/pub/85-002-x/2016001 /article/14642-eng.htm
10. Douglas Fields, *Why We Snap: Understanding the Rage Circuit in Your Brain* (Penguin Random House, 2015), 4. This actually gets at questions of how we define the self, decision-making, and causality and control more generally, all interesting topics but beyond our scope here!
11. Fields, *Why We Snap*, 145.
12. Craig Anderson et al., "Does the Gun Pull the Trigger? Automatic Priming Effects of Weapon Pictures and Weapon Names," *Psychological Science* 9, no. 4 (1998).
13. Fields, *Why We Snap*, 53.
14. Lisa Feldman Barrett, *How Emotions Are Made: The Secret Life of the Brain* (E-book, Houghton Mifflin Harcourt, 2017).
15. Christine Wickens et al., "Addressing Driver Aggression: Contributions from Psychological Science," *Current Directions in Psychological Science* 22, no. 5 (2013).
16. Fields, *Why We Snap*, 215.
17. David Rand and Ziv Epstein, "Risking Your Life Without a Second Thought: Intuitive Decision-Making and Extreme Altruism," *PLoS One* 9, no. 10 (2014).
18. Canadian Yearly Meeting of the Religious Society of Friends, Minute 93, 1981.

19. Sarah Chandler, "'Til the Cows Come Home: What Kind of Neighbour Do You Want?" *Quaker Concern*, Spring 2014, 1.

20. Samira Shackle, "Should We Treat Crime as Something to be Cured Rather than Punished?" *The Guardian*, July 24, 2018, theguardian.com /news/2018/jul/24/violent-crime-cured-rather-than-punished-scottish -violence-reduction-unit

21. See, for example, the documentary film *The Interrupters*, directed by Steve James, 2011.

22. Stephen Michaud and Hugh Aynesworth, *The Only Living Witness: The True Story of Serial Sex Killer Ted Bundy* (Authorlink, 2012).

23. Peter Vronsky, *Female Serial Killers: How and Why Women Become Monsters* (Berkley Books, 2007).

24. Center for Disease Control and Prevention, "Adverse Childhood Experiences Journal Articles," *Violence Prevention*, April 1, 2016, cdc.gov /violenceprevention/acestudy/journal.html

25. David Brooks, "The Psych Approach," *The New York Times*, September 27, 2012, nytimes.com/2012/09/28/opinion/brooks-the-psych-approach .html

26. Nadine Burke Harris in Jeremy Adam Smith, "How to Reduce the Impact of Childhood Trauma," *Greater Good Magazine*, March 30, 2018, greatergood.berkeley.edu/article/item/how_to_reduce_the_impact_of _childhood_trauma

27. Gabor Maté, *In the Realm of Hungry Ghosts: Close Encounters with Addiction* (Vintage Canada, 2008), 171, 194, 291–292.

28. Morgan Kelly, "Poor Concentration: Poverty Reduces Brainpower Needed for Navigating Other Areas of Life," *Princeton University*, August 29, 2013, princeton.edu/news/2013/08/29/poor-concentration-poverty-reduces -brainpower-needed-navigating-other-areas-life

29. Kent Shifferd et al., *A Global Security System: An Alternative to War* (World Beyond War, 2018).

30. Documentary film *A Force More Powerful*, directed by Steve York, 1999.

31. Quoted in Jamiles Lartey, "Diane Nash: 'Non-violent Protest was the Most Important Invention of the 20th Century'," *The Guardian*, April 6, 2017, theguardian.com/global-development-professionals-network/2017/apr /06/diane-nash-non-violent-protest-civil-rights-gandhi-martin-luther -king

## Chapter 13: When Hate Rises

1. *Transforming Ourselves, Transforming the World* (Fernwood Publishing, 1999), 25.

2. See, for example, one activist calling white supremacists "rabid dogs" as quoted in Wes Enzinna, "This Is a War and We Intend To Win," *Mother Jones*, May/June, 2017, motherjones.com/politics/2017/04/anti-racist -antifa-tinley-park-five/

3. Natasha Lennard, "Is Antifa Counterproductive? White Nationalist Richard Spencer Would Beg to Differ," *The Intercept*, March 17, 2018,

theintercept.com/2018/03/17/richard-spencer-college-tour-antifa-alt
-right/

4. Eric Heinze, "Ten Arguments for—and Against—'No-Platforming',"
*Free Speech Debate*, March 1, 2016, freespeechdebate.com/discuss/ten
-arguments-for-and-against-no-platforming/

5. Enzinna, "This Is a War and We Intend To Win."

6. Faiza Patel and Michael German, "Countering Violent Extremism," *New
York University*, brennancenter.org/sites/default/files/analysis/102915
%20Final%20CVE%20Fact%20Sheet.pdf

7. Wiktor Soral et al., "Exposure to Hate Speech Increases Prejudice
Through Desensitization," *Aggressive Behaviour* 44, no. 2 (2018).

8. See, for example, Thant Sin, "Facebook Bans Racist Word 'Kalar' in Myanmar, Triggers Collateral Censorship," *Global Voices Advox*, June 2, 2017,
advox.globalvoices.org/2017/06/02/facebook-bans-racist-word-kalar-in
-myanmar-triggers-collateral-censorship/

9. Mack Lamoureux, "Here Are the Far-Right Conspiracists the Quebec City
Mosque Shooter Followed," *Vice*, April 16, 2018, vice.com/en_ca/article
/ywxeyg/here-are-the-far-right-conspiracists-the-quebec-city-mosque
-shooter-followed

10. Conor Gaffey, "Neo-Nazi Site The Daily Stormer Tried To Go Online in
Albania. It Failed," *Newsweek*, August 31, 2017, newsweek.com/daily
-stormer-andrew-anglin-charlottesville-657468

11. Maura Conway et al., "Disrupting Daesh," *VOX-Pol*, 2017, voxpol.eu/down
load/vox-pol_publication/DCUJ5528-Disrupting-DAESH-1706-WEB-v2
.pdf, 19

12. Tom Huddleston Jr., "YouTube Is Using Machine Learning to Combat Terror Content," *Fortune*, August 1, 2017, fortune.com/2017/08/01/youtube
-machine-learning-terror-content/

13. Angela Moscaritolo, "YouTube Redirecting Potential ISIS Recruits to
Anti-Terrorist Content," *PC Mag*, July 21, 2017, pcmag.com/news/355085
/youtube-redirecting-potential-isis-recruits-to-anti-terroris

14. Kevan Feshami, "What Happens When the Internet Tries to Silence
White Supremacy," *Yes! Magazine*, August 28, 2017, yesmagazine.org
/people-power/what-happens-when-the-internet-tries-to-silence-white
-supremacy-20170828

15. Quoted in Enzinna, "This Is a War and We Intend To Win."

16. İbrahim Kalın, "Daesh, Dabiq and the Follies of an Apocalyptic Ideology," *Daily Sabah*, October 17, 2016, dailysabah.com/columns/ibrahim
-kalin/2016/10/18/daesh-dabiq-and-the-follies-of-an-apocalyptic
-ideology

17. Jessica West, "Changing the War on Terror Script," *Project Ploughshares*,
April 4, 2017, ploughshares.ca/2017/04/changing-the-war-on-terror
-script/

18. Erin Kearns et al., "Why Do Some Terrorist Attacks Receive More Media
Attention Than Others?" *SSRN*, March 5, 2017, papers.ssrn.com/sol3
/papers.cfm?abstract_id=2928138

19. Mack Lamoureux, "Nearly Half of Canadians Have Negative Feelings Towards Islam," *Vice*, November 17, 2017, vice.com/en_ca/article/gyj97x/nearly-half-of-canadians-have-negative-feelings-towards-islam-poll

20. Marie-Danielle Smith, "Weak Link Found Between Religion, Terrorism for Canada," *Embassy*, May 20, 2015, embassynews.ca/news/2015/05/20/Weak-link-between-religion-terrorism-Canada/47109

21. Scott Plous and Philip Zimbardo, "How Social Science Can Reduce Terrorism," *The Chronicle of Higher Education*, September 10, 2004, socialpsychology.org/pdf/chronicle04.pdf

22. Tom Engelhardt, "How America Made ISIS," *Tom Dispatch*, September 2, 2014, tomdispatch.com/blog/175888/; Martin Chulov, "ISIS: The Inside Story," *The Guardian*, December 11, 2014, theguardian.com/world/2014/dec/11/-sp-isis-the-inside-story

23. Murtaza Hussain, "Trauma and Deprivation Lead Syrian Youths to Extremist Groups, Says New Report," *The Intercept*, May 19, 2016, theintercept.com/2016/05/19/trauma-and-deprivation-lead-syrian-youths-to-extremist-groups-says-new-report/

24. Alex Wilner and Claire-Jehanne Dubouloz, "Homegrown Terrorism and Transformative Learning," *Canadian Political Science Association Conference*, University of Ottawa, May, 2009, cpsa-acsp.ca/papers-2009/Wilner-Dubouloz.pdf

25. Plous and Zimbardo, "How Social Science Can Reduce Terrorism."

26. Glenna Gordon, "American Women of the Far Right," *The New York Review of Books*, December 13, 2018, nybooks.com/daily/2018/12/13/american-women-of-the-far-right/

27. Michael Kimmel, "Almost All Violent Extremists Share One Thing: Their Gender," *The Guardian*, April 8, 2018, theguardian.com/world/2018/apr/08/violent-extremists-share-one-thing-gender-michael-kimmel

28. The Sunday Edition, "Former Quebec Neo-Nazi Speaks Out About How He Learned to Hate Minorities," *CBC*, August 27, 2017, cbc.ca/radio/thesundayedition/august-27-2017-the-sunday-edition-1.4260430/former-quebec-neo-nazi-speaks-out-about-how-he-learned-to-hate-minorities-1.4260438

29. Robert Sampson et al., "Does Marriage Reduce Crime? A Counterfactual Approach to Within-individual Causal Effects" *Criminology* 44, no. 3 (2006).

30. Tom Jacobs, "Using Art Therapy to Open the Minds of Jihadists," *Pacific Standard*, May 8, 2015, psmag.com/social-justice/using-art-therapy-to-open-the-minds-of-jihadists

31. Search for Common Ground, "Transforming Violent Extremism: A Peacebuilders Guide," 2017, sfcg.org/transforming-violent-extremism-peacebuilders-guide/, 30.

32. Zak Ebrahim, *The Forgiveness Project*, June 2, 2016, theforgivenessproject.com/zak-ebrahim

33. Moises Velasquez-Manoff, "How to Make Fun of Nazis," *The New York Times*, August 17, 2017, nytimes.com/2017/08/17/opinion/how-to-make-fun-of-nazis.html

34. Janey Stephenson, "Fight Fascism With a Dance Party," *Yes! Magazine*, August 11, 2017, yesmagazine.org/people-power/fight-fascism-with-a -dance-party-20170811

35. Jack Ross, *Nonviolence for Elfin Spirits* (Argenta Friends Press, 1992), 18–19.

36. Ross, *Nonviolence for Elfin Spirits*, 52.

37. Sammy Rangel, *The Forgiveness Project*, July 4, 2011, theforgivenessproject .com/stories/sammy-rangel-usa/

38. Zaid Jilani, "This Group Has Successfully Converted White Supremacists Using Compassion. Trump Defunded It," *The Intercept*, August 17, 2017, theintercept.com/2017/08/17/this-group-has-successfully-converted -white-supremacists-using-compassion-trump-defunded-it/

39. Sammy Rangel, "The Power of Forgiveness," *TEDxDanubia*, June 23, 2015, youtube.com/watch?v=iOzJO6HRIuA&feature=youtu.be

## Chapter 14: Violence in Social Change

1. *Peter* Gelderloos, *How Nonviolence Protects the State* (South End Press, 2007).

2. Gelderloos, *How Nonviolence Protects the State.*

3. Adam Shatz, "The Doctor Prescribed Violence," *The New York Times*, September 2, 2001, nytimes.com/2001/09/02/books/the-doctor-prescribed -violence.html

4. Erica Chenoweth, "The Success of Nonviolent Civil Resistance," *TEDxBoulder*, Nov 4, 2013, youtube.com/watch?v=YJSehRlU34w

5. Erica Chenoweth and Maria Stephan, *Why Civil Resistance Works: The Strategic Logic of Nonviolent Conflict* (Columbia University Press, 2011). The raw dataset used is publicly available: Erica Chenoweth, "NAVCO Data Project," *University of Denver*, du.edu/korbel/sie/research/chenow_navco _data.html; Chenoweth, "The Success of Nonviolent Civil Resistance."

6. Chenoweth and Stephan, *Why Civil Resistance Works*, 10.

7. Erica Chenoweth and Maria Stephan, "How the World is Proving Martin Luther King Right about Nonviolence," *The Washington Post*, January 18, 2016, washingtonpost.com/news/monkey-cage/wp/2016/01/18/how-the -world-is-proving-mlk-right-about-nonviolence/

8. Avram Alpert, "Why the Greatest Advocates of Nonviolence Didn't Condemn Anti-Racist, Anti-Fascist Acts of Violence," *Truthout*, September 12, 2017, truth-out.org/opinion/item/41902-why-the-greatest-advocates-of -nonviolence-didn-t-condemn-anti-racist-anti-fascist-acts-of-violence

9. Ben Case, "Beyond Violence and Nonviolence," *ROAR Magazine*, April 2, 2017, roarmag.org/magazine/beyond-violence-nonviolence-antifascism/

10. Erica Chenoweth and Kurt Schock, "Do Contemporaneous Armed Challenges Affect the Outcomes of Mass Nonviolent Campaigns?" *Mobilization* 2, no. 4 (2015).

11. Chenoweth and Schock, "Do Contemporaneous Armed Challenges Affect the Outcomes?"

12. For example, Jonathan Montpetit, "Far-right Group Claims PR Victory After Duelling Protests in Quebec City," *CBC*, August 20, 2017, cbc.ca /news/canada/montreal/quebec-far-right-la-meute-1.4254792

13. Chenoweth and Stephan, "How the World is Proving Martin Luther King Right."
14. Laurie Marhoefer, "How to Protest Neo-Nazis Without Adding to the Violence," *Yes! Magazine*, August 29, 2017, yesmagazine.org/peace-justice /how-to-protest-neo-nazis-without-adding-to-the-violence-20170829
15. Emma Thomas and Winnifred Louis, "When Will Collective Action be Effective?: Violent and Non-violent Protests Differentially Influence Perceptions of Legitimacy and Efficacy Among Sympathizers," *Personality & Social Psychology Bulletin* 40, no. 2 (2014).
16. Robert Levering, "How Anti-Vietnam War Activists Stopped Violent Protest from Hijacking their Movement," *Waging Nonviolence*, March 7, 2017, wagingnonviolence.org/feature/vietnam-antiwar-protests-weathermen -resist-black-bloc/
17. Levering, "How Anti-Vietnam War Activists Stopped Violent Protest."
18. Wendy Pearlman, *Violence, Nonviolence, and the Palestinian National Movement* (Cambridge University Press, 2011).
19. Elaine Fox, *Rainy Brain, Sunny Brain: The New Science of Optimism and Pessimism* (HarperCollins, 2012), 56.
20. Heather Wadlinger and Derek Isaacowitz, "Positive Mood Broadens Visual Attention to Positive Stimuli," *Motivation and Emotion* 30, no. 1 (2003).
21. Matthew Lieberman et al., "Putting Feelings into Words," *Psychological Science* 18, no. 5 (2007).
22. Calum Marsh, "Rough Day? Time to Visit the Rage Room, Where Destruction is Encouraged," *The Guardian*, August 12, 2015, theguardian.com /travel/2015/aug/12/rage-room-toronto
23. Brad Bushman et al., "Catharsis, Aggression, and Persuasive Influence: Self-fulfilling or Self-defeating Prophecies?" *Journal of Personality and Social Psychology* 76, no. 3 (1999).
24. Brad Bushman, "Does Venting Anger Feed or Extinguish the Flame?" *Personality and Social Psychology Bulletin* 28, no. 6 (2002).
25. Brad Bushman, "Do People Aggress to Improve their Mood?" *Journal of Personality and Social Psychology* 81, no. 1 (2001).
26. Jeffrey Goldstein et al., "Escalation of Aggression: Experimental Studies," *Journal of Personality and Social Psychology* 31, no. 1 (1975).
27. Andy Martens et al., "Killing Begets Killing: Evidence From a Bug-Killing Paradigm That Initial Killing Fuels Subsequent Killing," *Personality and Social Psychology Bulletin* 33, no. 9 (2007).
28. Gianne Broughton, "Canadian Quakers and 'Just Peace'," January 31, 2012, quakerservice.ca/wp-content/uploads/2013/05/12.01.31.Just-Peace -Seminar-presentation.1.pdf, 1.
29. Gianne Broughton, *The Four Elements of Peacebuilding: How to Protect Nonviolently* (Canadian Friends Service Committee, 2013).
30. Enuga Reddy ed., "Apartheid, South Africa and International Law," from "Notes and Documents," no. 13/85, *United Nations Centre against Apartheid*, December, 1985, sahistory.org.za/sites/default/files/Apartheid,%20 South%20Africa%20and%20International%20Law.pdf

31. Jo Vellacott in Matthew Legge, "Peace and the Commemoration of World War I," *Quaker Concern*, Fall 2014, 3, 7.
32. Michael Randle, *Civil Resistance* (Fontana Press, 1994).
33. The methods are listed on the website of the Albert Einstein Institute, founded by Gene Sharp. "198 Methods of Nonviolent Action," aeinstein.org/nonviolentaction/198-methods-of-nonviolent-action/
34. Erica Chenoweth et al., "Days of Rage: Introducing the NAVCO 3.0 Dataset," *Journal of Peace Research* 55, no. 4 (2018).
35. Stephanie Van Hook, "Conflict Escalation Curve," *Metta Centre for Nonviolence*, October 6, 2012, mettacenter.org/conceptual-models/conflict-escalation-curve
36. Gene Sharp, *The Politics of Nonviolent Action* (Porter Sargent, 1973).
37. Julia Taleb, "Syrians Roll Back Extremism in Idlib Without Military Intervention," *Waging Nonviolence*, May 23, 2017, wagingnonviolence.org/feature/syrians-roll-back-extremism-idlib/. My thanks also to Jobran Kanji for his help in writing this example.
38. This activity is adapted from an exercise first developed by Augusto Boal, one of many activities used in Theatre of the Oppressed.

**Chapter 15: Who Benefits?**
1. *Peace by Peaceful Means: Peace and Conflict, Development and Civilization* (SAGE Publications, 1996), 116.
2. Andrew Feinstein, *The Shadow World: Inside the Global Arms Trade* (Penguin, 2012).
3. Mark Duffield, "Globalization, Transborder Trade, and War Economies," eds. Mats Berdal and David Malone in *Greed and Grievance: Economic Agendas in Civil Wars*, (Lynne Rienner, 2000), 74.
4. David Keen, *The Economic Functions of Violence in Civil Wars* (Routledge, 2005).
5. Cristina Bicchieri and Hugo Mercier, "Norms and Beliefs: How Change Occurs," *The Jerusalem Philosophical Quarterly* 63 (2014): 63.
6. John Jost, "The End of the End of Ideology," *American Psychologist* 61, no. 7 (2006): 655.
7. Kristin Laurin quoted in Tom Jacobs, "How the Intolerable Becomes Acceptable," *Pacific Standard*, February 19, 2018, psmag.com/news/how-the-intolerable-becomes-acceptable
8. David Gal and Derek Rucker, "When in Doubt, Shout! Paradoxical Influences of Doubt on Proselytizing," *Psychological Science* 21, no. 11 (2010).
9. Mark Snyder and William Swann Jr., "Behavioral Confirmation in Social Interaction: From Social Perception to Social Reality," *Journal of Experimental Social Psychology* 14, no. 2 (1978).
10. Christopher Hsee and Bowen Ruan, "The Pandora Effect: The Power and Peril of Curiosity," *Psychological Science* 27, no. 5 (2016).
11. Vanessa Bohns, "You're Already More Persuasive than You Think," *Harvard Business Review*, August 3, 2015, hbr.org/2015/08/research-were-much-more-powerful-and-persuasive-than-we-know

12. Katherine Phillips, "How Diversity Makes Us Smarter," *Scientific American*, October 1, 2014, scientificamerican.com/article/how-diversity-makes-us-smarter/

13. Mary Mahoney, "My Life in the Cult: How 'Serving God' Unraveled into Sex Abuse, Child Neglect and a Waking Nightmare," *Salon*, October 25, 2015, salon.com/2015/10/25/my_life_in_the_cult_how_serving_god_unraveled_into_sex_abuse_child_neglect_and_a_waking_nightmare/

14. Solomon Asch, "Studies of Independence and Conformity: A Minority of One Against a Unanimous Majority," *Psychological Monographs* 70, no. 9 (1956).

15. Bicchieri and Mercier, "Norms and Beliefs," 63.

16. Daniel Hunter, "Mainstream/Margin in Groups," *Training for Change*, 2009, trainingforchange.org/sites/default/files/Mainstream%3AMargin%20in%20Groups.pdf, 1.

17. John Paul Lederarch, *Preparing for Peace: Conflict Transformation Across Cultures* (Syracuse University Press, 1996), 60.

18. Psychologists for Social Responsibility, "Groupthink Vaccine," 2004, psysr.org/about/pubs_resources/gt/vaccination%20flicker%202004.swf

19. The Moral Injury Project, "What is Moral Injury," moralinjuryproject.syr.edu/about-moral-injury/

20. Martin Luther King Jr., *A Testament of Hope: The Essential Writings and Speeches* (HarperOne, 2003).

21. Kazu Haga, "Why Black Bloc Tactics Won't Build a Successful Movement," *Waging Nonviolence*, February 13, 2017, wagingnonviolence.org/feature/why-black-bloc-wont-build-successful-movement/

22. Eric Brahm, "Hurting Stalemate Stage," *Beyond Intractability*, September, 2003, beyondintractability.org/essay/stalemate

23. Michael Nagler, "Six Principles of Nonviolence," *Nonviolence Magazine*, October 18, 2016, nonviolencemag.org/six-principles-of-nonviolence-be7f7a48cfac

24. Jarem Sawatsky, Peacebuilding lecture series (delivered online), 2015.

25. Duke Today, "Most Teen Psychiatric Disorders Go Untreated," November 18, 2013, today.duke.edu/2013/11/costello

26. Rebecca Solnit quoted in Keziah Weir, "The Philosopher Queen," *Elle*, March 2, 2017, elle.com/culture/books/a42862/the-philosopher-queen-rebecca-solnit/

27. Adapted from Training for Change, "Walking Across the Room," trainingforchange.org/tools/walking-across-room

## Chapter 16: Oppressors and Victims

1. *A Collection of the Works of William Penn* (J. Sowle, 1726), 827.

2. William Brennan, *Dehumanizing the Vulnerable: When Word Games Take Lives* (Life Cycle Books, 2000).

3. Symon Hill, "White Poppies Don't 'Indoctrinate' Children, They Open Up Debate," *Huffington Post*, October 16, 2017, huffingtonpost.co.uk/symon-hill/white-poppy_b_18282732.html

4. Rachel MacNair, *The Psychology of Peace* (Praeger, 2011), 93–94.

5. Albert Bandura et al., "Mechanisms of Moral Disengagement in the Exercise of Moral Agency," *Journal of Personality and Social Psychology* 71, no. 2 (1996).

6. Cathy Spatz Widom and Helen Wilson, "How Victims Become Offenders," in eds. Bette Bottoms et al., *Children as Victims, Witnesses, and Offenders* (Guilford Press, 2009).

7. George Lakey, "Do 'Safe Spaces' and 'Trigger Warnings' Weaken Us?" *Waging Nonviolence*, January 6, 2016, wagingnonviolence.org/feature/do -safe-spaces-and-trigger-warnings-weaken-us/

8. For one good summary of some fascinating findings about this, see the chapter "How You Obtain Power by Letting Go: The Joy of Agency and the Fear of Losing Control" in Tali Sharot, *The Influential Mind: What the Brain Reveals About Our Power to Change Others* (E-book, Henry Holt and Co., 2017).

9. John Bargh et al., "Automaticity of Social Behavior: Direct Effects of Trait Construct and Stereotype Priming on Action," *Journal of Personality and Social Psychology* 71, no. 2 (1996).

10. Rob Holland et al., "Smells Like Clean Spirit: Nonconscious Effects of Scent on Cognition and Behavior," *Psychological Science* 16, no. 9 (2005).

11. Lakey, "Do 'Safe Spaces' and 'Trigger Warnings' Weaken Us?"

12. Jeannie Suk Gersen, "The Trouble with Teaching Rape Law," *The New Yorker*, December 15, 2014, newyorker.com/news/news-desk/trouble -teaching-rape-law

13. Greg Lukianoff and Jonathan Haidt, "The Coddling of the American Mind," *The Atlantic*, September, 2015, theatlantic.com/magazine/archive /2015/09/the-coddling-of-the-american-mind/399356/

14. Peter Norton and Esther Price, "A Meta-analytic Review of Adult Cognitive-behavioral Treatment Outcome Across the Anxiety Disorders," *Journal of Nervous & Mental Disease* 195, no. 6 (2007).

15. Debra Soh, "We Need to Protect Free Speech on Campus," *The Globe and Mail*, June 28, 2017, beta.theglobeandmail.com/opinion/we-need-to -protect-free-speech-on-campus/article35476933/

16. Lukianoff and Haidt, "The Coddling of the American Mind."

17. Benedict Carey, "The Psychology of Cheating," *The New York Times*, April 16, 2011, nytimes.com/2011/04/17/weekinreview/17chump.html

18. Anis Shivani, "Notes on the Ascendancy of Identity Politics in Literary Writing," *Subtropics*, June 12, 2017, subtropics.english.ufl.edu/index.php /2017/06/12/notes-ascendancy-identity-politics-literary-writing/

19. Phakyab Rinpoche and Sofia Stril-Rever, "Gratitude for My Torturers," *Tricycle*, May 9, 2017, tricycle.org/trikedaily/gratitude-for-my-torturers/

20. Amelia Goranson et al., "Dying is Unexpectedly Positive," *Psychological Science* 28, no. 7 (2017).

21. Benedict Cary, "Down and Out—or Up," *The New York Times*, January 10, 2009, nytimes.com/2009/01/11/weekinreview/11carey.html

22. George Bonanno, "Loss, Trauma, and Human Resilience," *American Psychologist* 59, no. 1 (2004), 21.

23. Bonanno, "Loss, Trauma, and Human Resilience," 22.

24. Bonanno, "Loss, Trauma, and Human Resilience," 23–24.

25. Southern Connecticut State University, "Rape Culture, Victim Blaming, and the Facts," southernct.edu/sexual-misconduct/facts.html

26. Jordan Peterson in Jason Tucker and Jason Vanden Beukel, "'We're Teaching University Students Lies'—An Interview with Dr Jordan Peterson." *C2C Journal*, December 1, 2016, c2cjournal.ca/2016/12/were-teaching-university-students-lies-an-interview-with-dr-jordan-peterson/

27. Jordan Peterson, "Genders, Rights and Freedom of Speech," *The Agenda with Steve Paikin*, October 26, 2016, youtube.com/watch?v=kasiovoytEc

28. Simona Chiose, "University of Toronto Professor Defends Right to Use Gender-specific Pronouns," *The Globe and Mail*, November 19, 2016, beta.theglobeandmail.com/news/national/university-of-toronto-professor-defends-right-to-use-gender-specific-pronouns/article32946675/

29. Peterson in Tucker and Vanden Beukel, "'We're Teaching University Students Lies.'"

30. Nellie Bowles, "Jordan Peterson, Custodian of the Patriarchy," *The New York Times*, May 18, 2018, nytimes.com/2018/05/18/style/jordan-peterson-12-rules-for-life.html

31. Common Cause Foundation, "Common Cause Communication," 2015, valuesandframes.org/resources/CCF_communications_toolkit.pdf, 122.

32. Peterson in Tucker and Vanden Beukel, "'We're Teaching University Students Lies.'"

33. Will Roscoe, *Changing Ones: Third and Fourth Genders in Native North America* (Palgrave Macmillan, 1998).

34. Chiose, "University of Toronto Professor Defends Right to Use Gender-specific Pronouns."

35. Laura Rodriguez and Donald Gaitlin, "New Study Suggests Link Between Experiences of Discrimination and Suicide Attempts Among Transgender People," *University of California Los Angeles*, January 28, 2014, williamsinstitute.law.ucla.edu/press/press-releases/28-jan-201/

36. Peterson in Tucker and Vanden Beukel, "'We're Teaching University Students Lies.'"

37. James Lindsay et al., "Academic Grievance Studies and the Corruption of Scholarship," *Aero*, October 2, 2018, areomagazine.com/2018/10/02/academic-grievance-studies-and-the-corruption-of-scholarship/

38. Daniel Engber, "What the 'Grievance Studies' Hoax Actually Reveals," *Slate*, October 5, 2018, slate.com/technology/2018/10/grievance-studies-hoax-not-academic-scandal.html

39. Steven Sloman and Philip Fernbach, *The Knowledge Illusion: Why We Never Think Alone* (E-book, Riverhead Books, 2017).

40. Tabatha Southey, "Is Jordan Peterson the Stupid Man's Smart Person?" *MacLean's*, November 17, 2017, macleans.ca/opinion/is-jordan-peterson-the-stupid-mans-smart-person/

41. Peterson states that he mostly appeals to men and that many are lost and need a sense of direction in "Joe Rogan Experience #1208—Jordan Peterson," *YouTube*, youtube.com/watch?v=vIeFt88Hm8s; see also

Peterson supporters profiled in Bowles, "Jordan Peterson, Custodian of the Patriarchy."

42. Jack Brehm, "Control, Its Loss, and Psychological Reactance," in eds. Gifford Weary et al., *Control Motivation and Social Cognition* (Springer-Verlag, 1993).

43. Geoffrey Cohen et al., "Bridging the Partisan Divide: Self-affirmation Reduces Ideological Closed-mindedness and Inflexibility in Negotiation," *Journal of Personality and Social Psychology* 93, no. 3 (2007).

44. Ben Brimelow, "The Incredible True Story of When WWI Stopped for Enemy Armies to Celebrate Christmas Together," *Business Insider*, December 25, 2017, businessinsider.fr/us/christmas-truce-1914-world-war-i-2017-12/

## Chapter 17: Connection

1. Quoted in *Faith and Practice* (Canadian Yearly Meeting of the Religious Society of Friends, 2011), 16.

2. Rachel Feltman, "Most Men Would Rather Shock Themselves than be Alone with Their Thoughts," *The Washington Post*, July 3, 2014, washingtonpost.com/news/to-your-health/wp/2014/07/03/most-men-would-rather-shock-themselves-than-be-alone-with-their-thoughts/

3. Sendhil Mullainathan, "The Mental Strain of Making Do With Less," *The New York Times*, September 21, 2013, nytimes.com/2013/09/22/business/the-mental-strain-of-making-do-with-less.html

4. Larry Kim, "Multitasking is Killing Your Brain," *Observer*, February 2, 2016, observer.com/2016/02/multitasking-is-killing-your-brain/

5. Jean Twenge, "With Teen Mental Health Deteriorating Over Five Years, There's a Likely Culprit," *The Conversation*, November 14, 2017, theconversation.com/with-teen-mental-health-deteriorating-over-five-years-theres-a-likely-culprit-86996

6. David Gessner quoted in Phillip Judd, "Science Shows this Popular Swiss Activity Increases Brain Power and Life Expectancy," January 21, 2016, lenews.ch/2016/01/21/science-suggests-this-popular-swiss-activity-could-increase-life-expectancy/

7. United Nations Department of Economic and Social Affairs, "World's Population Increasingly Urban with More than Half Living in Urban Areas," July 10, 2014, un.org/development/desa/en/news/population/world-urbanization-prospects.html

8. Alex Korb, *The Upward Spiral: Using Neuroscience to Reverse the Course of Depression, One Small Change at a Time* (E-Book, New Harbinger Publications, 2015).

9. Florian Lederbogen et al., "City Living and Urban Upbringing Affect Neural Social Stress Processing in Humans," *Nature* 474, no. 7352 (2011).

10. Douglas Fields, *Why We Snap: Understanding the Rage Circuit in Your Brain* (Penguin Random House, 2015), 341–342.

11. Craig Anderson, "Heat and Violence," *Current Directions in Psychological Science* 10, no. 1 (2001).

12. Irving Spiegel, "Man Pulled From Ledge as Crowd Yells 'Jump!'," *The New*

*York Times*, June 8, 1964, nytimes.com/1964/06/08/man-pulled-from -ledge-as-crowd-yells-jump.html

13. Jon Ronson, *So You've Been Publicly Shamed* (Riverhead Books, 2015).

14. Chen-Bo Zhong et al., "Good Lamps Are the Best Police," *Psychological Science* 21, no. 3 (2010).

15. Emma Jane, *Misogyny Online: A Short (and Brutish) History* (SAGE Publications, 2017).

16. Tom Postmes and Russell Spears, "Deindividuation and Antinormative Behaviour: A Meta-Analysis," *Psychological Bulletin* 123, no. 3 (1998).

17. Melissa Bateson et al., "Cues of Being Watched Enhance Cooperation in a Real-World Setting," *Biological Letters* 2, no. 3 (2006).

18. Dan Gilbert, "The Surprising Science of Happiness," *TED*, February, 2004, ted.com/talks/dan_gilbert_asks_why_are_we_happy

19. Marc Berman et al., "The Cognitive Benefits of Interacting With Nature," *Psychological Science* 19, no. 12 (2008).

20. Florence Williams, "This is Your Brain on Nature," *National Geographic*, January, 2016, nationalgeographic.com/magazine/2016/01/call-to-wild/

21. Kristophe Green and Dacher Keltner, "Nature is So Good for You That Even Watching It on TV Improves Well-Being," *Yes! Magazine*, December 25, 2017, yesmagazine.org/happiness/nature-is-so-good-for-you-that -even-watching-it-on-tv-improves-well-being-20171225

22. Jos Brosschot et al., "The Perseverative Cognition Hypothesis: A Review of Worry, Prolonged Stress-related Physiological Activation, and Health," *Journal of Psychosomatic Research* 60, no. 2 (2006).

23. Lauren Friedman and Kevin Loria, "11 Scientifically Proven Reasons You Should be Spending Less Time in the Office," *Business Insider UK*, June 30, 2016, uk.businessinsider.com/why-being-outside-in-nature-is-healthy -2015-6

24. Tan Ee Lyn, "15 Minutes of Exercise a Day Can Extend Life by Three Years," *Reuters*, August 16, 2011, reuters.com/article/us-exercise-taiwan /15-minutes-of-exercise-a-day-can-extend-life-by-three-years-idUSTRE 77E69L20110816

25. Paul Piff et al., "Awe, the Small Self, and Prosocial Behavior," *Journal of Personality and Social Psychology* 108, no. 6 (2015).

26. See, for example, Mark Burch, *Stepping Lightly: Simplicity for People and the Planet* (New Society Publishers, 2011).

27. Mark Burch, "CYM Quaker Studies Series," *Canadian Yearly Meeting*, 2014, quaker.ca/resources/audio-video/

28. Ruut Veenhoven, "Hedonism and Happiness," *Journal of Happiness Studies* 4, no. 4 (2003).

29. Government of Framingham, "About Framingham," *Government of Framingham*, framinghamma.gov/58/About-Framingham

30. James Fowler and Nicholas Christakis, "The Dynamic Spread of Happiness in a Large Social Network," *British Medical Journal* 337, no. 768 (2008).

31. Tobias Greitemeyer, "The Spreading Impact of Playing Violent Video Games on Aggression," *Computers in Human Behaviour* 80 (2018).

32. "Depressive Thinking Can Be Contagious," *Time*, April 24, 2013, health land.time.com/2013/04/24/depressive-thinking-can-be-infectious/

33. James Fowler and Nicholas Christakis, "Cooperative Behavior Cascades in Human Social Networks," *PNAS* 107, no. 12 (2010).

34. Postmes and Spears, "Deindividuation and Antinormative Behaviour."

**Chapter 18: Changing Ourselves**

1. In *Technology and the Image of God* (Canadian Council of Churches, 2017), 9.

2. Margot Van Sluytman, *The Forgiveness Project*, January 23, 2017, theforgive nessproject.com/stories/margot-van-sluytman-canada/

3. Charlotte van Oyen Witvliet et al., "Granting Forgiveness or Harboring Grudges: Implications for Emotion, Physiology, and Health," *Psychological Science* 12, no. 2 (2001).

4. Saima Noreen, "Forgiving You Is Hard, but Forgetting Seems Easy: Can Forgiveness Facilitate Forgetting?" *Psychological Science* 25, no. 7 (2014).

5. Charlotte van Oyen Witvliet et al., "Compassionate Reappraisal and Emotion Suppression as Alternatives to Offense-focused Rumination," *The Journal of Positive Psychology* 6, no. 4 (2011).

6. Daniel Wegner et al., "Paradoxical Effects of Thought Suppression," *Journal of Personality and Social Psychology* 53, no. 1 (1987).

7. Kate Kelland, "One in 12 Teenagers Self Harm, Study Finds," *Reuters*, November 16, 2011, reuters.com/article/us-self-harm/one-in-12-teen agers-self-harm-study-finds-idUSTRE7AG02520111117

8. Yoel Inbar et al., "Moral Masochism: On the Connection Between Guilt and Self-Punishment," *Emotion* 13, no. 1 (2012); Alex Korb, *The Upward Spiral: Using Neuroscience to Reverse the Course of Depression, One Small Change at a Time* (E-Book, New Harbinger Publications, 2015).

9. Alexandra Michel, "Burnout and the Brain," *Association for Psychological Science*, January 29, 2016, psychologicalscience.org/observer/burnout -and-the-brain

10. David Nowell, "Manage Procrastination With the Pomodoro Technique," *Psychology Today*, July 2, 2013, psychologytoday.com/ca/blog/intrinsic -motivation-and-magical-unicorns/201307/manage-procrastination-the -pomodoro-technique

11. Alison Kodjak, "In Ads, Tobacco Companies Admit They Made Cigarettes More Addictive," *NPR*, November 27, 2017, npr.org/sections/health-shots /2017/11/27/566014966/in-ads-tobacco-companies-admit-they-made -cigarettes-more-addictive

12. Fred Bass, personal communication and "Helping Patients to Quit Smoking," *Canadian Family Physician* 35 (1989).

13. Chip and Dan Heath, *The Power of Moments: Why Certain Experiences Have Extraordinary Impact* (E-book, Simon & Shulster, 2017).

14. Judson Brewer, "A Simple Way to Break a Bad Habit," *Mindful*, November 10, 2017, mindful.org/simple-way-break-bad-habit/

15. Jacoba Urist, "What the Marshmallow Test Really Teaches About Self-Control," *The Atlantic*, September 24, 2014, theatlantic.com/health /archive/2014/09/what-the-marshmallow-test-really-teaches-about-self -control/380673/

16. Most recently see Tyler Watts et al., "Revisiting the Marshmallow Test: A Conceptual Replication Investigating Links Between Early Delay of Gratification and Later Outcomes," *Psychological Science* 29, no. 7 (2018).

17. Urist, "What the Marshmallow Test Really Teaches About Self-Control."

18. Peter Giancola and Michelle Corman, "Alcohol and Aggression: A Test of the Attention-Allocation Model," *Psychological Science* 18, no. 7 (2007); Adrianna Jenkins and Ming Hsu, "Dissociable Contributions of Imagination and Willpower to the Malleability of Human Patience," *Psychological Science* 28, no. 7 (2017); Anna Christiansen, "Can We Wire Children's Brains to Not Crave Junk Food?" *PBS*, September 9, 2014, pbs.org/newshour/science/can-wire-childrens-brains-crave-candy

19. Roy Baumeister in Leslie Carr, "How to Increase Willpower and Follow Through With Resolutions," *The Atlantic*, January 30, 2012, theatlantic.com/health/archive/2012/01/how-to-increase-willpower-and-follow-through-with-resolutions/252043/

20. Baumeister in Carr "How to Increase Willpower."

21. Kristin Neff, "Self-esteem Might Boost Our Egos, But Self-compassion Opens Our Hearts," *Yes! Magazine*, April 4, 2017, yesmagazine.org/happiness/self-esteem-might-boost-our-egos-but-self-compassion-opens-our-hearts-20170404

22. Joanne Wood et al., "Positive Self-statements: Power for Some, Peril for Others," *Psychological Science* 20, no. 7 (2009).

23. Neff, "Self-esteem Might Boost Our Egos, But Self-compassion Opens Our Hearts."

24. Kristin Neff, "The Space Between Self-esteem and Self-compassion," *TEDx Talks*, February 6, 2013, youtube.com/watch?v=IvtZBUSplr4&feature=youtu.be

25. Joel Wong et al., "Does Gratitude Writing Improve the Mental Health of Psychotherapy Clients? Evidence from a Randomized Controlled Trial," *Psychotherapy Research* 28, no. 2 (2018).

26. Robert Emmons and Michael McCullough, "Counting Blessings versus Burdens: An Experimental Investigation of Gratitude and Subjective Well-being in Daily Life," *Journal of Personality and Social Psychology* 84, no. 2 (2003).

27. Barbara Fredrickson et al., "What Good are Positive Emotions in Crisis? A Prospective Study of Resilience and Emotions Following the Terrorist Attacks on the United States on September 11th, 2001," *Journal of Personality and Social Psychology* 84, no. 2 (2003).

28. Barbara Fredrickson, "The Value of Positive Emotions," *American Scientist* 91, no. 4 (2003).

29. Korb, *The Upward Spiral.*

30. Fredrickson, "The Value of Positive Emotions."

31. Emmons and McCullough, "Counting Blessings versus Burdens."

32. Helen Weng et al., "Compassion Training Alters Altruism and Neural Responses to Suffering," *Psychological Science* 24, no. 7 (2013).

33. Barbara Fredrickson quoted in Angela Winter, "The One You're With: Barbara Fredrickson On Why We Should Rethink Love," *The Sun Magazine*, July, 2014, thesunmagazine.org/issues/463/the-one-youre-with

34. Barbara Fredrickson et al., "Open Hearts Build Lives: Positive Emotions, Induced through Loving-kindness Meditation, Build Consequential Personal Resources," *Journal of Personality and Social Psychology* 95, no. 5 (2008).

35. Fredrickson et al., "Open Hearts Build Lives," 1059.

36. This version of the meditation may not be exactly the same as Fredrickson used in the study mentioned. It is adapted from Barbara Fredrickson, Lectures: "Loving-Kindness Introduced" and "Loving-Kindness Meditation," *Positive Psychology*, The University of North Carolina at Chapel Hill, coursera.org/learn/positive-psychology

## Chapter 19: Who's Dreaming?

1. London Yearly Meeting Minutes, 1919, 123–4.

2. "Grenada, 1983," *Population Pyramid*, populationpyramid.net/grenada /1983/

3. Jorge Domínguez, *To Make a World Safe for Revolution* (Harvard University Press, 1989), 168.

4. "United Nations General Assembly Resolution 38/7," *United Nations*, November 2, 1983, un.org/documents/ga/res/38/a38r007.htm

5. Ronald Cole, "Operation Urgent Fury: The Planning and Execution of Joint Operations in Grenada," 1997, dtic.mil/doctrine/doctrine/history /urgfury.pdf, 62, 4.

6. Alex Ward, "Why America Doesn't Win Wars Anymore: An Expert Explains Why the US Struggles with Modern Wars," *Vox*, August 23, 2018, vox.com/2018/2/15/17007678/syria-trump-war-win-interview

7. Jennifer Llewellyn and Daniel Philpott, *Restorative Justice, Reconciliation, and Peacebuilding* (Oxford University Press, 2014), 4–5.

8. "Global Terrorism Index 2015," *Institute for Economics and Peace*, 2015, economicsandpeace.org/wp-content/uploads/2015/11/Global-Terrorism -Index-2015.pdf; Don Winslow, "U.S. War on Drugs Empowers Mexico Cartels," *CNN*, June 28, 2015, cnn.com/2015/06/28/opinions/winslow -drug-war-folly/index.html

9. Alleen Brown et al., "Leaked Documents Reveal Counterterrorism Tactics Used at Standing Rock to 'Defeat Pipeline Insurgencies,'" *The Intercept*, May 27, 2017, theintercept.com/2017/05/27/leaked-documents-reveal -security-firms-counterterrorism-tactics-at-standing-rock-to-defeat -pipeline-insurgencies/

10. Kevin Walby and Brendan Roziere, "Rise of the SWAT Team: Routine Police Work in Canada is Now Militarized," *The Conversation*, January 24, 2018, theconversation.com/rise-of-the-swat-team-routine-police-work -in-canada-is-now-militarized-90073

11. Tomáš Weiss, "The Blurring Border Between the Police and the Military," *Cooperation and Conflict* 46, no. 3 (2011).

12. Institute for Economics and Peace, "Global Peace Index 2018," June, 2018, visionofhumanity.org/app/uploads/2018/06/Global-Peace-Index-2018-2 .pdf, 3.

13. World Bank Group and United Nations, "Pathways to Peace: Inclusive

Approaches to Preventing Violent Conflict," 2018, openknowledge.world
bank.org/handle/10986/28337, 4–5.

14. Alexander Nazaryan, "The US Department of Defense Is One of the
World's Biggest Polluters," *Newsweek*, July 17, 2014, newsweek.com/2014
/07/25/us-department-defence-one-worlds-biggest-polluters-259456
.html; Executive Office of the President, "The President's Climate Action
Plan," June, 2013, obamawhitehouse.archives.gov/sites/default/files
/image/president27sclimateactionplan.pdf, 7.

15. Aaron Hoffman et al. "Norms, Diplomatic Alternatives, and the Social
Psychology of War Support," *Journal of Conflict Resolution* 59, no. 1 (2015).

16. The Abolition Project, "Arguments and Justifications," *The Abolition Project*, abolition.e2bn.org/slavery_112.html

17. See, for ,example Canada's arguments when selling arms to a country with
one of the worst human rights records in the world: Steven Chase, "Dion
Quietly Approved Arms Sale to Saudi Arabia in April," *The Globe and
Mail*, April 12, 2016, theglobeandmail.com/news/politics/liberals-quietly
-approved-arms-sale-to-saudis-in-april-documents/article29612233/

18. Stuart Russell et al., "Why We Really Should Ban Autonomous Weapons: A Response," *IEEE Spectrum*, August 3, 2015, spectrum.ieee.org
/automaton/robotics/artificial-intelligence/why-we-really-should-ban
-autonomous-weapons

## Chapter 20: Just War, Just Peace, and Responsibility

1. *Achieving Security in Sub-Saharan Africa* (Institute for Security Studies, 2004), vii.

2. Brad Bushman et al., "When God Sanctions Killing: Effect of Scriptural
Violence on Aggression," *Psychological Science* 18, no. 3 (2007).

3. Rudy Giuliani quoted in Michael Cooper, "Giuliani Questioned on Torture," *The New York Times*, October 25, 2007, nytimes.com/2007/10/25/us
/politics/25torture.html

4. Heather Kirk, *Seeking Peace: The Quakers* (Borealis Press, 2017), 52, 22, 32.

5. Michael Jerryson, "Monks with Guns: Westerners Think That Buddhism
is About Peace and Non-violence. So How Come Buddhist Monks are in
Arms Against Islam?" *Aeon*, April 26, 2017, aeon.co/essays/buddhism-can
-be-as-violent-as-any-other-religion; Poppy McPherson, "'We Must Protect Our Country': Extremist Buddhists Target Mandalay's Muslims," *The
Guardian*, May 8, 2017, theguardian.com/cities/2017/may/08/buddhist
-extremists-anti-muslim-mandalay-ma-ba-tha; Brian Victoria, "Zen as
a Cult of Death in the Wartime Writings of D. T. Suzuki," *The Asia Pacific
Journal* 11, issue 30, no. 4 (2013).

6. Dan Smith, "Obama in Power: Is the War in Afghanistan a Just War?"
*Open Democracy*, December 17, 2009, opendemocracy.net/dan-smith
/obama-in-power-is-war-in-afghanistan-just-war

7. World Bank Group and United Nations, "Pathways to Peace: Inclusive Approaches to Preventing Violent Conflict—Main Messages and
Emerging Policy Directions," 2018, openknowledge.worldbank.org
/handle/10986/28337, 9.

8. Diana Francis, "War: Justifiable or Simply Catastrophic?" *Open Democracy*, January 21, 2010, opendemocracy.net/5050/diana-francis/war-justifiable -or-simply-catastrophic

9. *Just Peace Companion* (World Council of Churches, 2012), 94.

10. Séverine Autesserre, "Constructing Peace: Collective Understandings of Peace, Peacemaking, Peacekeeping, and Peacebuilding," *Columbia University Academic Commons*, 2011, academiccommons.columbia.edu/catalog /ac:145128, 5.

11. Saferworld and Conciliation Resources, "Effective Local Action: From Early Warning to Peacebuilding," 2016, saferworld.org.uk/resources /publications/1042-effective-local-action-from-early-warning-to-peace building

12. Camilla Campisi and Laura Ribeiro Rodrigues Pereira, "Filling the Gap: How Civil Society Engagement Can Help the UN's Peacebuilding Architecture Meet its Purpose," *The Global Partnership for the Prevention of Armed Conflict and The Quaker United Nations Office*, April, 2015, gppac .net/documents/130492842/131146243/Filling+the+Gap.pdf/f90e9b00 -36f6-4d65-acb7-d071f4156a86

13. William Harris, "Why Can't Scientists Accurately Predict the Weather?" *How Stuff Works*, science.howstuffworks.com/nature/climate-weather /atmospheric/scientists-predict-weather.htm

14. Robert Ricigliano, *Making Peace Last: A Toolbox for Sustainable Peace-building* (Routledge, 2015).

15. Carnegie Commission on Preventing Deadly Conflict, *Preventing Deadly Conflict* (Carnegie Corporation of New York, 1997), 54.

16. Barbara Crossette, "Iraq Sanctions Kill Children, U.N. Reports," *The New York Times*, December 1, 1995, nytimes.com/1995/12/01/world/iraq -sanctions-kill-children-un-reports.html

17. For example, "Commerzbank Fined $1.5bn for Doing Business with Sanctioned Iran and Sudan," RT, March 13, 2015, rt.com/business/240353 -commerzbank-billion-fine-sanctions/

18. Peggy Mason, "Alternatives to War with Iraq," *Carleton University*, December, 2002, carleton.ca/csds/docs/occasional_papers/npsia-34.pdf

19. Amnesty International, "Iraq: US Military Admits Failures to Monitor Over $1 Billion Worth of Arms Transfers," May 24, 2017, amnesty.org/en /latest/news/2017/05/us-military-admits-failures-to-monitor-over-1 -billion-worth-of-arms-transfers/

20. Jennifer Welsh, "The Challenge of Peace," CBC, August 14, 2017, cbc.ca/player/play/872643651511/

21. Carnegie Commission on Preventing Deadly Conflict, *Preventing Deadly Conflict*, 6.

22. Carnegie Commission on Preventing Deadly Conflict, *Preventing Deadly Conflict*, 39.

23. Paul Heinbecker, "Letter Dated 26 July 2002 from the Permanent Representative of Canada to the United Nations Addressed to the Secretary-General," *United Nations*, August 14, 2002, 5/57/303, 27.

24. Noam Chomsky, "Statement by Professor Noam Chomsky to the United Nations General Assembly Thematic Dialogue on the Responsibility to

Protect," *United Nations*, July 23, 2009, un.org/ga/president/63/inter active/protect/noam.pdf

25. Canadian Yearly Meeting of the Religious Society of Friends, Minute 57, 2007.

26. United Nations General Assembly, "Resolution 60/1," *United Nations*, October 24, 2005, A/RES/60/1, unpan1.un.org/intradoc/groups/public /documents/UN/UNPAN021752.pdf, 30 (emphasis added); Carl Stieren in Gianne Broughton, *The Four Elements of Peacebuilding: How to Protect Nonviolently* (Canadian Friends Service Committee, 2013), 4.

27. Heinbecker, "Letter Dated 26 July 2002," 36, xii.

28. See, for example, Asia-Pacific Centre for the Responsibility to Protect, r2pasiapacific.org/

29. United Nations Department of Public Information, "The Responsibility to Protect," April, 2013, un.org/en/preventgenocide/rwanda/about/bg responsibility.shtml

30. UN News Service, "Security Council Authorizes 'All Necessary Measures' to Protect Civilians in Libya," March 17, 2011, un.org/apps/news/story.asp ?NewsID=37808&Cr=libya&Cr1=#.UgfvHazfLTo

31. Eric Bailey, "An Interview with Noam Chomsky—Nothing Can Justify Torture," *Torture Magazine*, December 14, 2012, humanrights.asia/news /ahrc-news/AHRC-ART-146-2012/

32. United Nations Security Council, "6498th Meeting," March 17, 2011, S/PV .6498, daccess-ddsny.un.org/doc/UNDOC/PRO/N11/267/18/PDF/N112 6718.pdf?OpenElement

33. Bailey, "An Interview with Noam Chomsky."

34. Jeffery Simpson, "NATO Bombs Cleared the Path for IS in Libya," *The Globe and Mail*, February 18, 2015, theglobeandmail.com/opinion/nato -bombs-cleared-the-path-for-is-in-libya/article23044006/

35. Seumas Milne, "Coups and Terror are the Fruit of NATO's War in Libya," *The Guardian*, May 22, 2014, theguardian.com/commentisfree/2014 /may/22/coups-terror-nato-war-in-libya-west-intervention-boko-haram -nigeria

36. Lynne Jones, "The Moral Failure of the Peace Movement," *Peace and Democracy News* 7, no. 1 (Summer 1993), reprinted at civilresistance.info /challenge/1-Bosnia

37. Diana Francis, "Lessons From Kosovo/a: Alternatives To War," December, 2000, dianafrancis.info/other-publications/lessons-from-kosovo-a -alternatives-to-war/

38. Francis, "Lessons From Kosovo/a."

39. For example, United Nations, "General Assembly Concludes High-Level Debate on Sustaining Peace with Consensus Resolution Encouraging Further Action by United Nations, Member States," April 26, 2018, GA/12014, un.org/press/en/2018/ga12014.doc.htm

40. World Bank Group and United Nations, "Pathways to Peace," 23–43.

41. See, for example, the Canadian Peace Initiative, canadianpeaceinitiative.ca

42. Scott Strauss, "Fundamentals of Genocide and Mass Atrocities Prevention," *United States Holocaust Memorial Museum*, 2016, ushmm.org/m /pdfs/Fundamentals-of-Genocide-and-Mass-Atrocity-Prevention.pdf

43. John Shuford, "AVP: An Instrument of Peace," *Friends Journal*, January 1, 2009, friendsjournal.org/avp-instrument-peace/
44. Quoted in Bethany Mahler et al., "Now I Am Human: Testimonies from the Healing Companions Program in Rwanda and Burundi," *Peace Ways* 2, no. 2 (2007), aglifpt.org/publications/articles/hroc/pdf/PWfall2007.pdf, 18–19.
45. Quoted in ed. Laura Shipler Chico, *This Light That Pushes Me: Stories of African Peacebuilders* (Quaker Books, 2014), 3.
46. David Zarembka, "Healing and Rebuilding our Communities (HROC) Update," Email, July 20, 2017.

## Chapter 21: Unarmed Civilian Protection

1. "Citizen Diplomacy," *Beyond Intractability*, 2013, beyondintractability.org/coreknowledge/citizen-diplomacy
2. World Bank Group and United Nations, "Pathways to Peace: Inclusive Approaches to Preventing Violent Conflict—Main Messages and Emerging Policy Directions," 2018, openknowledge.worldbank.org/handle/10986/28337, 35.
3. Lisa Hultman et al., "Beyond Keeping Peace: United Nations Effectiveness in the Midst of Fighting," *American Political Science Review* 108, no. 4 (2014).
4. "Unarmed Civilian Protection: Expanding the Protection of Civilians Tool Kit," *United Nations Web TV*, October 19, 2016, webtv.un.org/watch/unarmed-civilian-protection-expanding-the-protection-of-civilians-tool-kit/5177505946001
5. Madelyn MacKay, "People Power and the Environment," *Kootenay Co-Op Radio*, May 16, 2017, cjlypodcast.net/cchange/Climate_of_Change_Ep_42_for_Podcast_stereo.mp3
6. For example Selkirk College, "Unarmed Civilian Peacekeeping," selkirk.ca/unarmed-civilian-peacekeeping; United Nations Institute for Training and Research, "Unarmed Civilian Peacekeeping," unitar.org/ptp/unarmed-civilian-peacekeeping; Merrimack College, "Unarmed Civilian Protection," merrimack.edu/academics/professional-studies/unarmed-civilian-protection/
7. Mica Stumpf, "The Future of Security," *Open Democracy*, August 7, 2017, opendemocracy.net/transformation/mica-stumpf/future-of-security
8. Quoted in Elizabeth Boardman, *Taking a Stand: A Guide to Peace Teams and Accompaniment Projects* (New Society Publishers, 2005), 45.
9. Adam Curle, *Another Way: Positive Response to Contemporary Violence* (Jon Carpenter Publishing, 1995), 106.
10. One example of this is the program Turning the Tide developed by British Quakers, turningtide.org.uk
11. Gianne Broughton, *The Four Elements of Peacebuilding: How to Protect Nonviolently* (Canadian Friends Service Committee, 2013), 17.
12. Nonviolent Peaceforce, "Frequently Asked Questions," nonviolentpeaceforce.org/background/2014-09-10-18-33-03; Tiffany Easthom, "Unarmed Civilian Protection," *United Nations Web TV*.
13. Easthom, "Unarmed Civilian Protection."

14. Sarah Thompson, "CPT United States: Christian Peacemaker Teams Supports Clergy and Community Members in Charlottesville through Trainings in Nonviolent Action," *Christian Peacemaker Teams*, August 18, 2017, cpt.org/cptnet/2017/08/18/cpt-united-states-christian-peacemaker-teams-support-clergy-and-community-members-

15. Boardman, *Taking a Stand*, 88.

16. Hannah Redekop, "Palestine/Colombia Reflection: Made in the USA—Take Action to Stop Military Aid," *Christian Peacemaker Teams*, September 10, 2017, cpt.org/cptnet/2017/09/08/palestinecolombia-reflection-made-usa-take-action-stop-military-aid

17. Thompson, "CPT United States."

18. Christian Peacemaker Teams, "Weapons: Security Precautions," cpt.org/files/PP%20-%20Security%20-%20Weapons.pdf

19. Boardman, *Taking a Stand*, 12–14.

20. George Lakey, "Laboratories for Nonviolent Defense," *Waging Nonviolence*, July 23, 2013, wagingnonviolence.org/feature/laboratories-for-non violent-defense/

21. Peace Brigades International Canada, "The Four Areas of Work," pbicanada.org/index.php/en/what-we-do-2/the-four-areas-of-work

22. Michael Nagler and Karen Ridd, "Humor but not Humiliation: Finding the Sweet Spot in Nonviolent Conflict Resolution," *Open Democracy*, May 7, 2014, opendemocracy.net/transformation/michael-nagler-karen-ridd /humor-but-not-humiliation-finding-sweet-spot-in-nonviolent-

23. Annie Hewitt, "Why Unarmed Civilian Protection is the Best Path to Sustainable Peace," *Waging Nonviolence*, July 6, 2018, wagingnonviolence .org/feature/unarmed-civilian-protection-sustainable-peace/

24. James Favel, "Face To Face: Dennis Ward Sits Down with Bear Clan Patrol Executive Director, James Favel," *Aboriginal Peoples Television Network*, April 18, 2017, aptnnews.ca/2017/04/18/face-to-face-dennis-ward-sits -down-with-bear-clan-patrol-executive-director-james-favel/

25. Bear Clan Patrol Inc., "History of Bear Clan Patrol," Bear Clan Patrol Inc., bearclanpatrolinc.com/history

26. Bear Clan Patrol Inc., "About Bear Clan Patrol," Bear Clan Patrol Inc., bearclanpatrolinc.com/about-bear-clan

27. Favel, "Face To Face."

28. Peter Gollwitzer and Paschal Sheeran, "Implementation Intentions and Goal Achievement: A Meta-analysis of Effects and Processes," *Advances in Experimental Social Psychology* 38 (2006).

29. Bakari Akil II, "What to Do When No One's Doing Anything," *Psychology Today*, May 16, 2016, psychologytoday.com/blog/communication-central /201605/what-do-when-no-one-s-doing-anything

30. The People's Response Team, "Bystander Intervention 101," March, 2017, peoplesresponseteamchicago.org/uploads/8/7/9/8/87981704/bystander _intervention_final.pdf, 9.

31. Adapted from The People's Response Team, "Bystander Intervention 101."

32. Christopher Bergland, "The Neurobiology of Grace Under Pressure," *Psychology Today*, February 2, 2013, psychologytoday.com/blog/the-athletes -way/201302/the-neurobiology-grace-under-pressure

## Chapter 22: Mediation

1. *Tools for Transformation: A Personal Study* (Hawthorn Press, 1990), 32.
2. Jennifer Beer and Caroline Packard, *The Mediator's Handbook* (New Society Publishers, 2012), 34.
3. Quaker Council for European Affairs, "Building Peace Together: A Practical Resource," February, 2018, qcea.org/wp-content/uploads/2018/03/Building-Peace-Together.pdf, 30.
4. Adam Curle, *Another Way: Positive Response to Contemporary Violence* (Jon Carpenter Publishing, 1995), 86.
5. Curle, *Tools for Transformation*, 76.
6. Teresa Wakeen, "Pioneer Series: Being Neutral is a Myth—Video," *Mediate*, March, 2010, mediate.com/articles/wakeendvd05.cfm
7. Curle, *Another Way*.
8. Teresa Whitfield, "External Actors in Mediation: Dilemmas and Options for Mediators," 2010, peacemaker.un.org/sites/peacemaker.un.org/files/ExternalActorsinMediation_HDCenter2010.pdf
9. Curle, *Another Way*, 81.
10. Scott Strauss, "Fundamentals of Genocide and Mass Atrocities Prevention," *United States Holocaust Memorial Museum*, 2016, ushmm.org/m/pdfs/Fundamentals-of-Genocide-and-Mass-Atrocity-Prevention.pdf, 153–154.
11. Curle, *Another Way*, 77, 84.
12. Curle, *Another Way*, 87–88.
13. Andrew Marshall in the documentary film *In Pursuit of Peace*, directed by Garry Beitel, reFrame Films, 2015.
14. Curle, *Another Way*, 107.
15. William Ury, "The Walk from 'No' to 'Yes'," *TED*, October, 2010, ted.com/talks/william_ury
16. Sammy Rangel quoted in Sarah Freeman-Woolpert, "Why Reconciliation and Redemption are Central to Countering White Supremacy," *Waging Nonviolence*, January 17, 2018, wagingnonviolence.org/2018/01/life-after-hate-sammy-rangel-countering-white-supremacy/
17. Curle, *Another Way*, 86.
18. Evan Hoffman, "Addressing Terrorism: Does Conflict Resolution Have a Role?" *Canadian International Institute of Applied Negotiation*, 2006, ciian.org/PDF%20Docs/cancraddressterrorism.pdf
19. Joshua Weiss, "Why Has Negotiation Gotten a Bad Name?" *Mediate*, February, 2003, mediate.com/articles/weissj.cfm
20. Beer and Packard, *The Mediator's Handbook*, 5.
21. "Protest and Persist: Why Giving Up Hope is Not an Option," *The Guardian*, March 13, 2017, theguardian.com/world/2017/mar/13/protest-persist-hope-trump-activism-anti-nuclear-movement
22. Amb Kiplagat Bethuel in George Wachira, "Citizens in Action: Making Peace in the Post-election Crisis in Kenya—2008," *Nairobi Peace Initiative-Africa*, January, 2010, kroc.nd.edu/assets/229294/wachira_e_book.pdf, iv.
23. Wachira, "Citizens in Action," xvii.
24. Wachira, "Citizens in Action," v.

25. Dekha Ibrahim Abdi, "Concerned Citizens for Peace," *Right Livelihood Award*, January, 2008, rightlivelihoodaward.org/fileadmin/Files/PDF /Literature_Recipients/Dekha_Abdi/Concerned_Citizens_for_peace .pdf, 4.

26. Harold Miller, "Concerned Citizens for Peace in Kenya," *Kenya News blog*, January 11, 2008, updatesonkenya.blogspot.ca/2008/01/concerned -citizens-for-peace-in-kenya.html

27. Wachira, "Citizens in Action," xi–xii.

**Chapter 23: Peace Education**

1. *Faith and Practice* (Britain Yearly Meeting of the Religious Society of Friends, 1990), 24.54.

2. Rita Verma, *Critical Peace Education and Global Citizenship: Narratives From the Unofficial Curriculum* (Routledge, 2017).

3. Emily Holland, "Can 'Mindfulness' Help Students Do Better in School?" *The Wall Street Journal*, February 16, 2015, wsj.com/articles/can-mindful ness-help-students-do-better-in-school-1424145647

4. Parker Palmer, *The Courage to Teach: Exploring the Inner Landscape of a Teacher's Life* (E-Book, Jossey Bass, 2017).

5. For an example of what this can look like, see Eric Butler in the documentary film *Circles*, directed by Cassidy Friedman, 2018.

6. Rachel Pinney, *Creative Listening* (Annick Press, 1976), 12.

7. For example, Baruch Nevo and Iris Brem, "Peace Education Programs and the Evaluation of Their Effectiveness," in eds. Gavriel Salomon and Baruch Nevo, *Peace Education: The Concept, Principles, and Practices Around the World* (Psychology Press, 2005).

8. Claire O'Kane and Michael McGill, "Evaluation of Child and Youth Participation in Peacebuilding," *Global Partnership for Children and Youth in Peacebuilding*, 2015, sfcg.org/wp-content/uploads/2014/11/2015July_Eval -of-ChildYouth-Peacebuilding-DRC.pdf

9. Mercy Corps, "Youth and Consequences: Unemployment, Injustice, and Violence," 2015, mercycorps.org/sites/default/files/MercyCorps_Youth ConsequencesReport_2015.pdf, 2.

10. Gilles-Philippe Pagé, "Greenpeace's Campaign Strategies," *Peace Magazine*, July-September, 2004, peacemagazine.org/archive/v20n3p13.htm

11. Jake Lynch, "What is Peace Journalism?" *Transcend Media Service*, transcend.org/tms/about-peace-journalism/1-what-is-peace-journalism/

12. Dietrich Fischer, "What is Peace Journalism?" *Transcend Media Service*, transcend.org/tms/about-peace-journalism/1-what-is-peace-journalism/

13. Amanda Ripley, "Complicating the Narratives," *Solutions Journalism Network*, July 27, 2018, thewholestory.solutionsjournalism.org/complicating -the-narratives-b91ea06ddf63

14. Ann Mason, "Peace-building Stories," *Global Campaign for Peace Education*, March 9, 2017, peace-ed-campaign.org/peace-building-stories -connecting-children-young-people-peace-building-ideas/

15. Maria Montessori, *Education and Peace* (Kalakshetra Publications, 1972), 23.

16. Maria Montessori, *The Absorbent Mind* (Dell Publishing Co., 1967), 283.

17. Montessori Observer, "Authentic Montessori," montessoriobserver.com /montessori-education/authentic-montessori/
18. Maria Montessori quoted in Elizabeth Hainstock, *The Essential Montessori: An Introduction to the Woman, the Writings, the Method, and the Movement* (New American Library, 1986), 81.
19. Angeline Lillard, *Montessori: The Science Behind the Genius* (Oxford University Press, 2016).
20. Angeline Lillard and Nicole Else-Quest, "Evaluating Montessori Education," *Science* 313, no. 5795 (2006); My thanks also to Meg Gunsar, an Association Montessori Internationale-trained Montessori teacher, for her help in writing this example.

## Chapter 24: What Peace *Is*

1. "Shared Security: Building Peace in an Interdependent World," December 1, 2015, afsc.org/sites/default/files/documents/Shared%20Security%20 booklet_WEB_0.pdf, 6.
2. Oxford Learner's Dictionary, "Peace," oxfordlearnersdictionaries.com /definition/english/peace
3. Merriam-Webster Dictionary, "Peace," merriam-webster.com/dictionary /peace
4. United Nations Peacebuilding Support Office, "Peacebuilding and the United Nations," un.org/en/peacebuilding/pbso/pbun.shtml
5. UNESCO, "Peace in the Minds of Men and Women," September 24, 2014, unesco.org/new/en/africa/priority-africa/culture-of-peace-in-africa /yamoussoukro/
6. Johan Galtung, *Peace by Peaceful Means: Peace and Conflict, Development and Civilization* (SAGE Publications, 1996), 265.
7. Johan Galtung in eds. Paul Smoker et al., *A Reader in Peace Studies* (Pergamon Press, 1990), 9.
8. Galtung, *Peace by Peaceful Means*, 35.
9. Adam Curle, *Another Way: Positive Response to Contemporary Violence* (Jon Carpenter Publishing, 1995), 10.
10. Simon Fisher et al., *Working with Conflict: Skills and Strategies for Action* (Zed Books, 2000), 49.
11. Johns Hopkins School of Advanced International Studies, "Peacebuilding," sais-jhu.edu/content/peacebuilding
12. Quoted in Alliance for Peacebuilding, "Selected Definitions of Peacebuilding," August 12, 2013, allianceforpeacebuilding.org/2013/08/selected -definitions-of-peacebuilding/
13. Ellie Roberts and Alexandra Pluss Encarnacion, "Building Peace through Principle 10," *Quaker United Nations Office*, April, 2015, quno.org/sites /default/files/resources/building%20peace_pr10.pdf
14. Scott Strauss, "Fundamentals of Genocide and Mass Atrocities Prevention," *United States Holocaust Memorial Museum*, 2016, ushmm.org/m /pdfs/Fundamentals-of-Genocide-and-Mass-Atrocity-Prevention.pdf, 135.

15. United Nations, "Security Council Unanimously Adopts Resolution 2282 (2016) on Review of United Nations Peacebuilding Architecture," April 27, 2016, SC/12340, un.org/press/en/2016/sc12340.doc.htm
16. Quoted in Canadian Friends Service Committee, "Summary of Canadian Quaker Discernment on 'The Responsibility to Protect,' 2006–7," 5.

## Appendix 1: What We Mean by a Culture of Peacebuildin

1. Eve Schmitz-Hertzberg in particular helped to develop an earlier version of this statement.

## Appendix 2: The Basics of Facilitation

1. Amy Edmondson, "Psychological Safety, Trust, and Learning in Organizations: A Group-level Lens," *ResearchGate*, October, 2011, researchgate.net /publication/268328210_Psychological_Safety_Trust_and_Learning_in _Organizations_A_Group-level_Lens
2. This idea is adapted from Leonard Joy in Gray Cox, *A Quaker Approach to Research* (Quaker Institute for the Future, 2014), 39–40.
3. Quaker Peace and Service, "The Quaker Peace Testimony," 1993, 79.
4. Quaker Peace and Service, "The Quaker Peace Testimony," 80.
5. Quaker Peace and Service, "The Quaker Peace Testimony," 77.
6. Aside from the places otherwise noted, this appendix draws heavily from Sam Kaner, *Facilitator's Guide to Participatory Decision-Making* (New Society Publishers, 1996).

# Index

Responsibility to Pro-
tect doctrine (RtoP),
225–226
unarmed civilian
protection, 234
urban living, 194, 195, 199
*Urgent Fury*, 215
Ury, William, 246

**V**
validation, 89
Van Hook, Stephanie, 158
Van Sluytman, Margot,
200
victimhood, 174, 177, 180
victimization, 177, 178
victims, 174, 175, 176, 177,
180–188
Vietnam War, 154–155
vindictive protective-
ness, 177
violence
adverse childhood
experiences (ACEs)
and, 134–135
archeological evidence
of, 125
catharsis and, 156–157
causes of, 134, 253
counter-productive-
ness, 156
crime and, 131, 133
cultural differences,
125–126, 129
economic cost of, 218
engaging, 118–119,
120, 122
extremism, 143
gender and, 81–82,
84–85
human evolution
and behavior and,
124–125
inherent in life, 115
internal factions and,
155, 159
interpersonal, 123–124,
129, 132

love of, 123, 124
media and, 127–128
as motivator, 25–26, 27
normalization of, 157
political, 253
responding to, 119
responsibility for,
120–121
self-harm, 201
self-interest and, 165
shame as cause of, 103
slow, 118
snapping, 132–133, 136
in social activism,
151–162
stress and, 135
temperature and, 194
unavoidability of, 117,
121–122
war on drugs and, 217
war on terror and, 217
warfare, 123–124, 129
who benefits, 163
volunteering, 121

**W**
Wachira, George, 250
Wakeen, Teresa, 244
war
among Indigenous
peoples, 125
archeological evidence
of, 124, 125
causes of, 78–79
on drugs, 217
economic cost of, 218
as institutional vio-
lence, 123–124
outcomes, 215–217, 220
pollution and, 218
prevention of, 218, 220,
228–229
religious faith and,
221–223, 228
support for, 33, 218–
219
on terror, 217
who benefits, 163

Ware, Bronnie, xiii
waterboarding, 222
ways of being, 195
weapons, 25, 27
weather reports, 223
The Weathermen,
154–155
Weiss, Joshua, 247
Welsh, Jennifer, 224
West Bank, 235
White, Douglas, 32
"white genocide," 142
white powder, 146
white supremacists, 139,
140, 142, 144
Williams, Gerry, 26
Wilson, Elwin, 41
Wink, Walter, 105
women
in Nonviolent Peace-
force, 236
online hatred toward,
195
in peace process,
82–83
resisting oppression in
Syria, 160
word puzzles, 174
workplace, 29, 31
World Council of
Churches, 223, 228
worldviews
confirmation bias
and, 55–56. *see also*
beliefs
described, 53
implicit nature of,
54–55
influence of, 70
power-over and, 54

**Y**
Yugoslavia, 227

**Z**
zeros, 24, 33
zero-sum thinking, 25,
30

## ABOUT NEW SOCIETY PUBLISHERS

New Society Publishers is an activist, solutions-oriented publisher focused on publishing books for a world of change. Our books offer tips, tools, and insights from leading experts in sustainable building, homesteading, climate change, environment, conscientious commerce, renewable energy, and more—positive solutions for troubled times.

We're proud to hold to the highest environmental and social standards of any publisher in North America. This is why some of our books might cost a little more. We think it's worth it!

- We print all our books in North America, never overseas

- All our books are printed on **100% post-consumer recycled paper**, processed chlorine-free, with low-VOC vegetable-based inks (since 2002)

- Our corporate structure is an innovative employee shareholder agreement, so we're one-third employee-owned (since 2015)

- We're carbon-neutral (since 2006)

- We're certified as a B Corporation (since 2016)

At New Society Publishers, we care deeply about *what* we publish—but also about *how* we do business.

Download our catalog at https://newsociety.com/Our-Catalog or for a printed copy please email info@newsocietypub.com or call 1-800-567-6772 ext 111.

---

### New Society Publishers
#### ENVIRONMENTAL BENEFITS STATEMENT

For every 5,000 books printed, New Society saves the following resources:[1]

| | |
|---:|---|
| 36 | Trees |
| 3,270 | Pounds of Solid Waste |
| 3,598 | Gallons of Water |
| 4,692 | Kilowatt Hours of Electricity |
| 5,944 | Pounds of Greenhouse Gases |
| 26 | Pounds of HAPs, VOCs, and AOX Combined |
| 9 | Cubic Yards of Landfill Space |

[1]Environmental benefits are calculated based on research done by the Environmental Defense Fund and other members of the Paper Task Force who study the environmental impacts of the paper industry.

---

Certified B Corporation

FSC
www.fsc.org
MIX
Paper from responsible sources
FSC® C016245

new society
PUBLISHERS
www.newsociety.com